Advance Praise for *Finding Solid Ground*

Finding Solid Ground is easily one of the most helpful books available on the treatment of clinical dissociation. Based on an extended clinical research study, this guide is highly recommended for those who seek concrete, evidence-based guidance in this area. Equally recommended is the associated workbook, which provides detailed and compassionate information and exercises for clients struggling with dissociative challenges.

—**John Briere**, PhD, Professor Emeritus of Psychiatry, Keck School of Medicine, University of Southern California, author, *Treating Risky and Compulsive Behavior in Trauma Survivors.* NY: Guilford (2019)

Finding Solid Ground is an enormous contribution to the field of trauma: the first book on trauma and dissociation written by authors who are both scholars and clinicians. They build a solid ground of research evidence to support an understanding of dissociation combined with practical applications that can be easily integrated into psychotherapy or serve as a stand-alone treatment. Well done!

—**Janina Fisher**, PhD, author of Healing the *Fragmented Selves of Trauma Survivors, Transforming the Living Legacy of Trauma,* and *The Living Legacy Flip Chart*

Finding Solid Ground provides invaluable resources on the treatment of dissociative trauma-related disorders. The authors are educators *par excellence* who have used their expertise as researchers and clinicians to produce a highly readable overview of dissociation along with treatment guidelines and exercises. Their innovative TOP DD studies offer empirical support for their approach. A major contribution!

—**Christine A. Courtois**, PhD, ABPP, Licensed Psychologist, Consultant/Trainer, Author, Co-Editor, *The Treatment of Complex Traumatic Stress Disorders* (2020)

learn together, heal together

Finding Solid Ground

Overcoming Obstacles in Trauma Treatment

BETHANY L. BRAND, HUGO J. SCHIELKE,

FRANCESCA SCHIAVONE,

AND RUTH A. LANIUS

OXFORD
UNIVERSITY PRESS

Oxford University Press is a department of the University of Oxford. It furthers
the University's objective of excellence in research, scholarship, and education
by publishing worldwide. Oxford is a registered trade mark of Oxford University
Press in the UK and certain other countries.

Published in the United States of America by Oxford University Press
198 Madison Avenue, New York, NY 10016, United States of America.

Library of Congress Cataloging-in-Publication Data
Names: Brand, Bethany L., author. | Schielke, Hugo J., author. |
Schiavone, Francesca, author. | Lanius Ruth A., author.
Title: Finding solid ground : overcoming obstacles in trauma treatment /
Bethany L. Brand, Hugo J. Schielke, Francesca Schiavone, Ruth A. Lanius.
Description: New York : Oxford University Press, 2022. |
Includes bibliographical references and index.
Identifiers: LCCN 2022010860 (print) | LCCN 2022010861 (ebook) |
ISBN 9780190636081 (paperback) | ISBN 9780190670160 (epub) |
ISBN 9780190636104
Subjects: LCSH: Post-traumatic stress disorder—Treatment. |
Dissociative disorders—Treatment.
Classification: LCC RC552.P67 B728 2022 (print) | LCC RC552.P67 (ebook) |
DDC 616.85/21—dc23/eng/20220511
LC record available at https://lccn.loc.gov/2022010860
LC ebook record available at https://lccn.loc.gov/2022010861

DOI: 10.1093/med-psych/9780190636081.001.0001

Printed by Marquis, Canada

CONTENTS

Foreword—Frank Putnam vii
Preface xi
Acknowledgments xvii

1. Trauma-Related Disorders and Dissociation: Hidden in Plain Sight at Great Cost 1

2. Assessment of Dissociation, Trauma-Related Disorders, and Dissociative Disorders 19

3. The Neurobiology of Trauma-Related Disorders: What Patients and Therapists Need to Know 39

4. An Overview of Complex Trauma-Related Disorder Treatment and the Treatment of Patients with Dissociative Disorders (TOP DD) Studies' Research Findings 62

5. Understanding and Addressing the Impact of Trauma on Relational Functioning 82

6. Addressing Challenges Related to Dissociation, Emotions, and Somatic Symptoms 100

7. Understanding and Working with Dissociative Self-States 124

8. Stabilizing Unhealthy and Unsafe Behaviors 142

9. The Finding Solid Ground Program and How to Use It in Individual and Group Settings 149

Appendix A: Assessment Measures: PITQ-t and PITQ-p 171
Appendix B: Grounding Script 181
Appendix C: Resources, Training, and Suggested Readings 183
Books and Guidelines About Complex Trauma-Related Disorders with an Emphasis on Dissociation 185
References 189
About the Authors 213
Index 215

FOREWORD

FRANK PUTNAM

The year 2020 marks the 40th anniversary of the third edition of the *Diagnostic and Statistical Manual of Mental Disorders*, commonly referred to as "DSM-III" (1980). Unveiled to cries of acclaim and alarm from the establishment, the DSM-III's atheoretical, symptom-driven, multi-axial, descriptive approach to psychiatric diagnosis was a significant departure from earlier nosology based on outdated theories of personality reaction formation. The DSM-III's delineation of specific symptom constellations, irrespective of theory or etiology, helped to refocus clinicians on the clients in front of them.

While acute psychological effects of combat were recognized under labels such as WWI "shell shock" and WWII "combat fatigue/neurosis," there was a need for psychiatric diagnoses that encompassed delayed and/or chronic emotional, cognitive, somatic, and behavioral responses to past trauma. In the United States this was, in large measure, a response to a growing awareness of the serious mental health problems in Vietnam War veterans that often emerged years after their return from combat. To address this deficit, the DSM-III introduced the diagnosis of posttraumatic stress disorder (PTSD) as well as detailing a more accurate clinical profile of multiple personality disorder, subsequently renamed dissociative identity disorder (DID) in DSM-IV (1994). The DSM-III's recognition of delayed-onset posttraumatic disorders initiated a new field of research and clinical practice—although it would struggle to gain legitimacy and resources for years to come.

Forty years later, however, the existence of posttraumatic disorders is rarely questioned, although a lively debate continues about subtypes. As additional, noncombat forms of trauma were studied (e.g., rape, child abuse, first responders, and natural disasters), it became clear that there is a range of posttraumatic responses that are complexly influenced by variables such as age, gender, type(s) and duration of trauma, and relationship to perpetrator(s), as well as factors such as degree of social support, synergistic interactions among different types of trauma, and individual differences. One of the posttraumatic psychological processes that critically influences clinical presentation and treatment response is the client's degree of dissociation. The recent addition of the diagnosis, PTSD—dissociative subtype in DSM-5, for example, reflects a growing appreciation of the importance of dissociation in influencing clinical features of trauma-related disorders (TRDs).

Despite an initial lack of professional awareness and widespread skepticism about the existence of dissociative disorders, much has been learned over the past four decades that demystifies these conditions. Dissociation is now measured with the same psychometric precision as depression and anxiety. Epidemiological studies in general population and clinical samples find that the dissociative disorders are common psychiatric conditions (see Chapter 1 of this book). High levels of dissociation are correlated with refractoriness to standard treatments for a variety of psychiatric conditions, including PTSD, eating disorders, and borderline personality disorder.

Pathological dissociation is strongly linked to a history of severe trauma. This etiological relationship of severe trauma and subsequently increased levels of dissociation holds for a wide range of types of trauma across culture and time. Severe, repetitive, often early-life traumas such as childhood sexual abuse are recognized as a necessary—but not sufficient—cause of dissociative disorders.

Longitudinal parent–child dyad studies outline a generational dissociative trajectory in which certain parental deficits in caretaking, together with early-life trauma, are associated with Type D attachment in infants. Type D attachment in infancy, in turn, predicts increased levels of dissociation later in adolescence and early adulthood, which is associated with emotional dysregulation and impaired executive functions. Impaired executive functions are linked to difficulties learning from life experiences, problems controlling strong emotions, and failure to consolidate a unified sense of self. Adults with high levels of dissociation are more likely to use harsh parenting tactics associated with having Type D offspring. Thus, far more than for many psychiatric disorders, there is an empirically supported etiology and developmental theory for how early trauma and impaired caregiving produce pathological dissociation and identity fragmentation. Few other psychiatric disorders can marshal equivalent levels of evidence for their putative etiologies and developmental trajectories.

Research on the underlying neurobiology of TRDs in general and dissociative disorders in particular has been remarkably productive, despite low levels of funding. Brain imaging studies find activation patterns that differentiate classic PTSD hyperarousal from dissociative responses to traumatic reminders (see Chapter 3 of this book). Multiple studies using an array of imaging technologies detect reliable brain state differences associated with the identity states of individual DID subjects. Research with a variety of types of trauma finds that experimental activation of dissociative responses to recall of past trauma is associated with decreased autonomic arousal, especially decreased heart rate. This is consistent with theories that analogize human dissociative reactions to the "freezing" behaviors seen in young animals such as fawns and baby rabbits in response to predators.

Posttraumatic effects on memory, cognitive associations, and logical reasoning are now well documented for different forms of trauma. Emotional dysregulation manifest by rapid shifts in affect and mental state produces disruptions in an individual's continuous sense of self. Longitudinal and cross-sectional studies find that severe early trauma alters the long-term development of adrenal and gonadal hormonal systems as well as acute responses to stressors. Prepubertal sexual abuse, for example, accelerates the onset of puberty in females. Even a victim's genes may be altered by trauma through epigenetic mechanisms such as stress-induced DNA methylation. These trauma-induced genetic changes may be transmitted to future generations, providing a genetic contribution to the tragic cycles of family violence.

Progress in the treatment and prevention of TRDs, especially the dissociative disorders, has lagged behind developmental, cognitive, and neurobiological scientific advances. Treatments for classic PTSD that have been proven by randomized clinical trials (RCTs) exist, including psychotherapies, exposure and desensitization models, and pharmacotherapies. Until recently, however, treatment models for DID and other dissociative disorders were, at best, limited to the descriptive case series level, usually reflecting the experience of a single clinician's practice.

By systematically following the progress of hundreds of independent client–therapist dyads with longitudinal evaluations, the Treatment of Patients with Dissociative Disorders (TOP DD) studies have significantly advanced our therapeutic knowledge of the dissociative disorders. While short of gold-standard RCTs, the TOP DD Network study findings are based on repeated, independent client and therapist assessments with standard self- and therapist-report measures. After viewing a set of safety-oriented videos, TOP DD Network clients scoring in the higher ranges on dissociation measures (previously associated with clinical failure) showed clinically relevant improvements on behaviors such as nonsuicidal self-injury, number of hospitalizations, and degree of emotional and impulse control. In contrast to prior studies, clients with higher levels of dissociation showed faster rates of improvement than subjects with lower (but still abnormal) levels of dissociation, indicting a specificity of TOP DD therapeutic approaches for highly dissociative clients.

Finding Solid Ground: Overcoming Obstacles in Trauma Treatment and the accompanying workbook distill the lessons of the TOP DD studies into a coherent therapeutic approach. Because dissociative clients are likely to read this text, it is sprinkled with motivational encouragement to practice the TOP DD-tested interventions. In addition to the TOP DD insights, the authors add their own wealth of therapeutic expertise from years of working with patients with dissociative TRDs. As individuals, they have all achieved recognition for their contributions to the field. Together, the authors present an inclusive and comprehensive therapeutic approach to dissociative TRDs. While more remains to be learned, this volume and workbook translate 40 years of progress into a new, evidence-informed, generalizable approach to the treatment of dissociative TRDs surpassing many of the limitations inherent in earlier individual clinician-based case series.

This book grew out of our determination to help people with complex trauma-related reactions and symptoms, a group of patients who are often overlooked, misunderstood, and underserved by the mental health field. This book describes the Finding Solid Ground educational program and treatment approach for individuals who have experienced interpersonal trauma and, as a result, struggle with trauma-related reactions and symptoms, including dissociative reactions.

A RESEARCH-INFORMED AND RESEARCH-REFINED PROGRAM FOR SURVIVORS AND TREATMENT PROVIDERS

The Finding Solid Ground program is based on what we and our colleagues in the trauma field have learned over decades of trauma treatment and research, including our series of studies on the Treatment of Patients with Dissociative Disorders (the TOP DD studies; TOPDDstudy.com).

We developed this program, this book, and the companion workbook to address the alarming gap between the limited number of therapists who have been trained in treating complex trauma-related reactions and the vast number of individuals who urgently want and need treatment. This gap is particularly pronounced for patients struggling with trauma-related dissociation. We often heard from individuals who had tried to find a therapist who understood and could help them with trauma-related dissociation, only to find out that "no one in my area knows how to treat dissociation" or "the therapists who know how to treat dissociation are so busy they can't take on new patients."

Out of this urgent need was born the idea of creating an online program that patients and their therapists could participate in together that would help stabilize patients' struggles while also teaching therapists an approach to stabilizing these individuals. The TOP DD researchers, a subset of whom are the authors of this book and the accompanying workbook, are researchers in addition to therapists with expertise in treating severely traumatized, dissociative individuals. Based on our treatment research and clinical experience, and with feedback from trauma survivors, we developed an online educational study that therapists and dissociative patients could engage in as research participants for 2 years, which we called the TOP DD Network study.

The results of the study were very encouraging. As Chapter 4 will discuss in greater detail, participating patients showed significant improvements in symptoms and in their daily living. Specifically, they showed significant decreases in PTSD and dissociation symptoms, significant increases in emotion regulation ability, and reductions in self-injury (called nonsuicidal self-injury [NSSI] throughout this book), suicide attempts, and hospitalizations (Brand et al., 2019). The individuals who had been engaging in NSSI over 6 months showed they could stabilize and dramatically improve their safety, including many of those who had engaged in NSSI hundreds of times. No treatment study had shown improvements with individuals who struggled with such frequent, severe dissociation along with NSSI, PTSD, depression, and related difficulties. Furthermore, both patient and therapist participants demonstrated large changes in stabilization-related knowledge at study completion (Schielke & Brand, 2019), offering validation of the joint patient/therapist education program approach. (A brief disclaimer and research update: Although participants showed meaningful improvements and offered comments attributing improvements to participating in the program, only studies that use random assignment of participants to a control group and treatment group can prove convincingly that the intervention caused the changes. With this in mind, we are conducting additional research to determine with certainty whether these changes can be attributed to patients' participation in the educational program.)

Because it is important to us to keep learning from the people we aim to help (the TOP DD slogan is "work together, learn together, heal together"), the study's materials have been refined based on feedback from the patients and therapists who participated in the TOP DD Network study and participants in subsequent in-person trauma symptom management treatment groups that made use of these materials. The refined educational program is called the Finding Solid Ground program. The exercises and handouts are presented in the workbook that accompanies this book, *The Finding Solid Ground Program Workbook: Overcoming Obstacles in Trauma Recovery* (Schielke et al., 2022).

THE GOALS OF THE FINDING SOLID GROUND PROGRAM AND THIS BOOK

Our overarching goal in publishing this book and its companion workbook is to help trauma patients and their therapists find solid ground for successful collaboration toward healing and recovering from trauma. We share this information to help therapists provide research-informed encouragement and guidance as their patients work to learn how to manage and reduce complex trauma-related reactions and symptoms, including dissociation.

The Finding Solid Ground program workbook presents patient informa-tion and techniques that can increase patients' ability to manage trauma-related symptoms and reactions in recovery-focused ways, and help them develop com-passionate curiosity about themselves as they come to gradually understand how to help themselves get and feel safer. Most importantly, it presents this informa-tion in a sequence aimed at giving patients the most practical, useful information first, and in a way that is designed to be as understandable, easy to follow, and manageable as possible given the many interlocking challenges and dynamics in-volved in treatment for these underserved individuals.

Our specific goal with this book is to discuss the individual and group therapy implications and application of this information so that providers can have some sense of solid ground in the face of the sometimes seemingly overwhelming challenges their patients (and, therefore, they themselves) face in this work. Toward these ends, we have strived to make this book and the program work-book practical and accessible so that therapists and patients alike can benefit from them regardless of their level of experience or knowledge about trauma and dissociation, in a way that is hopefully applicable across many cultures. (Note: The TOP DD studies have been conducted with participants from around the world, so the approach has demonstrated some evidence of cross-cultural applicability.)

Trauma is overwhelming and terrifying. For most individuals with recur-rent dissociation, multiple traumas occurred over time, repeatedly causing dysregulation and overwhelm. Many such individuals first experienced trauma in childhood, and the related emotional and physiological overwhelm continually recurred and reverberated in the person's life. Although trauma-related reactions may have waxed and waned over the years (often in response to retraumatization or progress in recovery, respectively), they tend to continue to echo across the lifespan in the form of "flooding" emotion ("feeling too much") or "shutdown" moments of freeze or other forms of dissociation ("feeling too little") when faced with internal or external reminders of trauma. In these states, people with com-plex trauma histories are at risk of engaging in behavioral reenacts and/or unhealthy, risky, or unsafe behaviors. We view each of these as attempts to manage situations that may have felt, and may continue to feel, life-threatening. Safety problems are attempts at self-regulation; sometimes they are also attempts at regulating relationships with others. Thus, they are adaptations to trauma—adaptations that can be especially difficult to shift when trauma is continuing to occur or when trauma reminders continue to overwhelm.

As you will see in these books, this is why the Finding Solid Ground program places a strong emphasis on helping survivors (1) learn and make use of recovery- and healing-focused coping skills (to reduce overwhelm) and (2) work toward getting their healthy needs met safely (to increase health and safety). This work is approached with a sense of compassion for the understandable reasons survivors may have developed and maintained trauma-driven adaptations that helped them survive the past alongside a goal of identifying and moving away from adaptations that now place them at increased risk for retraumatization and/or inadvertently prolong their pain and suffering.

THE FOUR CORE SKILLSETS

The Finding Solid Ground program views unhealthy and unsafe behaviors and relationship patterns through a trauma- and attachment-informed lens: Often, these patterns and behaviors have been powerfully shaped by dysfunctional or abusive relationships. Early relationships, in particular, are especially influential in our lives; when caretakers or other adults neglect or abuse children, children develop trauma-based senses of themselves and expectations of others and view abuse, neglect, and unhealthy patterns as expected and/or unavoidable. Viewing trauma survivors' problems through these lenses clarifies why changing these patterns is often so difficult.

The Finding Solid Ground program presents the rationale and steps for developing healing-focused recovery skills in four crucial, interrelated capacities; these are foundational for healing from complex trauma, especially for dissociative individuals:

- *Grounding* when first beginning to feel too much or too little to prevent emotional overwhelm and/or dissociation
- *Separating past from present* (Rothschild, 2000; Loewenstein, 2006), including containment of intrusive imagery, recollections, and bodily sensations, and interrupting cognitive and behavioral reenactments related to trauma (e.g., trauma-based beliefs and behavioral "scripts")
- *Emotion regulation* (including self-compassionate use of grounding and other recovery-focused skills) as alternatives to unhealthy, risky, or unsafe behaviors, dissociation, trauma-related reactions that are no longer necessary, and/or habitual avoidance of emotions
- *Getting healthy needs met safely*, including through the use of healing-focused recovery skills and the development of distress management plans to help patients recognize and interrupt patterns of risky, unhealthy, or unsafe behavior that are no longer adaptive.

It is crucial for therapists and individuals who have experienced trauma to realize that, for some patients, decreasing their use of unhealthy methods of managing trauma-related feelings, memories, and symptoms can be terrifying and may feel downright dangerous—even more dangerous than using risky or unsafe methods of coping such as NSSI. For individuals who may have never known safety, the idea of "getting safe" can feel entirely unconceivable, and "getting safer" can seem like a trick and/or feel impossible. Many of these individuals may feel they do not have the right to feel good or to have a good, safe, stable life.

The good news is that the approach outlined in Finding Solid Ground has helped many people make these changes. Related comments from Network study participants have included:

- "Hearing that many other people have the same symptoms as I have supports me in believing more strongly that these symptoms are consequences of trauma."
- "It's like you wrote the program based on my struggles! This was very validating."
- "It was astonishing for me how personal and encouraging this program was."
- "This program makes me believe that it is possible to heal from trauma."

In summary, we developed this program, this book, and the accompanying workbook to provide a foundation to help trauma patients and their therapists find solid ground for successful collaboration toward getting and feeling safer and healing and recovering from trauma. This work can help trauma patients manageably work toward reclaiming all of who they are (rather than seeing themselves strictly in relation to, and through the lenses of, their trauma history), increase their capacity to feel peaceful and safe, and create a life that they can feel good about. By working, learning, and healing together, patients, therapists, and researchers can help people who have experienced trauma find solid, safe ground.

ACKNOWLEDGMENTS

We are able to treat, research, consult, and provide training about working with individuals with interpersonal trauma histories because we have been extremely fortunate to have been able to start our careers with training from some of the contemporary masters in the trauma field. First, we would not have been able to develop and carry out the TOP DD studies without the wise input, consistent support, statistical acumen, and depth of knowledge about treating trauma and dissociation we found among our "dream team" of TOP DD collaborators and consultants, so with deep gratitude we acknowledge and thank Suzette Boon, Catherine Classen, Paul A. Frewen., Ellen K. K. Jepsen, Willemien Langeland, Richard J. Loewenstein, Amie Myrick, Clare Pain, Frank W. Putnam, Karen Putnam, and Kathy Steele. This incredible group of researchers are gifted clinicians, superb writers, and unfailing cheerleaders and friends. We are also indebted to the colleagues and mentors who have most deeply inspired, supervised, supported, and taught us, notably Pamela Alexander, Judith Armstrong, Christine Courtois, Nel Draijer, Barton Evans, Catherine Fine, Richard Kluft, Richard Loewenstein, Frank Putnam, Joyanna Silberg, Kathy Steele, and Bessel van der Kolk.

We have been able to continue our learning and deepen our knowledge through the collegial discussions, research partnerships, and consultations with incredibly gifted, wise, and compassionate clinicians and researchers. We owe them our gratitude. Our clinical work with traumatized individuals and our conceptualization of assessment and treatment, our publications, and our research have been strongly shaped and influenced by many inspirational colleagues, authors, and researchers who are too numerous to name. These individuals include, but are not limited to, Su Baker, Peter Barach, Ruth Blizard, John Briere, Dan Brown, Laura Brown, Lisa Butler, Eve Carlson, Richard Chefetz, James Chu, Constance Dalenberg, Paul Dell, Martin Dorahy, Brad Foote, Julian Ford, Steve Frankel, Jennifer Freyd, David Gleaves, Steve Gold, Naomi Halpern, Judith Herman, Ingunn Holbæk, Elizabeth Howell, Phil Kinsler, Peter Levine, Roberto Lewis-Fernandez, Giovanni Liotti, Karlen Lyons-Ruth, Alfonso Martínez-Taboas, Warwick Middleton, Andrew Moskowitz, Ellert Nijenhuis, John O'Neil, Simone Reinders, Colin Ross, Vedat

Sar, Alan Schore, Daniel Siegel, Daphne Simeon, Eli Somer, David Spiegel, Joan Turkus, Onno van der Hart, and Eric Vermetten.

We have learned a tremendous amount from the individuals we have worked with in treatment over the decades. Their creativity, resilience, and courage in the face of the depth of their pain and struggles have moved and inspired us beyond what we can convey in words. Thank you for taking the risk of trusting us to work with you on your healing journeys, and for helping us learn how to be of better help to you and others. We feel humbled by the time we have spent with you, and earnestly hope to share what we learned together with others who have also felt the searing angst of being neglected and harmed.

We are also deeply indebted to the participants in our TOP DD studies, those hard-working and thoughtful patients and therapists who completed hours of surveys, watched our educational videos, completed the practice exercises, and gave us invaluable feedback along the way that shaped and improved the Finding Solid Ground program and the TOP DD research studies.

We would also like to express our sincere gratitude to our panel of people who live with the impact of trauma and dissociation who generously reviewed our materials and gave us insightful suggestions about making the program more user-friendly and beneficial. Your input has contributed to making this program useful to people around the world.

On a more personal level, we would like to give our warm thanks to our dearest friends and family members who tolerated our enthusiastic (and perhaps some-times nonstop?) talk about our research and this book, and who have tolerated the times when we disappeared into our offices to produce this book. Thank you for not giving up on us during what surely must have felt like a long journey.

Trauma-Related Disorders and Dissociation

Hidden in Plain Sight at Great Cost

In this chapter, we provide a brief overview of the relationships between trauma-related disorders (TRDs) and dissociation, describe the prevalence and presentations of dissociation among trauma survivors, and discuss the challenges that contribute to TRDs and dissociative disorders (DDs) being "hidden in plain sight." Please note that throughout this book we use the term "trauma-related disorders" as an overarching term that includes those who have a diagnosable trauma-related DD, which means that dissociation is typically severe, frequent, and disabling. Thus, our use of TRD in this book includes individuals with posttraumatic stress disorder (PTSD), acute stress disorder, the dissociative subtype of PTSD (DPTSD) complex PTSD (CPTSD), and persons with trauma-related DDs. Since many authors consider borderline personality disorder (BPD) a TRD due to the frequent occurrence of trauma, childhood maltreatment, and attachment problems in this population, we include those with trauma histories in our use of TRD as well. We also use the terms "patient" and "client" interchangeably.

PREDICTING TRAUMA-RELATED DISORDERS

Trauma-related disorders are predicted by dissociation. A review of 1,647 studies examining PTSD risk factors (Ozer et al., 2003) found that the presence of one or more symptoms of dissociation during or immediately after a traumatic event (i.e., *peritraumatic dissociation*) was the strongest studied predictor of meeting criteria for a PTSD diagnosis, stronger than perceived life threat, prior psychological adjustment, and prior trauma. Dissociative reactions, such as feeling dazed or numb around the time of a motor vehicle accident, for example, have been found to predict PTSD symptom severity 3 years later (Mayou et al., 2002). Research also suggests that dissociation that is present more than a month after a traumatic event is an even stronger predictor of PTSD (Halligan et al., 2003; van der Velden & Wittmann, 2008) and that persistent dissociation plays a role in maintaining PTSD (Ehlers, 2006; Ehlers & Clark, 2000). Similarly, most cases of complex DDs develop in response to trauma, typically in the context of a vulnerable individual who has insecure attachment.

RESPONSES TO POTENTIALLY TRAUMATIC SITUATIONS

Most people initially respond to danger by exhibiting an "orienting freeze" associated with a decrease in heart rate, during which they locate and gather further information about the threat. Next, they execute a series of survival strategies to end the threatening situation with minimal harm. Schauer and Elbert (2010) refer to this progression of self-protective strategies as the *defense cascade*. As we will review in more detail in Chapter 3, these reactions are the result of hard-wired neurological pathways. In other words, people do not consciously choose to have these defensive responses. The use of these defenses is impacted by previous traumas the person may have experienced, if any. Some of these defenses are intimately linked with dissociative symptomatology.

Most people who have not previously been exposed to trauma will initially respond with active attempts to protect themselves (often referred to as "fight or flight," though the reverse order [i.e., "flight or fight"] is the norm; see, e.g., Schauer & Elbert, 2010). However, when such responses are not possible, or when the individual has learned that they are unlikely to be effective, the individual is more likely to use immobilizing defenses—that is, those involving stillness and/or emotional disconnection (i.e., dissociation) rather than active engagement with the threat. Tonic immobility, which is akin to feigning death, may occur (note that this is a different type of stillness than the initial orienting freeze during which an individual attempts to orient toward and locate the threat). Tonic immobility is associated with high arousal, increased autonomic reactivity, and increased muscle tone, preventing the individual from moving all or part of their body (Nijenhuis et al., 1998b; Schauer & Elbert, 2010). Animal research indicates that predators may become disinterested in dead prey, which may permit the prey to escape if the predator shifts attention away from the animal. If the threat is inescapable, this sequence may proceed to emotional collapse/shutdown, which involves further parasympathetic activation, loss of motor tone, anesthesia, and apnea (for further details, see Chapter 3).

There are also two relational stances that frequently occur in the face of highly stressful/potentially traumatic situations that cannot be escaped or interrupted, both of which can co-occur alongside (and with the benefit of) dissociation: "going along" with what is going on to reduce the risk of greater/further harm (*submission*) and, especially when faced with extended/repeated exposure to trauma by a person or group of people, *identification* with the perspective of the abuser(s) alongside dissociation of the person's own perspective (i.e., what has come to be known as "Stockholm syndrome"). These self-protective reactions that allow a person to continue to feel agency in the face of this being taken from them can be confusing to observers and trauma survivors alike and can lead to unfair "victim blaming" and/or self-shaming.

Tonic immobility and emotional shutdown/collapse have parallels with dissociative states (Kluft, 1985; Nijenhuis et al., 1998a; Spiegel, 1984). Profoundly dissociative states may be associated with disturbances in the encoding, consolidation, storage, and retrieval of memory, which can contribute to the fragmentation and compartmentalization of traumatic memory over time (Spiegel, 1991; Spiegel et al., 2011). Researchers are increasingly interested in investigating the role of these immobilizing responses in trauma-related symptomatology: For example, the Scale for Tonic Immobility Occurring Post Trauma (STOP) is a new assessment measure with good psychometric properties that was designed to help clinicians assess tonic immobility (Lloyd et al., 2019).

Due to extensive research showing that most complex DDs develop in response to childhood trauma, most cases of complex DDs are considered childhood trauma disorders, with dissociative identity disorder (DID) being the disorder that has been most strongly linked to childhood abuse and neglect. Almost all (95% to 97%) individuals with DID report severe, chronic antecedent childhood sexual or childhood physical abuse or both, typically perpetrated by caregivers (e.g., Putnam et al., 1986; Ross et al., 1991). The strong connection between severe child abuse and DID has been replicated in clinical and epidemiological studies in Australia, Canada, the United States, the Netherlands, Germany, Turkey, and Puerto Rico. In contrast, depersonalization/derealization disorder is often linked with emotional abuse rather than physical or sexual abuse, although it sometimes begins during a panic attack or as a reaction to a drug, and does not resolve even when the panic attack or intoxication has subsided (Simeon & Loewenstein, 2009). There is a greater risk for dissociative amnesia with more repeated exposure to adverse childhood experiences including trauma and severe, frequent violence (Dalenberg et al., 2007).[1]

1. The fact that trauma can cause dissociation is the premise of the Trauma Model of Dissociation. Some authors challenge the Trauma Model of Dissociation. They argue that dissociation is caused by a variety of cognitive characteristics, including fantasy proneness, suggestibility, and symptom exaggeration; this perspective is called the Fantasy Model of Dissociation. Extensive reviews have found that research evidence supports the Trauma Model and have noted that Fantasy Model research generally does not include participants with DDs, or it employs measures that have not been validated for use with people with DDs. Rigorous reviews of these models, including meta-analyses and controlled research designs, are available for interested readers (Dalenberg et al., 2012, 2014; c.f. Lynn et al., 2014).

ATTACHMENT DIFFICULTIES AND TRDs

Attachment difficulties also contribute to the development of complex TRDs, including DDs. We summarize this work in the section below. (Detailed discussions that describe the connection among attachment, dissociation, and trauma include Barach, 1991; Blizard, 2003; Brown & Elliott, 2016; Liotti, 1992, 1999; and Pasquini et al., 2002.)

John Bowlby (1969) proposed that the attachment system is an innate mechanism by which children seek proximity to a caregiver as a way to safety ensure from danger. Bowlby (1980) theorized that infants develop attachment models, or internal representations, of the patterns of relationship that emerge between themselves and primary caregivers, noting that children typically seek proximity to a primary caregiver, especially when distressed. Later, researchers developed methods and interviews to assess and identify attachment styles in children and adults.

Mary Ainsworth (Ainsworth et al., 1978) designed the Strange Situation as an experimental procedure to assess and categorize children's attachment styles based on their response to separation from the caregiver. Securely attached infants were distressed by separation but could be consoled by the parent upon their return. Insecure-avoidant infants did not protest at separation or seek consolation upon the parent's return. Insecure-ambivalent infants were distressed and resistant to being consoled, at times appearing angry. While the pattern displayed by the securely attached infants is the most adaptive, all three behavior patterns represent organized and internally coherent responses to separation.

Some infants, however, behaved in ways that were not easily categorized into a single organized strategy. Main and Hesse (1990) described an additional type of insecure attachment called "disorganized attachment" (sometimes referred to as "Type D" attachment), which develops when a young child seeks comfort and protection from a primary caregiver who is frightening or whom the child inadvertently frightens (usually the caregiver in such cases has an unresolved history of trauma and so is prone to being frightened by emotions and/ or others). Contradictory internal working models of the caregivers can develop from these disorganizing experiences. A disorganized individual holds deeply contradictory viewpoints of an attachment figure such as "my mother protects me and is predictable and loving" that sharply contradicts with another belief that they also hold, such as "my mother is unpredictable and causes me extreme pain and humiliation." Hesse and Main (2000) described a variety of these behaviors that characterize the disorganized style, including simultaneous or sequential displays of contradictory behavior (e.g., approaching the caregiver while turning away, or approaching and then retreating); incomplete, misdirected, or asymmetrical movements; confusion or disorientation; and expressions of apprehension regarding the parent. Thus, the infant can show disorganization as they need to simultaneously escape from, and yet seek protection from, the caregiver.

In the Adult Attachment Interview, which is intended to classify attachment style in adults, those who value relationships and can describe their caregivers in organized, coherent ways with examples that clarify their positive or negative feelings about the caregiver are described as having a secure attachment style. Alternatively, insecurely attached individuals can be "dismissive" or "preoccupied" with regards to attachment relationships. In addition to these attachment styles, adults who show unresolved trauma or loss of an attachment figure are classified as having "unresolved attachment."

Behaviors that are typically coded as disorganized in children in the Strange Situation (e.g., periods of trancing, staring spells, contradictory actions executed sequentially or simultaneously) as well as those coded as "unresolved" (e.g., staring, incoherent speech, intrusion of decontextualized traumatic content) or "cannot classify" (e.g., abrupt switches between narratives consistent with dismissing or preoccupied styles during the same interview) in the Adult Attachment Interview appear dissociative in nature. Disorganized and unresolved attachment has been theorized as providing a foundation for the development of dissociative self-states (DSS; Barach, 1991; Blizard, 2003; Liotti, 1992), and some cases are theorized to represent switching between self-states (Liotti, 2004).

Research verifies that attachment problems are strongly linked to trauma and dissociation. Disorganized and unresolved attachment, problematic family communication, and neglect have been linked to dissociation in children as well as in adults (Byun et al., 2016; Lyons-Ruth et al., 2006; Ogawa et al., 1997), including DDs. A review of over 200 studies of adult attachment found that "adults with abuse experiences or PTSD were mostly unresolved" (p. 223) in attachment (Bakermans-Kranenburg & van Ijzendoorn, 2009).

The "gold standard" study of a longitudinal attachment study carefully assessed 186 high-risk mothers and their infants for three decades and found clearly that adult DDs occurred in cases in which infants with disorganized attachment were exposed to later childhood abuse (Carlson, 1998; Ogawa et al., 1997). Disorganized attachment in infants was associated with dissociation in childhood and adolescence that usually decreased by adulthood, unless the child was physically or sexually abused, in which cases the dissociation tended to shift into rigid compartmentalization of dissociative experiences and the emergence in adulthood of distinct dissociative personality states.

A study of 60 patients diagnosed with DID using the Structured Clinical Interview for Dissociative Disorders (SCID-D) found that over 90% had disorganized attachment as well as unresolved status related to trauma or loss (Brown & Elliott, 2016). The authors concluded that "we have come to understand each alter personality state as an expression of a specific unmet attachment need in a patient with severe disorganized attachment, and the switches from one alter personality state to another personality state as sequential manifestations of these unmet attachment needs" (Brown & Elliott, 2016, p. 192).

A study of 17 individuals who won settlements for the physical and sexual abuse that occurred at the Catholic orphanage in which they were raised sheds light on the attachment–trauma–dissociation links (Brown & Elliott, 2016). Each individual received 16 hours of testing by a forensic expert, Dr. Daniel Brown. These individuals experienced similar forms of abuse at the hands of the staff at the orphanage, many of whom had already had prior allegations of sexual abuse. About 60% of the adults had insecure attachment, primarily the disorganized type, and they came primarily from chaotic families characterized by violence, alcoholism, or a parent managing a drug or prostitution business from the home. The 40% who had secure attachment came from loving Catholic families that were large, were poor, and usually were forced to place their children in the orphanage following the death or disability of the father. The study found that despite all the adults having suffered repeated, often sadistic abuse at the orphanage, there were different attachment outcomes based on early family caregiving. To increase the power of the analyses, the orphanage sample was compared to a group of 28 adults who had been given the same comprehensive assessments as part of forensic evaluations for litigation against different alleged childhood sex offenders (Brown & Elliott, 2016). In the combined sample of 45 patients, three met SCID-D criteria for DID and 17 met criteria for DD not otherwise specified (DDNOS). The individuals with DDs showed significantly more disorganization in their attachment interviews, and depersonalization and derealization were more prevalent in those with insecure attachment compared to those with secure attachment.

The role of attachment and neglect in the etiology of DDs has been found cross-culturally. For example, in a study of Turkish college students, emotional neglect predicted a DD diagnosis (including DID; Şar et al., 2006). In a study in South Africa, emotional neglect by biological parents or siblings was the strongest predictor of an adult diagnosis of a DD, including DID, in psychiatric patients (Krüger & Fletcher, 2017).

In summary of this and other studies, Brown and Elliott (2016, p. 218) note that "the data clearly show that the combination of disorganized attachment aggravated by later childhood abuse predicts the development of dissociative disorders in adulthood (Carlson, 1998; Liotti, 1992; Ogawa et al., 1997)." This suggests that attachment patterns in relationships, including the one between the therapist and client, are crucial to address in treatment.

CONCEPTUALIZATIONS OF DISSOCIATION AND TRDs

What is dissociation?

Dissociation is defined in a multitude of ways and is a complex phenomenon. To be treatment focused, pragmatic, and accessible, we do not review the multitude of definitions and theories about dissociation and DDs here, nor the historical development of these theories; excellent overviews are available (e.g., Dell & O'Neil, 2009; Simeon & Loewenstein, 2009). Among the most prominent theories of trauma-related dissociation are Frank Putnam's (1997) discrete behavioral model, the structural model of dissociation (Nijenhuis & van der Hart, 2011), the "4-D

Model" of dissociation (Frewen & Lanius, 2015), and the corticolimbic model of dissociation (Fenster et al., 2018; Lanius et al., 2010).

Our clinical conceptualization of traumatized patients' dissociative symptoms, our research, and the foundation of the treatment approach described here are each rooted in these theoretical models. An individual who is "dissociated" is in a discrete state of consciousness, or as Putnam describes it, a "discrete behavioral state." Therefore, throughout this book and in the workbook, we refer often to dissociative "states."

Trauma creates states of overwhelm that are strikingly different from normal states of being (Frewen & Lanius, 2015; Lanius et al., 2010; Putnam, 1989, 1997, 2016). Trauma-based states differ in terms of the intensity and types of physiological arousal, emotion, neurobiological patterns, level of self-awareness and awareness of others (sometimes called "metacognitive" or "reflective" abilities), access to autobiographical memory, and patterns of thinking, perceiving, and behaving (Frewen & Lanius, 2015; Lanius et al., 2010; Putnam, 1997, 2016).

As they mature, children are supposed to gradually develop awareness and control over what are initially uncontrolled shifts in state. It is common for an infant or toddler to rapidly shift from being alert and playful to whining, crying, or having a tantrum when overwhelmed with the physiological and emotional distress of intense hunger or exhaustion. The rapidity of this type of state change and the intense dyscontrol of emotion and behavior are normal in very young children but are not typical of older children or adults. Older children and adults do not typically shift states that rapidly or intensely or with that level of dyscontrol.

Maltreatment interferes with a child developing control over behavioral states as well as the integration and organization of these trauma-based states. Maltreatment can create unintegrated states of extreme distress that can unpredictably intrude into the person's thinking, behavior, and emotions, even decades after the maltreatment has ended. For example, an adult survivor may suddenly become utterly terrified and urgently want to run and hide. Sometimes, the adult has no idea what caused their utter terror, which makes them feel weak, vulnerable, and/or "crazy." People with severe DDs may become so terrified that they shift to a traumatized state and then behave like a terrified child. They may find themselves under a table as if they were still a child attempting to escape an abusive adult. They may or may not have control over what they do in such a trauma-based state. Afterwards, they may clearly remember hiding, they may remember it only vaguely, or they may have complete lack of memory (i.e., dissociative amnesia) for hiding.

Dissociative amnesia occurs from trauma creating trauma-dependent states that can lead to the development of "profound forms of state-dependent learning and memory retrieval" (Putnam, 1997, p 179). Said differently, the adult survivor may not recall what they did or how they felt when in a traumatized state once they shift back to a nontraumatized state due to memory being less accessible between states. As a result, a maltreated child may develop a sense of self (or selves) that is/ are unintegrated. That is, as the child matures, they may retain "discrete behavioral states" rather than integrate these states. The child may compartmentalize and avoid thinking about "that bad thing that happened to that bad child," thereby distancing themselves from the profound betrayal, shame, hurt, anger, and terror that they experienced during the abuse and even the memory of the maltreatment. Over time, particularly if traumatization occurs repeatedly and the child is not comforted or protected by caregivers, the disruption to the child's development can be amplified. The child may develop difficulty accessing memories about themselves and have increasingly elaborated, divergent rather than integrated, dissociative states of self. In cases of severe and early abuse, these states may become elaborated and complex and ultimately develop into DID (Putnam, 1997, 2016).

The various conceptualizations of trauma-related dissociative symptoms "converge around the concept that dissociation involves a failure to integrate or associate information and experience in a normally expectable fashion" (Putnam, 1997, p. 7). Consistent with this idea of a lack of integration, the fifth edition of the *Diagnostic and Statistical Manual of Mental Disorders* (DSM-5) defines dissociation as "a disruption and/or discontinuity in the normal integration of consciousness, memory, identity, emotion, perception, body representation, motor control, and behavior" (American Psychiatric Association [APA], 2013, p. 291).

Dissociative states range from mild, nonpathological detachment, such as those occurring during peak athletic, religious, and artistic experiences (Butler, 2006; Butler et al., 1996); to derealization or depersonalization that occur transiently with stress; to the more chronic pathological forms of dissociation, including DPTSD and DDs. The concept of a continuum of dissociation ranging in severity is most fitting to individuals who do not fall into the most severe end of the continuum, sometimes referred to as belonging in the "dissociative taxon." The dissociative taxon includes those with the most severe DDs, which includes DID and some forms of "other specified dissociative disorder" (OSDD; previously referred to as "dissociative disorder not otherwise specified" [DDNOS] in the DSM-IV-R [APA, 2000]; Waller & Ross, 1997). Most commonly, OSDD/DDNOS patients experience identity fragmentation without amnesia across self-states. Some writers refer to people in the dissociative subtype of PTSD as belonging to a dissociative taxon (Lanius et al., 2014), although we prefer to reserve the term "dissociative taxon" for those with elevated scores on the Dissociative Experiences Scale taxon subscale (DES; see Chapter 2), who are frequently also diagnosed with a DD.

The DSM-5 describes dissociation as a "disruption and/or discontinuity" among a variety of psychological processes. Examples of what can be disrupted in each of these psychological processes clarify how broad the range of dissociative experiences can be. Dissociation can disrupt *perception*, such as when one's surroundings appear to be far away, blurry, surreal, two-dimensional, or otherwise distorted; this is referred to as "derealization." Perceptual dissociation can also result in a type of detachment from self (i.e., feeling numb or disconnected from one's body or emotions, such as feeling as if one's body does not belong to oneself or seeing oneself at a distance as if in a movie), which is called "depersonalization." A traumatized person may enter a trance-like state during which they may be less responsive or even nonresponsive to what is going on around them; this is an example of a disruption of *consciousness*. Amnesia for part or all of a traumatic event, or not being able to recall what one has done for minutes, hours, or even days at a time, is an example of disrupted *memory*. Dissociation can also result in a lack of integration between identity and memory, which is referred to as "compartmentalization" (Holmes et al., 2005). Abrupt shifting of emotions, such as when a person shifts inexplicably from calm to terrified or from very angry to silly, could be due to dissociative disruptions in *emotion*. Feeling as if one has a fragmented identity (e.g., behaving, feeling, and/or thinking so differently that one feels as if one is almost a different person) rather than having a cohesive, unified sense of self exemplifies a disruption of *identity*. Dissociative *body representations* occur when a person perceives their body to be much younger or older, or larger or smaller, or of a different sex than they are. Dissociative disruptions of *motor control* and *behavior* often occur simultaneously. (For example, an individual with a DD may experience having no control over their movements, such as seeing themselves engaging in self-harm and wanting to stop the behavior but being unable to do so.) These dissociative experiences can be so confusing and frightening that the individual may avoid thinking about them, and may avoid telling others, including mental health professionals, about them due to fear of sounding "crazy."

Dissociative detachment can be conceptualized as a process or mechanism ("I am dissociating"), whereas compartmentalization can be conceptualized as an outcome of the process of detachment or structural dissociation ("Another part of me said those angry words, not me"). In this book, we use the term "dissociation" to mean the act of dissociating, whether it is experienced as a trance state or as depersonalization or derealization. When referring to the process of shifting DSS that occurs in the more complex DD, we will explicitly state this. When we are referring to the disorder that involves DSS coupled with periods of amnesia, we will specifically refer to DID.

PREVALENCE AND COMORBIDITY OF TRDs

A high number of co-occurring ("comorbid") psychiatric disorders and symptoms are common among people who have experienced trauma. The National Comorbidity Study found strong relationships between trauma exposure, PTSD, depression, substance abuse, and suicidality (Kessler, 2000; Kessler et al., 1995). This comorbidity makes assessment and treatment of TRDs more challenging and generally necessitates longer treatment.

The following represent the most prevalent accurate "primary" DSM-5 diagnoses assigned to people with more complicated trauma histories, presented in order from typically least to typically most severe. (Note: We will discuss common diagnostic errors in Chapter 2.)

The dissociative subtype of PTSD

Introduced in the DSM-5 (APA, 2013), DPTSD refers to individuals who present with depersonalization and/or derealization in addition to other symptoms indicative of a PTSD diagnosis. The prevalence of DPTSD has varied between 6% and 30% of individuals with PTSD (Armour et al., 2014a, 2014b; Blevins et al., 2014; Steuwe et al., 2012; Wolf et al., 2012a, 2012b), and individuals with DPTSD can be distinguished from those with PTSD using a variety of methods (Ginzburg et al., 2006; Waelde & Fairbank, 2005; Wolf et al., 2012a), including neuroimaging patterns (reviewed by Lanius et al., 2010). In a World Health Organization (WHO) sample of 25,018 patients from 16 countries (Stein et al., 2013), 14.4% of individuals with PTSD were found to meet criteria for DPTSD. In this international sample, DPTSD was associated with exposure to childhood adversities and prior trauma, childhood onset of PTSD, history of separation anxiety disorder and phobia, and male gender. Individuals with DPTSD demonstrated severe role impairment and high suicidality. Although this general population study found DPTSD was higher in males, clinical studies typically find the highest prevalence in females (Steuwe et al., 2012; Wolf et al., 2012a).

Although the DSM-5 diagnosis and most research related to DPTSD have focused only on depersonalization and derealization, we believe it is important for clinicians and researchers to expand the assessment of dissociative symptoms more broadly, evaluating the full range of possible dissociative phenomena. For example, amnesia frequently accompanies DPTSD and has been found to be strongly associated with dissociation in DPTSD (Steuwe et al., 2012). Although some authors refer to DPTSD individuals as having "high" dissociation, it may be more accurate to consider the individuals as having *moderate* dissociation compared to PTSD samples without elevated dissociation and to DD samples who have severe and recurrent dissociative symptoms.

In the WHO's International Classification of Disorders-11 (ICD-11; WHO, 2020), a TRD is included called complex PTSD (CPTSD). CPTSD was included in recognition that a wider array of difficulties than those included in PTSD are experienced by many individuals who have experienced complex trauma. As currently conceptualized, CPTSD does not specifically include common dissociative symptoms (e.g., derealization, depersonalization, amnesia for part or all of the traumatic event), although it includes intrusive recollections and flashbacks of trauma, which are dissociative in nature. Despite not expressly including a range of dissociative symptoms, research has shown that high levels of dissociation strongly distinguish PTSD from CPTSD (Hyland et al., 2018). Although CPTSD has been recognized by many trauma experts for decades (e.g., Herman, 1997), it is not currently included in the DSM-5.

Borderline personality disorder

BPD is linked to trauma exposure and dissociation. Childhood maltreatment is reported by up to 80–96% of individuals with BPD (Battle et al., 2004; Korzekwa et al., 2009a; Sack et al., 2013; Zanarini et al., 1989). Between 35% and 79% of persons with BPD have comorbid PTSD (Sack et al., 2013; Zanarini et al., 1998), a rate that is considerably higher than among individuals with other personality disorders (Golier et al., 2003). There is overlap between complex presentations of PTSD, including DPTSD, and BPD (e.g., Brand & Frewen, 2017).

There are considerable similarities between BPD and DDs, which can lead to underdiagnosis of DDs. DSM-5 BPD symptom criteria include dissociative states under stress that are well documented (Ludascher et al., 2010; Stiglmayr et al., 2001, 2008). BPD criteria also include "impairments in identity" and "unstable self-image." Some individuals with BPD experience both structural dissociation and trauma-related altered states of consciousness (Frewen et al., 2014). In some cases, these symptoms imply a dissociative process, as evidenced in the frequent comorbidity between BPD and DDs (Ellason et al., 1996; Şar et al., 2003, 2006). DDs are comorbid in 41% to 72% of persons with BPD (Conklin et al., 2006; Sack et al., 2013; Şar et al., 2003, 2006; Zittel Conklin & Westen, 2005), and studies have found that as many as 53% to 72.5% of patients entering treatment for BPD have a comorbid DD (Şar et al., 2006; Zittel Conklin & Westen, 2005), with 11% meeting criteria for DID (Zittel Conklin & Westen, 2005). Misdiagnosis driven by symptom overlap may account for some cases of comorbidity. Individuals who meet full criteria for both BPD and DID are more symptomatic and impaired than persons with either diagnosis alone (Ross et al., 2014). More severe dissociation was a negative prognostic indicator for treatment of BPD (Kleindienst et al., 2011).

The dissociative disorders

The DSM-5 describes five DD diagnoses: (1) depersonalization/derealization disorder, (2) dissociative amnesia (which includes dissociative fugue), (3) DID, (4) OSDD, and (5) unspecified dissociative disorder (UDD). (In the DSM-IV, OSDD and UDD phenomena would have been categorized as DDNOS.) Depersonalization/derealization disorder involves recurrent or persistent feelings of being detached from oneself and/or one's surroundings while also understanding the reality of their situation. Dissociative amnesia is characterized by an "inability to recall important autobiographical information, usually of a traumatic or stressful nature, that is inconsistent with ordinary forgetting" (APA, 2013, p. 298). DID involves a "disruption of identity characterized by two or more distinct personality states" that in some cultures may be referred to as possession, combined with recurrent periods of dissociative amnesia. OSDD is the designation given to presentations in which the patient does not meet full criteria for another DD. The DSM-5 defines four subtypes of OSDD; within this book, our focus will be on OSDD-1, which we will define below.

Although less common than DPTSD, DDs are not rare. The lifetime prevalence of any DD ranges from approximately 9% to 18%, with DID estimated in approximately 1.5% of the general population (Johnson et al., 2006; Ross, 1991; Şar et al., 2007). The prevalence of DDs among psychiatric inpatients is approximately 19%, and the average prevalence of DID is 4%, according to a review that used average weighted prevalence rates (Friedl et al., 2000). Rates of DID do not seem to vary between Europe and North America (Friedl et al., 2000).

Comorbidity is common among patients with DDs. Depression is both treatment-resistant and the most commonly found comorbid diagnosis in individuals with DDs (Ellason et al., 1996; Johnson et al., 2006). BPD is comorbid in 30% to 70% of persons with DID (Boon & Draijer, 1991; Dell, 1998; Ellason et al., 1996; Horevitz & Braun, 1984; Korzekwa et al., 2009a, 2009b; Şar et al., 2003). CPTSD (Courtois & Ford, 2009; Ford & Courtois, 2009), substance abuse (Ellason et al., 1996; Evren et al., 2008; Karadag et al., 2005), self-destructiveness and suicidality (Brand et al., 2009b, 2019b; Foote et al., 2008; Putnam et al., 1986), treatment-resistant anxiety disorders (Morrison et al., 2003), and eating disorders (Gleaves & Eberenz, 1995; Johnson et al., 2006) are other comorbid disorders seen in DD patients. In addition to multiple psychiatric disorders, DD patients often have high levels of recent, adult victimization as well as frequent serious medical problems (Espirito-Santo & Pio-Abreu, 2009; Myrick et al., 2013; Şar et al., 2007; Saxe et al., 1994; Webermann et al., 2014). In summary, the DDs are characterized by high levels of dissociation along with a range of psychological symptoms and behavioral difficulties (Brand et al., 2009c, 2016a; Lyssenko et al., 2018) that often require extended treatment, including multiple inpatient hospitalizations.

In the Treatment of Patients with Dissociative Disorders (TOP DD) naturalistic study, participants struggled with DDs as well as many additional disorders: 89% also had PTSD, 83% had a mood disorder, 54% had a personality disorder from the dramatic cluster, 51% had a personality disorder from the anxious cluster, 50% had an anxiety disorder, 30% had an eating disorder, and 22% had a substance use disorder (Brand et al., 2009b). Additionally, these patients frequently present with psychiatric symptoms that may seem bizarre or impossible, and can be mistaken for psychosis, leading to incorrect diagnoses of schizophrenia or other psychotic disorders (Schiavone et al., 2018). This psychiatric complexity can be perplexing for therapists, as they may be unsure which disorder to focus on, or how to prioritize the patient's multitude of psychiatric problems and symptoms.

What may be most helpful in these cases is to understand these patients as suffering a set of core deficits that cross diagnostic categories (e.g., insecure attachment, difficulty regulating emotions, dissociation and disconnection from the body) yet share a common etiology, stemming from chronic and repeated experiences of victimization, often inflicted by important attachment figures during key developmental periods. Repeatedly assisting patients in noticing these patterns and learning healthy ways to deal with these myriad yet often interconnected struggles, as described in this program, can lead to gradually ameliorating these deficits.

THE UNDERDIAGNOSIS OF COMPLEX DISSOCIATION AND ITS MANY COSTS

Despite being at least as prevalent as many other types of mental illness, complex TRDs, and especially their dissociative symptomology, are underrecognized. Consequently, most individuals with these disorders do not receive treatment specifically targeting the dissociative symptoms that maintain them. For example, 29% of the patients at an urban clinic in the United States were diagnosed with DDs via structured diagnostic interviewing, yet according to the medical records, only 5% had been diagnosed with a DD (Foote et al., 2006). In a sample of 613 consecutively admitted outpatients in Switzerland, only 3.6% (1 out of 28) of the patients who met criteria for a DD had been assigned a DD diagnosis in their medical records (Mueller et al., 2007). This pattern of DD underrecognition and lack of dissociation-focused treatment is also found in nonclinical samples. Although almost 20% of women in a representative community sample in Turkey met criteria for having a DD at some point in their lives, only one third of those had received mental health treatment, leading the authors to conclude, "The majority of dissociative disorders cases in the community remain unrecognized and unserved" (Şar et al., 2007, p. 175).

Such findings are particularly disappointing given that individuals with dissociative symptoms often suffer from high impairment. Dissociative symptoms are strongly related to impairment in a range of psychiatric disorders. A longitudinal study assessing predictors of impairment found that dissociation was among the strongest predictors of impairment among patients with mood, substance use, anxiety, dissociative, somatoform, and personality disorders symptoms (Tanner et al., 2019). In a nationally representative sample of German youth, 34% of the youth diagnosed with DDNOS reported reduced work productivity; 10% were unable to work at all due to psychological problems (Lieb et al., 2000). Despite this level of impairment, only 16% had received mental health treatment. Similarly, in a random sample of adolescents and young adults in the Netherlands, those with DD had the highest level of functional impairment of any disorder studied, yet only 2.3% of those with a DD had been referred for psychiatric treatment (Ferdinand et al., 1995). Adults with DDs are also typically quite impaired. Impairment rates for DDs were 50% higher than they were among the other psychiatric disorders assessed in a representative sample of New York residents; after controlling for age, gender, and co-occurring disorders, those with DDs were still significantly impaired (Johnson et al., 2006). After finding similar results in a Swiss study, the authors argued that DDs should be considered a type of "serious mental illness" because DID and DDNOS/OSDD contributed to functional impairment beyond the impact of coexisting nondissociative disorders (Mueller-Pfeiffer et al., 2012).

The extraordinarily high levels of disability that can accompany complex TRDs greatly impede the quality of life of TRD individuals and negatively impact their loved ones. In cases where the impact of trauma is not recognized and diagnosis and treatment of trauma-related disorders is delayed, patients' suffering is unnecessarily prolonged. During this time, in addition to suffering from symptoms, they may get involved in relationships where they become retraumatized, and their children may be at heightened risk for emotional problems, neglect, abuse, and other negative outcomes (Cicchetti et al., 2015; Folger et al., 2017; Narang & Contreras, 2005; Noll et al., 2009; Yeager & Lewis, 1996).

Suicidality is one of the most dangerous difficulties experienced by people with DDs (Foote et al., 2008). A review of 53,769 psychiatric admissions of U.S. soldiers found that the number of inpatient days for those hospitalized with a diagnosis of a DD within the past 12 months was associated with a very high risk for suicide in the year following discharge (odds ratio = 5.6; Kessler et al., 2015). In addition, many DD patients have multiple medical disorders (International Society for the Study of Dissociation, 2011). As a result of the wide range of complex, severe symptoms, the course of treatment is likely to be more prolonged compared to patients with "only" acute or classic TRDs.

In summary, although complex TRDs are prevalent, they are often not accurately diagnosed or treated, resulting in these individuals being underrecognized and underserved despite many struggling with myriad chronic symptoms and psychological disorders, being highly impaired, and being at risk for disability and suicide.

What are the economic costs?

In addition to the significant emotional, psychological, and highly personal costs associated with having a complex TRD, there can be immense economic costs associated with TRDs, with particularly high economic and personal costs for DD patients (Brand et al., 2012a; Ferry et al., 2015; Langeland et al., 2020; Lloyd, 2011, 2015; Myrick et al., 2017a). In addition, the failure to properly diagnose and treat DDs results in significant challenges for health care systems due to health care and disability costs. Mansfield et al. (2010) found that DD patients who were spouses of active-duty military personnel used mental health services at a higher rate than individuals diagnosed with any of the other 16 psychiatric disorders they studied.

Furthermore, studies have found that DD patients spend an average of 6 to 12 years in treatment before being correctly diagnosed (e.g., Boon & Draijer, 1993a; Loewenstein & Putnam, 1990; Putnam et al., 1986). During that time, they typically receive costly evaluations, partake in lengthy and ineffective treatments, and are hospitalized multiple times (e.g., Boon & Draijer, 1993a; Loewenstein & Putnam, 1990). DD patients also frequently attempt suicide (Foote et al., 2008). Each individual suicide attempt among general psychiatric patients costs an estimated $2,000 to $68,000 when direct costs such as ambulatory care, medical tests, surgeries, and psychiatric treatment are considered (Yang & Lester, 2007).

Some preliminary studies have calculated that accurate diagnosis of DDs, followed by appropriate trauma- and dissociation-focused treatment, would substantially decrease the cost of DD patients' treatments, even in cases where patients are severely impaired (Fraser & Raine, 1992; Lloyd, 2011; Ross & Dua, 1993). For example, the TOP DD researchers found that phasic trauma treatment for DD was associated with a reduction in the burden of disease for DD patients in a wide range of clinical domains (Brand et al., 2009b, 2013). That study demonstrated substantial cost savings during 30 months of treatment, in large part due to reduction in need for inpatient treatment (Myrick et al., 2017a). Case studies support the savings that can occur when a DD diagnosis is made and DD-focused treatment is provided. For example, the mental health care costs for two patients were compared before and after diagnosis of, and treatment for, DID in the United Kingdom's National Health Service (Lloyd, 2015). Both patients showed substantial savings once DID was recognized and treated: One patient whose diagnosis had not been recognized for years showed an overall cost reduction of 68% in the 4 years of therapy (Lloyd, 2015). Overall costs were reduced by 25% for the second person after DID was diagnosed and treated.

WHAT CONTRIBUTES TO TRDs BEING UNDERRECOGNIZED AND UNDERSERVED?

The topic of trauma evokes strong feelings and debate within society, including the mental health field. In her classic book on complex PTSD, Judith Herman (1997) noted that cycles of interest in trauma have been followed by disinterest and even dismissal of trauma's prevalence and impact. Factors that contribute to cycles of awareness followed by denial of trauma include an early absence of research about the prevalence and impact of child abuse and other traumas, which contributed to a lack of understanding about the causal role that trauma plays in the development of psychopathology and a lack of systematic training about trauma for professionals. One of the most important turning points in the mental health field occurred with the inclusion of PTSD and a chapter on DDs in the DSM in 1980. The inclusion of these trauma-related diagnoses led to increased scientific and clinical attention. In this climate of increased awareness of trauma, research on TRD, dissociation, and DDs has begun to flourish, although more research about DDs is still urgently needed (Dalenberg et al., 2007; Dorahy et al., 2014).

At times, a willingness to acknowledge childhood trauma and resultant dissociation has been dampened by concerns about the possibility of false reports of child abuse and reluctance to interfere with families in childraising. In the late 1980s and early 1990s, for example, a great deal of media attention was given to what reporters, and even some researchers, called a "witch hunt" for child abusers. This supposed witch hunt was given much media attention. However, according to thorough and well-documented research by Ross Cheit (Cheit & Krishnaswami, 2014), few cases of day care and nursery school abuse were, in fact, false. Unfortunately, because the number of false accusations of child abuse in nursery schools and day care settings was greatly inflated in media reports, the *narrative* that false reports of child sexual abuse were common gained a foothold in the minds of many in the general population. Cheit's research documents that even some well-known memory researchers, reporters, and attorneys exaggerated the prevalence of false "recovered memories" (typically called "delayed recollections" or dissociated memories by trauma experts) of abuse, leading many to believe that false memories are far more prevalent than indicated by research.

Although the prevalence of false memories of child abuse in child care centers was largely exaggerated, the "witch hunt narrative" continues to be kept alive by some media, academic, and textbook discussions about dissociation and child abuse. Researchers who have analyzed textbooks have consistently concluded that much of the information about child maltreatment, child abuse memories, and DDs is inaccurate, biased, sensationalized, and/or not empirically based (Brand et al., 2019a; Kissee et al., 2014; Wilgus et al., 2015). Undergraduate and graduate psychology textbooks typically include relatively little coverage about TRDs and DDs, and many include factually inaccurate or sensationalized information rather than evidence-based research (Brand et al., 2019a; Wilgus et al., 2015). Some authors of psychology textbooks only present research that shows that memories can be inaccurate, failing to present research that documents that delayed recollections of child abuse are as likely to be accurate as they are inaccurate (Dalenberg, 1996, 2006; Williams, 1995). In fact, many of the most prominent authors who previously challenged the accuracy of delayed recollections of abuse have recently admitted they are now "open to the possibility that some recovered memories are genuine" (Lynn et al., 2014, p. 23). Recent reviews of this debate are available (e.g., Brand et al., 2017a, 2017b, 2018; Dalenberg et al., 2012, 2014; Lynn et al., 2014; Merckelbach & Patihis, 2018).

In a climate where many academics and textbooks tend to present sensationalized portrayals of DDs and only one side of the debate about the accuracy of child abuse memories, there is less open-minded discussion, training, and research about child abuse and its impact, including dissociation and DDs. One impact of this biased presentation is that people who have already been victimized in childhood and/ or adulthood may suffer longer with TRD, poor quality of life, and a host of other sequelae of trauma. They are also at risk for encountering mental health and health care professionals who challenge the validity of their symptoms and DD (Nester, Hawkins & Brand, 2022). For example, 80% of Australian patients diagnosed with a DD reported they had experienced skeptical or antagonistic attitudes from clinicians about their DD diagnosis or dissociative symptoms (Leonard et al., 2005). Survivors of childhood abuse often experience disbelief, being blamed for the abuse, or a lack of compassion and/or protection if they have the courage to reveal the abuse. For example, 52% of women who revealed to a parent that they were being incestuously abused in childhood reported that the abuse continued for 1 year or longer after disclosure (Roesler & Wind, 1994), and many received reactions that blamed them rather than the abuser (McTavish et al., 2019; Roesler & Wind, 1994; Romano et al., 2019). Trauma survivors should not encounter damaging reactions when they seek assistance from the very professionals who are supposed to help them, not further compound their distress.

Unfortunately, few clinicians receive much if any systematic training about complex trauma, dissociation, and DDs, despite indicating that they need, want, and benefit from such training (Cook et al., 2017; Hepworth & McGowan, 2013; Kumar et al., 2019), so it is not surprising that clinicians have difficulty accurately diagnosing these disorders (Dorahy et al., 2017). Many clinicians also report having little or no training in how to inquire about a history of abuse as a child (e.g., Hepworth & McGowan, 2013; Lab et al., 2000), and Lab et al. (2000) found that 70% of psychiatrists, psychologists, and nurses working in a teaching hospital had received no training in working with people who had experienced childhood sexual abuse.

This lack of training understandably reduces the likelihood that clinicians have confidence in their ability to inquire about trauma in a sensitive, evidence-informed manner and be able to help their patients manage any emerging reactions. With trauma training being sparse even among mental health and health care professionals, it is not surprising that many patients are not asked about trauma exposure and that only a small percentage of medical records note such histories (Rossiter et al., 2015). For example, a recent study found that 51% of 100 females admitted to a psychiatric unit in Melbourne had not been asked about a history of trauma (Xiao et al., 2016).

Given that childhood trauma exposure has been linked with heightened risk for most types of psychiatric disorders, this lack of training and inquiry is concerning (Brand et al., 2019a). The equivalent in the medical field would be patients not being asked about a history of smoking; smoking is causally linked to so many medical disorders that failing to ask about it could be considered to be providing treatment below the standard of care. Ultimately, traumatized clients and our health care systems pay the price for the lack of systematic trauma training among the mental health field. We join other experts in calling for systematic trauma training for mental health professionals, including the assessment of trauma exposure and TRDs, and the treatment of the myriad symptoms and problems found among traumatized individuals, including TRD (Brand, 2016; Brand et al., 2019a; Courtois & Gold, 2009; Hepworth & McGowan, 2013). Careful assessment of trauma exposure and related PTSD and dissociative symptoms needs to become the standard practice in mental health assessments. Indeed, all clinical interviews should routinely include assessment of trauma history and trauma-related difficulties including but not limited to dissociation and DDs, much like it has become routine to assess for suicidality and substance abuse.

Trauma experts (e.g., Courtois & Gold, 2009) urge therapists to obtain specialized training with TRD patients because without it, serious mistakes and negative treatment outcomes may occur. The approach described in these books is meant to support such training efforts and to offer evidence-informed guidance toward the assessment and treatment of complex trauma related reactions, including dissociation. Complex, chronic PTSD cases are at higher risk for poor outcomes (Courtois & Ford, 2009; Courtois et al., 2009), and those who frequently dissociate may require longer treatment than those without high dissociation, regardless of whether the individual is being treated for a trauma-based disorder or not (Jepsen et al., 2013; Lynch et al., 2008; Michelson et al., 1998; Rufer et al., 2006). For example, an inpatient treatment study found that patients with TRDs showed reductions in PTSD symptoms and some aspects of dissociation, yet symptoms suggestive of DID did not improve (e.g., amnesia and identity fragmentation; Jepsen et al., 2014). The authors suggested that treatment likely needs to directly target amnesia and identity fragmentation in order to impact those symptoms. In keeping with these findings and expert consensus, the Finding Solid Ground program includes information and approaches aimed at targeting high levels of dissociation and helping people with DSS improve their relationships with (and communication and collaboration between) their DSS. (See Chapter 7 for a discussion on working with DSS and Chapter 9 for an overview of the workbook contents.)

CONCLUSION

The prevalence of TRDs, including DDs, is high, as is the severity of the symptoms, functional impairment, and economic costs associated with complex trauma and dissociation. Individuals with TRDs are underdiagnosed and underserved for a multitude of reasons, including that most mental health professionals have little training in assessing and treating TRD. As a result of being underserved and struggling with myriad chronic symptoms and psychological disorders, individuals with DDs and other TRDs pay an unacceptably high price in terms of functioning and quality of life. In addition to helping those with TRDs reduce their suffering and improve their quality of life, there is reason to believe that improved assessment and treatment awareness and implementation would reduce costs to our systems of care.

Despite the challenges inherent in recognizing TRDs and DDs, empirically informed approaches to the assessment and treatment of these disorders exist. These will be the focus of the rest of this book.

2

Assessment of Dissociation, Trauma-Related Disorders, and Dissociative Disorders

INTRODUCTION

The assessment of trauma-related disorders (TRDs) and dissociative disorders (DDs) is not widely taught, and accurate assessment of dissociative symptoms can be particularly challenging without adequate training. Clinicians who have not been trained in assessing TRD and DD may attribute TRD and DD symptoms to psychosis, bipolar disorder, borderline personality disorder (BPD), or malingering. As a result, TRD and DD are frequently underdiagnosed and misdiagnosed, preventing these underrecognized and yet highly symptomatic individuals from receiving appropriate, timely treatment (Brand, 2016; Dorahy et al., 2014; Grubaugh et al., 2011).

In this chapter, we provide a practical overview of the assessment of trauma-related and dissociative symptoms, including self-report measures and structured assessment tools that can complement the clinical interview; the assessment of common comorbidities; methods of distinguishing TRD and DD from diagnoses with similar presentations; and potential alternative explanations for apparently dissociative experiences. We will also provide an overview of possible challenges and pitfalls in using "general" psychological assessment instruments that have not been validated with individuals with complex trauma histories.

ACCURATE, TRAUMA-INFORMED ASSESSMENT OF TRD

Questions about trauma should be included in all clinical and forensic assessment interviews. Individuals with trauma histories often do not disclose their trauma without being specifically asked. To allow development of a reasonable working alliance before going into topics that can be very difficult for people to talk about, however, we recommend sequencing interview content such that trauma-related questions are asked toward the end of the interview. (More on how to do this can be found in the "Assessing Trauma History" section below.)

While not all clients who meet criteria for TRDs experience dissociative symptoms, to ensure accurate diagnosis and appropriate treatment, assessment of TRDs must include screening for dissociation. Individuals who meet criteria for the dissociative subtype of posttraumatic stress disorder (i.e., DPTSD, as described by the criteria for the "with dissociative symptoms" specifier of PTSD), for example, may be inadvertently overwhelmed and possibly harmed if treated with the same protocols appropriate for the "classic" hyperaroused, reexperiencing presentation of PTSD. While some treatment literature focusing specifically on DPTSD has suggested that patients with the dissociative subtype respond equally well to exposure-based treatment without prior stabilization of dissociation, this body of work does not address the subpopulation of those with complex dissociative disorders (e.g., dissociative identity disorder [DID] and other specified dissociative disorder [OSDD]; Cloitre et al., 2012a; Resick et al., 2012, Schiavone et al., 2018a). If, based on screening, there is reason to believe that dissociation is part of the client's difficulties, the clinician should assess for the presence of a possible comorbid DDs.

The clinician should pay careful attention to the client's experience and maintaining the therapeutic relationship during the assessment, remembering that asking people to talk about experiences related to trauma means asking them to think about experiences they may find overwhelming. Clients with trauma histories may rightly fear becoming triggered. This can lead clients to avoid or curtail the assessment process, or to deny experiences in order to protect themselves from getting overwhelmed.

As a result, staying curious about and attuned to the client's experience throughout the assessment process and working with them to manage potential overwhelm are prerequisites for accurate assessment of TRDs and DDs. The assessor should especially watch for signs of reexperiencing and/or dysregulated arousal. It is important to be alert not just to symptoms of hyperarousal (e.g., shaking, hyperventilating, flushed face) but also to the presence of dissociation or hypoarousal (e.g., barely breathing, fixed staring, pallor, collapsed posture). If any of these occur, the assessor should stop and help the client ground themselves by using any or all of the following methods:

- Reorient the client to the current date and year and where they are.
- Remind the client that the trauma is not happening in the present moment.
- Encourage the client to look around the room and name and describe objects or colors that they see. (For additional guidance on grounding, see Appendix B: Grounding Script. Additional information on grounding techniques can be found in the accompanying workbook, *Finding Solid Ground Program Workbook: Overcoming Obstacles in Trauma Recovery* by Schielke et al., 2022)

- If the client is still having difficulty after reorienting to the present, consider asking them to list things and situations (especially positive developments and/or strengths) that are different in the here and now from the there and then. (For additional guidance on this, see Module 2, "Separating Past from Present," in the workbook.)

ASSESSING TRAUMA HISTORY

The presence of a trauma history is required for the diagnosis of a TRD, and having an understanding of the extent of a client's trauma history can help therapists plan and carry out effective treatment. At the same time, it is important to remember (and educate clients) that talking about details of traumatic experiences can be extraordinarily dysregulating and can trigger trauma-related symptoms (including reexperiencing, flashbacks, and other forms of dissociation) and/or intense emotions that last after the person leaves your office. This dysregulation may also lead a person who engages in risky behaviors aimed at distracting from and reducing overwhelm (e.g., substance use, self-harm) to engage in such behaviors. Therefore, discussions of trauma details are only recommended after a client has developed healthy coping skills adequate to the task of managing the inherently destabilizing process of talking about overwhelming experiences. For this reason, talking about the details of trauma is only recommended when it is clinically indicated or is legally necessary (such as in a forensic context) and should include a plan for how the person will manage possible dysregulation. Furthermore, inquiring about trauma history should come late in the assessment process, after asking about less difficult topics and a reasonable amount of rapport has been developed.

Clients who are not given guidance about the importance of carefully pacing discussions about trauma may feel obligated or pressured to disclose details of their trauma history. Providing education about the phases of trauma treatment, including that the first phase of treatment focuses on learning healthy ways to manage symptoms and emotions, can help clients learn the importance of self-care in healing from trauma. Clinicians should underscore the importance of staying grounded in the present while discussing the past and actively encourage clients to share only the amount of detail that they can tolerate.

To reduce clients' possible reluctance to engage in assessment for fear of getting triggered (and the risk of their talking about trauma in ways that trigger them), we recommend giving relevant education as part of the informed consent process. This includes letting clients know that they will *not* be asked to discuss trauma details; that questions about categories or kinds of trauma will be asked toward the end of the assessment, and the reasons for this; and that you want them to let you know if they are beginning to feel overwhelmed and need to stop or take a break.

It is our experience that most individuals experiencing acute trauma-related symptoms are relieved to hear this information. However, some people may interpret this to mean you "don't want to hear about it." This may trigger a trauma-related reaction to you, such as "you are just like all the other people who do not listen or care about me." The possibility of trauma-related reactions to the assessment process underscores the importance of informing traumatized individuals about this approach and its rationale before starting to ask trauma-related questions.

Some individuals may begin talking about traumatic experiences in response to questions about childhood, relational, and/or work history, however, and may become difficult to pause, interrupt, or redirect due to trauma-related reactions. If a client begins to share extensive detail about trauma at any point of an interview (which might mean they are getting increasingly "stuck in" and beginning to relive the past), compassionately interrupt and encourage them to keep their discussion of their history at a "headline level" (Loewenstein, 2006). For instance, the assessor could say, "Rather than go into details, which may lead you to feel overwhelmed or may even cause you to have difficulty later today, let's keep today's discussion at a 'headline level.' In other words, if you were to imagine the trauma as a news article, what would the title be? You don't have to share the whole story right now." (And if they need a reminder: "Try telling me just the title of the article, leaving out the details.")

We recommend that assessors initially focus on identifying whether the client has experienced trauma, using broad, open-ended questions, and gradually getting more specific if the client acknowledges trauma and can tolerate further questions. The assessor can inquire about categories of trauma and, if tolerable, ages of trauma incidence. Pause occasionally to ask the client how they are doing and to help them maintain grounding as indicated. Ask about experiences of childhood physical, sexual, and emotional abuse, neglect, and bullying as well as victimization in adulthood (e.g., sexual assault, interpersonal violence, stalking) and non-interpersonal trauma (e.g., car accidents, natural disasters, fires). One way to ensure comprehensive category coverage is to use a standardized trauma exposure measure (see next section). It is also useful to inquire about any history of substance abuse and mental illness in caregivers and family members.

The following are examples of broad questions about attachment relationships and caregiving experiences that can also help identify trauma history:

- Who did you turn to as a child when you were upset or hurt or sick? How would they typically respond?
- How was discipline handled in your household growing up? If you broke a rule, what would the consequences be?
- Have you ever had a sexual experience that made you feel uncomfortable or scared?
- Have you ever had any other experience that overwhelmed your ability to cope?

Note that some clients may not identify even the most severe experiences of childhood adversity as abusive, especially if these were framed as "normal" by those around them. This is why it can be useful to use phrases like "discipline" and "uncomfortable sexual experiences" as well as asking more directly about abuse and trauma. If a history of trauma is suspected or reported, the clinician can ask an open-ended question such as "How do you think that affected you?" and then move to a more structured exploration of PTSD symptoms, perhaps using a screening instrument such as the PTSD Checklist for DSM-5 (PCL-5, discussed below), which is available for free online through the National Center for PTSD.

ASSESSING DISSOCIATION

If a client has a trauma history, assessment for dissociation is warranted. When assessing dissociation, it is important to assess for each of the major types of dissociation, including depersonalization, derealization, dissociative amnesia (including fugue episodes), and identity alteration. We'll discuss each in turn below. General considerations for each type of dissociative symptom are as follows:

- Ensure that the symptoms reported do not occur solely in the context of substance intoxication or withdrawal, head injury, seizure, or other medical comorbidities.
- Follow up "yes" responses with requests for specific examples to ensure that the client is describing pathological dissociation rather than nonpathological dissociation (e.g., confusing "highway hypnosis" with dissociative amnesia or fugue) and is not misunderstanding the terminology (e.g., confusing auditory hallucinations with one's own thoughts).
- Clarify duration, frequency, and precipitants for reported symptoms.
- Give the client choice and control when possible. Some clients may feel obligated to disclose more detail than they can tolerate sharing unless explicitly encouraged to pay attention to and observe their own limits.
- Assist the client in getting regulated and/or grounded if they become overwhelmed or dissociated, as traumatized clients may react to clinicians with fear or automatic obedience as a result of past trauma.
- Be aware of the need to assess for dissociation multiple times during the course of treatment, as clients may be more aware of symptoms and/or more willing to disclose symptoms after a trusting therapeutic relationship has been established. Conversely, management of symptoms should improve with time, so ongoing assessment of dissociation is also a part of monitoring progress in therapy.
- Mirror the clients' own language when they describe dissociation (e.g., different terms for dissociative self-states or for traumatic experiences) unless there is a clear clinical rationale for doing otherwise, such as a concern that doing so would reinforce the perception that self-states are in fact separate people rather than aspects of one individual.

DEPERSONALIZATION AND DEREALIZATION

Depersonalization and derealization are experiences of disconnection or detachment, either from oneself (depersonalization) or the world (derealization).

Depersonalization questions

- Do you ever feel disconnected from your emotions?
- Do you ever feel like your thoughts are not your own?
- Do you ever feel detached from your body, as if it (or part of it) does not belong to you?
- Have you ever had the experience of watching yourself from outside your body (as if seeing yourself in a movie)?

Derealization questions

- Do you ever feel as if the world around you looks strange, unreal, or surreal?
- Do you ever feel like you're in a dream?

DISSOCIATIVE AMNESIA (INCLUDING FUGUE EXPERIENCES)

Dissociative amnesia refers to memory loss that is beyond the level of ordinary forgetfulness. However, not all amnesia is due to dissociation. In some cases, amnesia can result from failure to encode an event into memory, such as might occur if someone was so intoxicated that they could not encode what they did while drinking. *Dissociative* amnesia pertains to lack of memory for events that were encoded into memory but cannot be retrieved. Dissociative amnesia is not due to medical or organic causes such as intoxication or head injury. Dissociative amnesia can take many forms, including amnesia for traumatic events, for a period of one's life or significant life events (e.g., adolescence, one's wedding), for certain settings (e.g., school), or for day-to-day activities in the present. It is important to determine whether amnestic periods occurred solely in the past (e.g., around the time when a trauma was occurring) or are a part of the person's current day-to-day experience. When assessing for dissociative amnesia, the clinician should also assess for the presence of fugue states, where someone may travel to another place and not remember how they got there or why they went there.

Questions about present-day amnesia

- Do you ever have gaps in your memory or periods of time in day-to-day life that you can't account for?
- Do you ever find yourself somewhere and not know how you got there?
- Do you ever find things among your belongings and not know how you got them?
- Do people ever tell you that you have done or said things that you have no memory of doing or saying?

Questions about amnesia in the past

- Are there certain periods of your life (or important events) in the past that you don't remember?
- Do you have a clear memory of [past traumatic events] or are there pieces missing?

IDENTITY ALTERATION

Identity alteration refers to abrupt shifts between unintegrated self-states, or aspects of the self. These self-states exert influence over the individual's thoughts and behaviors such that those thoughts and behaviors are experienced as foreign or "not mine." While the experience of having different "sides," parts, or aspects of oneself is common across the lifespan and not pathological (e.g., having a "work side" and a "home side"), in complex DDs, internal self-states are typically experienced as more distinct and more foreign, and as exerting more control over the client's behavior counter to their stated wishes than would occur in someone without a DD. These self-states may be experienced as parts of the self, as alternate personalities, or, in some cultures where this is culturally normative, as experiences of supernatural possession. Clients may report a variety of types of self-states, including child states, internalized abuser/persecutor states, protector states, states with differing gender and/or sexual orientation, and nonhuman states.

When assessing for identity alteration, it is important to remember that, contrary to media portrayals suggesting that individuals with DID present with dramatic personality states and obvious state shifts, this view of DID is a myth. Although florid presentations occur in approximately 5% of DID patients (Kluft, 2009), typically DID patients present with a complicated mixture of psychiatric symptoms—mostly rather "hidden," unnoticed dissociative symptoms combined with PTSD, depression, anxiety, substance abuse, and eating disorders, as well as self-destructive and suicidal behavior, and somatoform and personality disorder symptoms (e.g., Brand et al., 2009b; Dell, 2002; Putnam et al., 1986; Rodewald et al., 2011).

Clinicians are also rarely aware that individuals with DID experience higher levels of first-rank symptoms (e.g., thought insertion or broadcasting, hearing voices, "made" impulses and actions) than do individuals with schizophrenia, with the exception of audible thoughts and thought broadcasting (Kluft, 1987; Ross et al., 1990). Clinicians are generally trained to associate hearing voices with psychosis, despite recent research showing that childhood trauma is frequently associated with hearing voices (Longden et al., 2012). Professionals should inquire about trauma history and dissociation as well as symptoms of psychosis when they assess patients reporting auditory hallucinations.

While some clients with complex DDs experience frank periods of amnesia during which another self-state takes full control, subtler manifestations of identity alteration are also possible and may be missed if the clinician is not aware of the broad range of ways dissociative self-states can intrude into the client's consciousness. This includes "passive influence phenomena" (feeling as if one is not fully in control over one's thoughts or behavior), where internal self-states may influence aspects of the client's experience and actions without assuming full executive control. These intrusions are often experienced in ways that may, on the surface, resemble symptoms of psychosis, such as "made" feelings, thoughts, and actions that occur seemingly out of the blue or out of the client's own control. Paul Dell has categorized dissociative intrusions as either partially excluded from consciousness (e.g., hearing voices, thought insertion/withdrawal, "made" actions/impulses) or fully excluded from consciousness (e.g., fugues, time loss) (Dell, 2006b; Dell & O'Neil, 2009). Intrusions can also be experienced as visual or auditory hallucinations. Clients may report hearing the voices of dissociative self-states from either inside or outside of their head; as will be discussed in greater detail later, hearing the voices of children is particularly suggestive of complex DDs rather than psychosis (Dorahy et al., 2009).

Should a person present with dissociative self-states, it is important to assess the degree of autonomy of the various self-states while being cautious not to ascribe more autonomy to them than they already possess. For example, clients may report that their self-states have names, but it is not advisable to encourage clients to name their self-states if they have not already done so.

The clinician should also be alert to more subtle cues that may indicate the presence of dissociation. Loewenstein (1991) describes a range of these, including:

- Micro-dissociations (briefly tuning out or losing track of the conversation)
- Contradictions in behavior or appearance (e.g., changes in tone of voice, pattern of speech, handedness, mannerisms, posture, or apparent age)
- Frequent blinking, eye fluttering, or eye rolling (may indicate the intrusion of other self-states)
- Fixed staring (may indicate spontaneous trancing)
- Referring to the self in the first-person plural ("we") or the body in a detached, depersonalized way ("the body" as opposed to "my body")

If any of these phenomena are observed, we recommend compassionately pointing these out and asking the client about their subjective experience. This line of questioning may yield further information about other self-states or dissociative symptoms. Questions may include the following:

- Do you ever feel as though there are multiple parts or sides of you that are so different that others might think you "seem like a different person"?
- Do you ever have thoughts (or feelings or actions) that seem out of your control or don't seem like yours?
- Do you ever feel like thoughts are being blocked or taken out of your head?
- Do you ever hear voices? If yes, do they seem to sound like children? Adults? Both? Are you hearing any voices now, as we're talking? If yes, what are they saying?

Assessing identity alteration can be particularly challenging. When identity dissociation is working as intended, clients may not have much awareness of dissociating. If they are aware of signs of their symptoms, they may not be aware that such experiences are abnormal and would be relevant to report. Conversely, they may be aware of their symptoms but actively deny or conceal these due to shame or lack of safety in the therapeutic relationship. They may worry that disclosing such symptoms will make them appear "crazy," and/or they may have had experiences of not being believed when they disclosed dissociative symptoms. Given the extent of relational trauma experienced by many dissociative clients, in the absence of efforts to cultivate safety, even skilled questioning may not elicit the necessary information.

For a semistructured interview that encompasses a wide range of dissociative phenomena (both observed and reported) and common comorbidities, see Loewenstein (1991).

ASSESSMENT OF DYSREGULATION

Dysregulation—of arousal, emotion, and behavior—is a pervasive issue in clients with TRDs and DDs (Brand & Lanius, 2014; Briere & Scott, 2015; Courtois & Ford, 2013; Frewen & Lanius, 2015; van der Kolk et al., 1996). Clients may be alternately overwhelmed by emotion and profoundly avoidant of emotion and/or may engage in a variety of unsafe behaviors to soothe intense emotion or punish themselves for having emotion. Emotion dysregulation often stems from developmental trauma and attachment difficulties, which may result in any or all of the following "rules" about emotions:

- Having emotions is wrong, bad, or a sign of weakness.
- Having emotions will lead to punishment or abuse from others.
- Emotions are unsafe and lead to violence, mockery, or abandonment.
- Emotions are untrustworthy.

- Emotions will not be met with empathy or understanding by others.
- Unsafe behaviors or dissociation are the only ways to manage strong emotions.

As a result of these experiences, many traumatized clients are alexithymic (unable to name or identify their emotions). They may not have an emotional vocabulary and/or may be accustomed to immediately numbing emotion through dissociation or distracting themselves through impulsive action or substance abuse. Their degree of disconnection from their bodies may impede their ability to sense somatic cues of various emotions (e.g., upset stomach indicating anxiety) early enough to successfully reregulate themselves before reaching a state of crisis. In clients with dissociative self-states, some emotions may be accessible to some self-states but not others, and self-states may have a limited range of emotional expression and tolerance.

If clients display nonverbal indicators of emotion during the assessment (e.g., smiling, sad facial expression, clenched fists) or are describing a situation that would be expected to provoke emotion, the clinician can ask what they are feeling in the moment or what they felt at the time. Some clients may use words like "upset" or "bad" and be unable to identify a more specific emotion, or may be unable to answer the question entirely, which provides valuable diagnostic information. In this case, they can be offered simple options (e.g., sad, mad, glad, afraid) to see if they can identify the emotion from a list. A handout with faces demonstrating what emotions "look like" can also be helpful.

SAFETY ASSESSMENT

Individuals with significant trauma histories are at increased risk for suicidal ideation, engaging in self-harm, and a range of unhealthy and/or unsafe behaviors as a means of reducing or distracting from overwhelm. As such, questions about these kinds of behaviors are an important part of understanding how a client is currently managing distress, their level of risk, and which unhealthy behaviors to target with replacement healthy coping skills such as those described in the program handouts.

It is important to remain nonjudgmental when discussing these behaviors. Clinicians need to be aware that unsafe behaviors may be the only way, or the only reliable way, the client knows how to manage and survive intense emotions, which can feel almost life-threatening to some traumatized individuals (Brand, 2001; Brand & Lanius, 2014). It can be helpful to explicitly talk about this in discussions with clients, underscoring that while these behaviors may not serve their best interests in the long term, these behaviors likely helped them survive and/or are the best strategies they've discovered so far—and that they can learn new ways of managing overwhelming emotion that support their health and recovery, such as those discussed in this program. It is important to know that the Treatment of Patients with Dissociative Disorders (TOP DD) Network research study recommended this approach to stabilizing safety struggles with DD participants. (Note: We use the phrase "the TOP DD Network study" to refer to the online research study that assessed the Finding Solid Ground program.) This study is discussed in detail in Chapter 4 of this book. The Finding Solid Ground program includes psychoeducational materials such as online videos and written and practice exercises. The written and practice exercises are available, as are handouts related to the topics covered in the TOP DD Network study, in the workbook that accompanies this book. Overall, the TOP DD Network patients showed improved emotion regulation, decreased dissociation, and reductions in self-injurious behavior, among other improvements; see Chapter 4 (Brand et al., 2019b).

Clients should be asked directly about a variety of potentially unsafe behaviors and their role in regulating emotion. Clients frequently experience shame about unsafe behaviors and are therefore less likely to talk about them unless asked in a compassionate, understanding manner. Important behaviors to ask about include alcohol use, substance use (including caffeine, nicotine, and misuse of prescriptions), disordered eating (overeating, restricting intake, purging), risky activities (related to sex, driving, etc.), excessive engagement in distraction/entertainment activities, shoplifting or other illegal activity, overspending, dysregulated sexual activity, and self-harm (including cutting, burning, hitting/banging, and skin picking). It is important to determine the context of these behaviors, including which emotions or situations tend to trigger them, and the consequences (both emotional and pragmatic). If the client is not aware of the triggers, the clinician can again offer options to determine if the unsafe behaviors are more often triggered by fear, anger, sadness, happiness, or shame (as we will discuss later, positive emotions such as joy or pride can also be potent triggers for those with TRD).

In clients with dissociative self-states, it is important to ask about the impact of these self-states on these behaviors and their safety, including dissociated self-injury, suicidality, aggression toward others, substance use, and other high-risk behaviors (Brand et al., 2019b). This should include an assessment of whether the client has a memory of engaging in the behaviors or if they occur during periods of amnesia, and if they have any sense of which self-states may be involved. It is also important to try to determine if any self-states are acting based on distorted beliefs about the impact of the actions of one self-state on the others or on "the body." Some highly dissociative clients have self-states that are experienced as so separate that those self-states may believe they can "kill" another self-state and then "take over control," not recognizing that a lethal suicide attempt will kill "the body" and all self-states. This belief can be held with close to delusional persistence in some individuals, therefore significantly increasing the client's risk for suicide attempts. As such, it is imperative to carefully assess for such "delusions of separateness" in treatment.

Questions that can be helpful include the following:

• Have you ever found injuries on your body or evidence of self-harm without knowing how it happened?

- Do you ever hear voices that tell you to harm yourself or anyone else? Do you ever do what they say?
- Do any of your self-states [or use client's words] threaten to harm any of the others? How would they do it?
- Do you ever lose time while driving or riding on public transportation? What happens?

In clients with dissociative self-states that engage in unsafe behaviors, discussion about unsafe behaviors can also provide an opportunity to model curiosity about, and compassion for, other self-states by validating the survival function of unsafe behaviors despite acknowledging that they are not serving the client well overall.

After the client's characteristic dysregulated behaviors have been identified, the intensity of urges, the frequency of engaging in the behaviors, and the severity of the outcomes should be monitored as the treatment progresses. Triggers for unsafe behaviors should be explored. It is also important to monitor whether clients who abuse substances are attending sessions under the influence, and if so, to address this with the client. As clients learn about, practice, and come to master new, recovery-focused coping skills (and those with dissociative self-states learn to communicate and cooperate across their self-states), these dysregulated behaviors tend to decrease in frequency (Brand et al., 2019b).

COMORBIDITY PROFILE

Trauma-related and dissociative disorders (including DID and OSDD), which are discussed below, are associated with a fairly wide range of possible comorbid symptoms and disorders (American Psychiatric Association, 2013; Brand et al., 2009b; Spiegel et al., 2011). It is particularly important to screen for the presence of mood and anxiety disorders, obsessive-compulsive disorder, substance use disorders, eating disorders, somatoform disorders, and personality disorders. It is often easier for clients to discuss these symptoms than those related specifically to trauma. Therefore, inquiring about symptoms related to these disorders should typically precede assessing for TRD.

ASSESSMENT TOOLS

Self-report measures

Because they are quick and easy to administer, self-report measures are an important tool in the assessment of TRD and DD. It is important to note, however, that self-report instruments are not diagnostic and should be used only to identify clients who would benefit from further assessment. It is crucial to know that self-report measures can produce false-positive findings, meaning that some clients who score above typical "cutoff scores" will not meet diagnostic criteria for the disorder in question. Some clients may misunderstand the items, may endorse largely nonpathological dissociative experiences, or may have another psychiatric condition that is associated with dissociative symptoms (e.g., PTSD). For these reasons, follow-up questions for symptoms endorsed (asking for descriptions of experiences of the symptoms) and/or use of a formal diagnostic interview (see below) is indicated when a person screens positive using self-assessment measures.

Conversely, people may underreport symptoms for a number of reasons. If you see what appears to be evidence of TRD or DD symptoms that are not endorsed, ask the person about what you observed in an open-ended, curious way that makes room for clarification.

LIFE EVENTS CHECKLIST FOR DSM-5 (LEC-5)

There are dozens of trauma exposure measures, and it is beyond the scope of this chapter to review more than one. The LEC-5 is one of the trauma exposure measures we recommend (Weathers et al., 2013). The LEC-5 is a self-report instrument that queries whether a person has been exposed to 16 kinds of events that can result in TRD. It also includes an item aimed at capturing whether a person has been exposed to any "very stressful" experiences not listed within the LEC-5's first 16 items. It is available for free online through the National Center for PTSD.

POSTTRAUMATIC STRESS DISORDER CHECKLIST FOR DSM-5 (PCL-5)

The PCL-5 (Blevins et al., 2015) is a 20-item self-report instrument that queries respondents about the DSM-5 criteria for "standard" PTSD. It is available for free online through the National Center for PTSD. A score of 33 has been suggested as indicative of a provisional positive screening result, and scores of 50 and above are considered suggestive of likely PTSD.

Notably, however, the PCL-5 does not ask about the dissociative symptoms of depersonalization or derealization, which are necessary to assess to ensure accurate subtype screening; the presence of either indicates that the "with dissociative symptoms" specifier (PTSD-D) is indicated. As such, this measure should be accompanied by interviewing about and/or administering a measure of dissociative symptoms.

Next, we review a few of the many tools used to assess dissociation.

DISSOCIATIVE EXPERIENCES SCALE (DES)

The DES-II (Bernstein & Putnam, 1986) is a 28-item self-report measure that inquires about various dissociative symptoms, including depersonalization, derealization, absorption, and amnesia. Patients are asked to indicate the percentage of time that this applies to them, from 0% (never) to 100% (always). The scores for each item are averaged to yield a final score between 0 and 100 for all 28 items.

A cutoff score of 30 identified patients with already diagnosed DID among a sample of general psychiatric patients (Carlson et al., 1993). The average DES score for patients with known DID was 42.8, which was significantly higher than all other patients, including those with PTSD. The majority of the patients with a DES score above 30 who were not diagnosed with DID (i.e., they were "false positives") met criteria for another DD or PTSD. Some of these high-scoring false-positive cases may have met criteria for DID if further testing had been done, but the study did not include formal diagnostic assessment. A subset of eight DES-II items makes up the DES taxon subscale (Waller & Ross, 1997). The DES-II is free and available at www.isst-d.org/resources.

Multiscale Dissociation Inventory (MDI)

The MDI (Briere et al., 2005) is a 30-item measure of six forms of dissociation: depersonalization, derealization, memory disturbance (dissociative amnesia), disengagement (disconnection from surroundings), emotional constriction (dissociation of emotions), and identity dissociation (identity alteration). The MDI is the only dissociation self-report measure that is population normed and yields T scores, making it particularly useful in forensic assessment and other contexts in which the assessor wants to compare an individual's reported level of dissociation to that of the general population. The MDI is free and available at www.isst-d.org/ resources.

Multidimensional Inventory of Dissociation

The Multidimensional Inventory of Dissociation 6.0 (MID-6) (Dell, 2006a) is a 218-item self-report measure of pathological dissociation. It does not specify a time frame for experiencing the dissociative experiences, so clinicians need to interpret the results with awareness that the client may not currently experience all of the items they endorsed. The MID is the only self-report measure that includes validity scales (e.g., Defensiveness, Rare Symptoms, Attention-Seeking Behavior, Factitious Behavior, and Emotional Suffering). As the longest self-report measure of dissociation, it assesses a wide range of pathological dissociative symptoms. In cases in which the MID-6's "I Have DID" subscale is elevated, the individual may be overly invested in having DID as a diagnosis or may feel that the disorder is a crucial element of their identity. The MID and its scoring guide are free and available at www.mid-assessment.com.

Somatoform Dissociation Questionnaire (SDQ-20 and SDQ-5)

The SDQ-20 (Nijenhuis et al., 1996) is a 20-item self-report measure that assesses the somatic, or "somatoform," experiences associated with dissociation within the past year. A score of 35 on the SDQ-20 is typically considered to indicate a high level of somatoform dissociation. A short five-item screen, the SDQ-5, can be useful in identifying possible DDs when a cutoff score of 8 is used (Nijenhuis, 2010). The DDQ-5 and SDQ-20 are free and available at www.isst-d.org/resources.

Scale for Tonic Immobility Occurring Post Trauma (STOP)

The STOP is a self-report measure designed to assess tonic immobility responses that persist following trauma (Lloyd et al., 2019). As we will discuss later, tonic immobility is a late-stage immobilizing defense mechanism that is activated when an individual perceives that more active defenses (i.e., flight, fight) are not available or will not succeed, as is frequently the case in the types of protracted childhood abuse experienced by many with TRD. It is characterized by simultaneous activation of the sympathetic and parasympathetic nervous systems. Chronic activation of this defense mechanism may underpin some symptoms seen in TRD, including tension, immobility, and some dissociative symptoms. This scale is available in the supplemental materials of Lloyd et al. (2019).

Structured and semistructured interviews

STRUCTURED CLINICAL INTERVIEW FOR DSM-IV
DISSOCIATIVE DISORDERS REVISED (SCID-D-R)

The SCID-D-R is a semistructured interview that clinicians can use to determine if an individual meets criteria for any of the DSM-IV-TR DD diagnoses (dissociative amnesia, dissociative fugue, depersonalization disorder, DID, and dissociative disorder not otherwise specified [DDNOS]) (Steinberg, 1994, 2000). The SCID-D-R assesses for five groups of dissociative symptoms (amnesia, depersonalization, derealization, identity alteration, and identity confusion). Because the SCID-D-R requires patients to provide examples and elaboration, and because interviewers score observations of dissociative behavior, the use of this interview results in fewer false-positive diagnoses than relying on self-report measures. Steinberg's field trial assessed the groups at baseline, 2 weeks, and 6 months. The weighted kappas for the presence as well as the severity of dissociative symptoms was good to excellent, as was agreement between raters about the presence of a DD (Steinberg, 2000). A recent meta-analysis of the SCID-D (i.e., the original version of the Structured Clinical Interview for Dissociative Disorders) and SCID-D-R found that the overall interview score as well as each of the five subscales, particularly amnesia and identity alteration, showed strong effect sizes in differentiating DD from non-DD disorders, thus establishing the interview as having a strong empirical basis for assessing DDs in clinical and forensic contexts (Mychailyszyn et al., 2021). Note: The SCID-D-R assesses DDs per DSM-IV-TR criteria, but the client's responses can be used to determine if the client meets criteria for a DD according to DSM-5 criteria. A reissued version of the SCID-D is being published (Steinberg, in press). It will include the SCID-D and SCID-D-R questions that are necessary for diagnosing DDs, as well as a limited number of optional questions to assist interviewers new to diagnosing DDs. The reissued version of the SCID-D will allow for making diagnoses based on DSM-5 as well as ICD-11 criteria for DDs (Marlene Steinberg, personal communication, January 1, 2020). The SCID-D-R is available for purchase at www.isst-d.org/resources.

DISSOCIATIVE DISORDERS INTERVIEW SCHEDULE (DDIS)

The DDIS (Ross, n.d.; Ross et al., 1989a) is a semistructured interview tool that can be used to diagnose OSDD (formerly DDNOS), DID, and dissociative amnesia. It also provides information on secondary symptoms and comorbidities of DID (e.g., substance abuse, somatic complaints, major depressive episodes, and BPD features), as well as childhood abuse history. Respondents answer questions

that are linked to DSM-IV or DSM-5 criteria for DDs using a "yes or no" response format. Although there are single close-ended (yes versus no) questions
related to most of the DSM DD criteria, no follow-up descriptions of symptoms
are elicited. This reduces administration time and the amount of clinician training
required, but the absence of follow-up inquiries about endorsed symptoms may
lead to false classifications, particularly in complicated diagnostic cases. The
DDIS had a sensitivity of 90% and a specificity of 100% for the diagnosis of DID
when administered to a mixed group of patients with DID, eating disorders, panic
disorder, and schizophrenia (Ross & Ellason, 2005).The DDIS is available free of
charge at www.isst-d.org/resources.

DIFFERENTIAL DIAGNOSIS OF DISSOCIATIVE DISORDERS

DDs are frequently confused with a range of other psychiatric disorders, particularly psychotic disorders and personality disorders. While these disorders have
some commonalities, there are also distinguishing features that can assist in the
differential diagnosis. These will be reviewed below.

DID and Other DDs

The hallmark of DID and OSDD-1 (i.e., Other Specified Dissociative Disorder-1)
is the presence of identity alteration due to dissociative self-states. DID is
characterized by the presence of both distinct self-states and the capacity for complete amnesia between self-states (though even clients with DID may not be consistently amnestic for all actions of all self-states). OSDD-1 presents similarly to
DID except that self-states are not as fully differentiated (e.g., self-states may be
experienced as the same individual at different ages) and/or the amnesia experienced between self-states may be more permeable (e.g., there may be a sense
of fogginess or "graying out" as opposed to frankly blacking out or losing time).
Some clients with DID may initially appear to have OSDD-1 until the full extent
of the symptoms experienced becomes clear. Both DID and OSDD-1 are associated with high levels of a broad range of dissociative symptoms, including depersonalization, derealization, and amnesia, but these symptoms are not specific
for DID and OSDD-1. In the absence of identity alteration, these symptoms are
more consistent with another DD, such as dissociative amnesia or depersonaliza-
tion/derealization disorder, or, in the presence of trauma and PTSD symptoms,
DPTSD.

Psychotic disorders

Some of the symptoms of DID and OSDD-1 can be confused with those of primary psychotic disorders. As will be described below, there are some hallmark

features that can help make the differential diagnosis and some that are less helpful (Dorahy et al., 2009; Ellason & Ross, 1995; Kluft, 1987; Laddis & Dell, 2012; Schiavone et al., 2018b).

Both patients with complex DDs and those with psychotic disorders may present with the following:

- Dissociative symptoms
- Histories of trauma
- Schneiderian first-rank symptoms, such as commenting or arguing voices, passive influence phenomena (e.g., "made" thoughts, behaviors), and thought withdrawal and broadcasting)[1]
- Hearing voices (either from inside or from outside the head)

There are, however, several overall differences in phenomenology in patients with DID and OSDD-1 compared to psychotic patients. Those with DID and OSDD-1 typically present with:

- More severe dissociative symptoms
- Absence of negative symptoms (e.g., flat affect, amotivation, anhedonia)
- Passive influence experiences (e.g., thoughts, feelings, and behaviors that feel as though they are being imposed by an outside force) in the absence of associated delusional beliefs about the source or nature of the experiences (e.g., delusions that their body is being controlled by God, or by a celebrity via social media)
- Auditory hallucinations that involve multiple voices, usually with an onset before age 18 and including child voices
- Nonauditory hallucinations (e.g., smelling sewage or feeling crawling sensations on the skin)

Finally, it is possible for individuals to meet criteria for both a DD and a psychotic disorder, although it is not common. Note, however, that per the DSM-5, DDs are more prevalent than psychotic disorders, and that a psychotic disorder should not be diagnosed if the symptoms are already accounted for or better explained by DD.

Borderline personality disorder

While BPD and complex DDs can and often do coexist, they may also be confused with each other. Both BPD and DID/OSDD-1 are associated with childhood trauma, identity confusion, dissociative symptoms, chronic suicidality, emotion dysregulation, and impulse dyscontrol, including self-harm and substance abuse.

---

1. These were once considered a hallmark of schizophrenia, but recent literature has suggested that they may in fact be more common in DID than in schizophrenia.

However, while dissociative symptoms are common to both disorders, they are typically more severe overall in DID/OSDD-1, and true dissociative amnesia for present-day events is not typical of BPD, whereas it is a hallmark of DID (Boon & Draijer, 1993b; Laddis et al., 2017). DID patients also typically report much more prominent identity alteration and the presence of markedly distinct self-states (Laddis et al., 2017). Identity changes in BPD are thought to be related more to emotion dysregulation and intense emotional flooding (e.g., an angry self and a happy self that behave differently) as opposed to the more fully elaborated and ego-dystonic self-states seen in DID and OSDD-1, some of which have recollections of behaviors or traumas that the individual does not recall during shifts in state.

From a psychosocial perspective, the trauma history found in DID/OSDD-1 tends to have an earlier onset and to be more severe and chronic than in BPD (Boon & Draijer, 1993a). Individuals with DID often have more organized thinking, greater capacity to form a working alliance, and greater capacity for self-reflection (Brand et al., 2009a). DID and OSDD-1 patients may have longstanding relationships or may be entirely avoidant of relationships but are not as prone to relational chaos as are individuals with BPD. They are at risk for ongoing abusive relationships, however.

PSYCHOLOGICAL TESTING

There are important considerations in the interpretation of commonly used psychological tests (e.g., the Minnesota Multiphasic Personality Inventory-2 [MMPI-2]) in patients with DID/OSDD. It has been repeatedly demonstrated that across a wide range of psychological instruments, highly traumatized individuals, including those with DID/OSDD, tend to produce profiles that can be misinterpreted as invalid or suggestive of malingering due to elevations on validity scales that include trauma-related symptoms and the wide range of endorsed clinical symptoms (Brand et al., 2016b, 2017a, 2017b). These scales typically include items that were considered to be either bizarre or unusual in the general population at the time when many tests were developed. However, when these validity scales are studied more closely with traumatized people, many of the endorsed items overlap substantially with known dissociative symptoms (identity alteration, depersonalization, derealization, amnesia) or other trauma-related phenomena such as mistrust of others, depression, and hearing dissociation-related voices. Many of the items endorsed by severely dissociative individuals also overlap substantially with symptoms of temporal lobe dysfunction (e.g., olfactory and visual hallucinations). A link between TRD, including DID and OSDD-1, and temporal lobe dysfunction has therefore been suggested (Schiavone et al., 2018b). Therefore, these seemingly invalid profiles may not indicate malingering in some cases. Rather, they may reflect an endorsement of genuine symptoms, many of which may be linked to trauma, with an established neurobiological origin. In light of this, caution should be used when interpreting the psychological profiles of complex trauma patients. For a recent detailed overview of relevant studies' guidance regarding the interpretation of specific measures, please see Brand et al. (2017a, 2017b, 2018).

ASSESSING TREATMENT PROGRESS

Patients' response to trauma treatment can be measured through repeated use of symptom measures, such as the PCL-5 and MDI (see above). Measurement of changes in symptoms is important in that it informs clinicians about the patient's symptomatology, which can impact daily functioning and may influence the focus and pacing of treatment. However, it is also crucial for therapists to be aware of a range of adaptive capacities that may be influenced by trauma and attachment history. To facilitate treatment planning and the monitoring of progress in treatment for individuals with complex and/or severe DD, we created the Progress in Treatment Questionnaires (PITQ; Schielke et al., 2017). Developed to evaluate therapeutic progress in terms of the development of adaptive capacities that are enhanced or developed over time in treatment, these measures assess progress toward expert-identified targets of treatment for complex trauma-related symptoms and reactions (Brand et al., 2012b; International Society for the Study of Dissociation, 2011). Although the measures were developed specifically for individuals with DDs, most of the adaptive capacities assessed in the measures are relevant for a wide range of trauma survivors.

The Progress in Treatment Questionnaire—Therapist (PITQ-t) is a therapist-completed measure; the Progress in Treatment Questionnaire—Patient (PITQ-p) is a patient self-report measure. Both are available free of charge at http://topddst udy.com/pitq.php and in Appendix A of this book. These measures are aimed at assessing the patient's ability to manage their safety, symptoms, emotions, relationships, and well-being.

Completing a PITQ-t enables therapists to consider multiple areas of functioning that may be challenging for DD patients, as well as the relative strength of a range of expert-identified abilities targeted in DD and complex trauma treatment. This information can guide treatment planning.

The PITQ-p enables therapists to quickly assess multiple areas of functioning that DD patients can find challenging and need assistance with managing. Patients can periodically complete a PITQ-p to provide important information that can focus treatment and the therapist's ability to individualize treatment according to the individual's current level of adaptive abilities. Completing the PITQ-p encourages patients to reflect on their progress toward treatment goals. We have found that periodically inviting patients to complete the PITQ-p increases their awareness of the extent to which they are using healthy coping techniques and often encourages them to increase their use of healthy coping skills assessed by the measure (e.g., grounding, distinguishing past versus present).

The PITQ-t and the PITQ-p have demonstrated good internal reliability and concurrent relationships with validated measures of emotion regulation, PTSD and dissociative symptoms, and quality of life (Schielke et al., 2017). Higher

scores are associated with patients experiencing greater levels of positive emotion
and lower levels of self-harm, dangerous behaviors, and impulsivity.

CONCLUSION

Psychological trauma should be routinely inquired about in all clinical and forensic contexts. Because it can be difficult for clients to discuss, interviewers
should generally assess trauma history toward the end of the interview with sensitivity to the possibility of dysregulation. The client may require assistance with
grounding and containment if they become overwhelmed during assessment. If
a history of trauma is reported, the information gathered from a combination
of validated self-report and/or clinician-administered tools will be useful along
with a thorough clinical interview to screen for and delineate the broad range of
symptoms, including dissociation, that are common in TRDs. Unsafe behaviors
need to be explored in a nonjudgmental way and acute safety issues addressed.
Clinicians should be aware of common comorbidities and differential diagnoses
for dissociative symptoms and of some of the key distinguishing indicators that
will allow for correct diagnosis of TRDs/DDs. Thorough trauma-informed assessment will allow for timely diagnosis and trauma-informed treatment of these
often highly impairing conditions.

3

The Neurobiology of Trauma-Related Disorders

What Patients and Therapists Need to Know

As we have discussed, individuals who have experienced severe and repeated trauma typically struggle with a range of serious physical and emotional symptoms. Some of these symptoms include feeling chronically on edge, chronically numb and flat, or alternating between the two; feeling like previously experienced traumas are happening again in the present (reexperiencing emotions and/or sensations); spacing out or detaching from reality; difficulties with thinking or attention; unusual sensory experiences; and physical experiences like pain, difficulty breathing, digestive problems, or sexual problems. Those who are not knowledgeable about complex trauma may conclude that such a severe and varied constellation of symptoms must be inexplicable, unrelated, exaggerated, or even completely made up. Many patients with trauma-related disorders (TRDs) have spent years hearing and believing such messages from health care providers and possibly friends and family. This often leaves them in a state of confusion and distress in which they may belittle and disrespect themselves and their experiences. They may feel they are "making it all up," are "too sensitive," or maybe are even "crazy." Therapists working with chronically traumatized individuals must have a coherent theoretical framework for understanding these symptoms in order to educate their patients and to guide their response to what can seem like a baffling level of wide-ranging problems.

Therapists come with a variety of theoretical backgrounds and preferred models for understanding and explaining TRDs. Some of these already explicitly incorporate the body (Ogden et al., 2006a; van der Kolk, 2014). A neurobiological understanding, drawn from the most recent scientific literature, is a vital underpinning to truly understanding and treating the enduring impact of complex trauma, and can complement a variety of other models and orientations, both explicitly body-oriented and otherwise (Cozolino, 2017). It is only through a fully trauma-informed and neurobiology-informed psychotherapeutic lens that therapists and patients can fully grasp why and how traumas that may have occurred decades earlier continue to haunt and "echo" through patients' day-to-day emotional and physiological response to current stressors and relationships, strongly impacting their sense of themselves, others, and the world. Such a lens can also help both the therapist and the patient to understand why change may occur so slowly, and to maintain hope in the face of setbacks and obstacles.

As we will review below, the scientific literature is increasingly demonstrating that the range of symptoms experienced by patients with TRDs is well explained by changes in the brain that have been repeatedly shown to occur in these patients. It is essential for therapists to have at least a basic understanding of the structures and processes that underlie common trauma-related symptoms and be able to explain these to patients in simple language. Providing an accessible introduction to the neurobiology of TRD is frequently an important intervention, which is why we include a very basic discussion about the neurobiology of trauma in the Finding Solid Ground program. Education about the neurobiology of trauma can reduce patients' shame by confirming that symptoms are understandable, are not consciously "made up," and are not unique to the patient. While some patients may feel discouraged by the idea that there is something "wrong" with their brain, this information can also instill hope by providing education that the patient can help their brain to heal from trauma with treatment, particularly if they practice self-care and symptom management techniques. As patients learn how important it is for them to actively work to help their brains and bodies heal from trauma by using the healthy methods of coping that therapists and the Finding Solid Ground program teach, their motivation to practice these methods typically increases. To this end, this chapter will present the recent literature on the neurobiology of TRD. We will pay particular attention to the clinical relevance of this literature, and how it can guide therapists in conceptualizing and understanding trauma-related presentations. We attempt to make this information easy to understand, yet admittedly this is challenging given the complexity of the human nervous system. We will end each section with a "Key Points" box written in patient-friendly language that will help therapists distill the most important aspects of each section and communicate these points to their patients in an accessible way.

BASIC NEUROBIOLOGY AND THE TRIUNE BRAIN MODEL

The nervous system, which includes the brain, the spinal cord, and nerves throughout the body, is responsible for almost everything we do, from complicated tasks, like problem-solving and daydreaming, to simple things, like a leg jerk in response to being tapped on the knee. The nervous system is divided into two components, called central and peripheral. Both components are essential in directing and maintaining trauma-related symptoms. Here, we will briefly overview both components and highlight their relevance to TRD.

The peripheral nervous system consists of those parts of the nervous system that are outside of the brain and spinal cord, such as the nerves that communicate with the heart, stomach, muscles, and other parts of the body. One part of the peripheral nervous system, called the autonomic nervous system, controls basic functions of the body like heart rate, breathing, digestion, and sweating. The autonomic nervous system helps to regulate the level of arousal, which can be broadly thought of as the difference between a tense, high-energy state and a low-energy one (this is often thought to be a relaxed state, but, as we will discuss below, can also represent another kind of survival response to trauma). Changes between these two states are managed by the two divisions of the autonomic nervous system: the sympathetic division, whose activation typically increases tension and energy to facilitate activity (such as flight or fight), and the parasympathetic division (often referred to as "rest and digest"), which typically decreases tension and energy (Kandel et al., 2000). In the context of TRD, the autonomic nervous system is involved in enacting the physiological/somatic response to danger: The sympathetic nervous system, when activated, produces increased heart rate, faster breathing, sweating, and shaking (as one might need if preparing to run away or fight back), whereas the parasympathetic nervous system coordinates the opposite response, including slowing down of the heartbeat and breath (as one might need if trying to escape danger by playing dead). As we will discuss, either of these can occur in response to threat depending on the nature of the threat, the past experiences of a particular person, and the survival strategies that have been perceived as most effective during previous traumas. Understanding these two divisions of the nervous system and their widespread effects on the body can help the clinician to more quickly notice subtle changes in their patients' level of arousal and understand how to intervene based on which part of the system is overactive.

Clinical Example: A patient begins discussing a memory of a past assault and becomes distressed. She does not respond when you ask her what is happening. You notice that her face is flushed, her hands are shaking, she appears tense, and her breath is very rapid. You realize that all of these body changes have the same underlying explanation—the sympathetic nervous system is being activated—and realize that her level of arousal is too high to process effectively. You engage her in a deep breathing exercise to regulate her breath, which helps her body to calm down through activation of the parasympathetic nervous system. The activation of the parasympathetic nervous system reverses some of these physiological changes and you are able to continue the session.

By contrast, another patient, also discussing a memory of a previous assault, becomes mute and very pale, slumps over, and seems to breathe in a very shallow manner. You realize that these are signs that her level of arousal is too low and engage her in an activity involving moving her limbs and standing up, which helps counter the physiological changes of parasympathetic activation.

In both cases, recognizing the characteristic changes associated with activation of the two branches of the peripheral nervous system allows you to better hypothesize about which extreme of arousal the patient is experiencing, and better choose an intervention to counter it. In other words, interventions that are optimal to target and resolve high levels of arousal may not be effective for regulating low levels of arousal, and vice versa.

The central nervous system is made up of the spinal cord, which transmits signals between the brain and the body, and the brain itself. The brain is made up of several different areas, including the brainstem, which is at the base of the brain and connects the brain to the spinal cord; the cerebellum, which is traditionally associated with motor coordination but also has other roles; and the cerebrum and its outermost layer, the cerebral cortex, which are divided into four lobes: frontal, parietal, occipital, and temporal. While all of these areas interact, and most things that people do require input from multiple brain areas, there are some broad associations between certain types of activities and certain parts of the brain. The frontal lobes are typically associated with complex thinking (including planning ahead) and personality; the parietal lobes with interpreting five sense information, particularly touch; the occipital lobes with sight; and the temporal lobes with hearing, language, memory, and emotion. Aside from the cerebral cortex, the cerebrum also contains various subcortical (or beneath the cortex) structures, including the structures of the limbic system (many people have heard of the amygdala, which is one of the parts of the limbic system) (Kandel et al., 2000). These structures are stereotypically associated with generating emotions, though, as we will discuss further below, other areas of the brain are increasingly thought to be equally important.

There are many ways of thinking about the how different parts of the brain interact to produce human experience. MacLean's (1990) triune brain model, which is particularly useful for understanding TRD, divides the parts of the brain into three interacting subsystems that, he proposes, evolved in sequence: the reptilian complex, the paleomammalian complex, and the neomammalian complex. Each subsystem is composed of several areas of the brain that, in his model, evolved around the same time.

The reptilian complex includes the brainstem and midbrain, has a diverse range of functions and structures, and includes many areas relevant to TRD, including the periaqueductal gray matter, which is involved in defensive behavior as well as some basic emotional systems (we will further discuss this later in this chapter). The reptilian complex, the most primitive subsystem, controls basic human survival needs. This includes functions necessary for life such as breathing and heart rate (via the autonomic nervous system as discussed above) as well as some aspects of emotional responses, particularly fast responses to basic emotions, and some aspects of our ability to notice and respond to dangerous situations even before we become consciously aware of them ("subliminal" triggers).

The paleomammalian complex, which includes the limbic system, is responsible for coordinating more complicated (though still relatively fast) emotional responses, including the social emotions involved in attachment and social bonding.

The neomammalian complex, which includes the cerebral cortex, is responsible for the most complicated thinking, such as planning and thinking abstractly, as well as symbolic language (using words to represent concepts) (MacLean, 1990; Panskepp, 2004).

The subsystems of the triune brain that we described above do not work separately from each other due to their dense interconnections. For example, in the context of painful but manageable emotions produced by other areas of the brain, the neomammalian complex, which is responsible for thinking and planning, can often provide a context and language for the emotion that allows the emotion to be used to provide information about how to respond appropriately to a situation (e.g., a feeling of anger might be used as a signal that it is necessary to set a boundary, and a person might then decide how to do so calmly and thoughtfully). The cerebral cortex can also "turn down the volume" on emotions by thinking about them and analyzing their context, which leads to a biological turning down of the emotional response in the areas of the brain where the emotion was produced (this is also referred to as "top-down processing"). However, as is particularly relevant in patients with TRD, this can occur the other way around ("bottom up") as well. Subcortical areas, including elements of the reptilian and paleomammalian complexes, can respond quickly to elements of a person's surroundings, including reminders of past traumas (locations, smells, people, etc.), and direct the entire system, leading to a "turning off" of the neomammalian complex, and powerful responses driven by strong emotion. A trauma survivor may respond by suddenly running away or exploding in anger, responses that may have been important for survival during the trauma but now no longer serve the person in the present. This turning off of the thinking parts of the brain leads to significant impairment in patients' ability to regulate the intensity of their emotions, put experiences into words, and respond flexibly and in a planned, logical way to stressful situations. Instead, there may be impulsive behaviors, such as anger outbursts or sudden flight, that patients themselves cannot consciously explain or understand. This inability to make sense of their own behavior, or to understand why they might have acted in ways that appear out of character despite "knowing" intellectually that another reaction would be more effective, can be incredibly distressing for patients, so this can be one particular area where psychoeducation grounded in neurobiology can be tremendously helpful in decreasing distress and self-judgment.

Clinical Example: A client is in the bathroom when her partner comes up behind her and unexpectedly touches her shoulder. It is very important to her to never perpetrate violence toward anyone, but she suddenly shoves him into the wall and runs out of the room. Later, she feels intense shame and cannot explain why she behaved aggressively, when she knows that her partner is a safe person who did not mean any harm toward her. You are able to explain to her that at times, subcortical areas of her brain might respond extremely quickly to cues related to past trauma, to the point where her cerebral cortex is not able to inhibit the automatic defensive reaction that comes from a more primitive brain area. You are able to help her see that while she is responsible for helping her nervous system to recover from trauma, her actions in that moment were not a reflection on her personality and do not mean that she is a violent person. This reduces her shame and confusion.

In people with TRD, there may also be dissociative responses involving excessive turning off of emotions and physical feelings, leading to dissociative shutdown, numbness, or collapse caused by excessive turning down of emotions in response to threat. Again, patients may be unable to consciously explain or make sense of these reactions, as they occur below the level of conscious awareness, leading to further confusion and distress for both the patient and those around them. Many of the behaviors and responses seen in TRD can therefore be seen not as reasoned strategies to respond to present-day events but as unconscious and primitive defensive responses to perceived imminent threat to survival (whether or not such a threat exists in the present day). Understanding these reactions as defensive responses allows for a way of making sense of where these reactions come from, and a way of approaching them without judgment or shame.

Clinical Example: A patient has a disagreement with his partner. His partner raises her voice, and the patient collapses into a chair and stops responding verbally. His partner becomes more upset with him, believing that he is ignoring her on purpose, which causes further tension in their relationship. The patient later insists that he was unable to speak or move in that moment, but cannot explain why. In your next session, you are able to educate the patient about defensive responses and help him to explain to his partner that in moments of distress, survival responses are activated by more primitive brain areas that are not under conscious control. This helps both of them to interpret his behavior from a trauma-informed lens and reduces conflict between them.

KEY POINTS

The brain, spinal cord, and peripheral nerves, which together make up the nervous system, are responsible for coordinating almost everything that happens in our minds and bodies, from simple things, like making your knee jerk when someone taps on it, to complicated things, like daydreaming or planning how to get to the grocery store. The central nervous system is made up of the brain and the nerves in the spinal cord. All of the other nerves, including the ones that communicate with body parts like the muscles, stomach, heart, and lungs, are in the peripheral nervous system. The peripheral nervous system controls what happens in our organs and muscles. It is called *peripheral* because it is outside of the central nervous system, and the central nervous system gives it directions. When something happens that might be dangerous, our peripheral nervous system can make changes to get us ready to run away or fight back. For example, our muscles get tight, our eyes get wide, our skin gets hot, our heart starts to race, and we start to breathe faster. The part of the peripheral nervous system that does this is the sympathetic nervous system. As we will talk about later, different people's nervous systems have learned to react differently to trauma. While some people react by getting very energetic and ready to escape or fight, other people's nervous systems have learned that it is safer to just shut down. Often, people who have been through a lot of trauma starting at a very young age react by shutting down; we will talk about this below. The peripheral nervous system helps with shutting down, too, by making the breathing rate and the heart rate very slow, making the skin pale, and making the muscles limp. The part of the peripheral nervous system that causes this shutdown is the parasympathetic nervous system.

The central nervous system, especially the brain, is responsible for coordinating these kinds of reactions and also for creating thoughts, emotions, and plans and processing information from the five senses. Different parts of the brain are more responsible for different types of activities. Some parts of the brain such as the reptilian brain are very old and evolved very early. These parts of the brain are responsible for controlling basic body functions like eating, sleeping, and breathing but are also responsible for reacting quickly to signs of danger and emotions like terror and fear. In addition, the reptilian brain in concert with the limbic brain is also involved in more complicated emotional processes, including seeking out other people for connection. Finally, the most recently evolved parts of the brain are the parts that are involved in complicated thoughts, planning, and making decisions. This is important because people who have been through trauma are often self-critical, believing that they should be able to "just think about things differently" or "be rational." However, thinking is only one small part of what the brain and nervous system know how to do, and only one small part of the information that directs our reactions. When earlier areas of the brain react to danger, people might act in ways that do not make sense to them, or that they do not have words for. We can understand these better when we recognize that these reactions are directed by other parts of the brain.

THE DEFENSE CASCADE

As noted above, many symptoms of TRD can be seen as instinctive attempts to defend against what a person's mind and body consider to be threats to their life (whether or not there are in fact objective threats in the present) rather than a voluntary way of engaging with the world. Schauer and Elbert (2010) propose the defense cascade model as a way of understanding how people try to survive in the face of trauma or reminders of trauma. They propose that most people who have not previously been conditioned by prior trauma to respond to trauma in any specific way will first notice a threat on a subconscious level and respond with an initial orienting freeze, which is a brief period of stillness during which the person tries to figure out what the danger is and where it is. This is followed by trying an orderly series of additional survival strategies to end the threatening situation with minimal harm to the person.

If the person perceives that they might be able to get away, there is an effort to flee or fight off the attacker, characterized by a burst of energy and activity in the sympathetic nervous system. These responses are called "mobilizing" responses because they involve increased activity and movement. If these strategies have been tried and have failed, or if the person perceives that escape is impossible (e.g., if they are already physically hurt or if the perpetrator is too close or too strong to allow for running away), there is a shift toward immobilizing defenses, which are characterized by stillness. First, there is a period of tonic immobility (tense, high-energy stillness), where the sympathetic and parasympathetic systems are working at the same time, and then a predominantly parasympathetic response called emotional collapse/shutdown, which is characterized by low energy, absence of pain, and emotional numbness. In a situation of overwhelming and unescapable trauma, numbing and separating from the traumatic experience in this way is a self-protective and essential survival strategy.

In individuals without TRD, the immobilizing defenses (those involving stillness and collapse) are usually not elicited until after more active responses have failed, because escape from danger is always preferable if it is possible. People who have experienced repeated or protracted trauma, however, have learned through long-term danger (e.g., ongoing abuse) that the immobilizing defenses are the safest and most effective response to inescapable threat. Thus, they may have developed a deeply held belief (in the body as well as in the mind) that it is never possible to successfully prevent, escape, or interrupt threatening situations. They may have been conditioned to believe that running away or fighting back in the face of inescapable danger is not effective (e.g., due to the far smaller size of a child compared to an adult perpetrator) or will even worsen the threat to survival (e.g., by drawing the attention of or further angering the perpetrator). Therefore, even if the situation in the present may be escapable, and a mobilizing defense would be more functional, the person may still automatically default to immobilizing defenses based on past learning.

Clinical Example: A patient with a history of severe physical abuse by her father is repeatedly verbally berated by a coworker. Others in her workplace typically respond to this coworker by leaving the room (a "flight" response) or telling him to stop (a "fight" response). The patient tells herself that the next time it happens, she will stand up to him, and she plans exactly what she can say or do. However, each time it happens, she begins to feel numb and unable to move her body, and she stays in her chair staring into space until he leaves (a "freeze" response). She feels shame and does not understand why she does not stand up for herself when everyone else seems to be able to. You explain to her that most people, when they face a threat that they believe they can overcome, will mobilize to escape or fight back, but that in her case, because of her childhood trauma history, it makes sense that she would be unable to move, because her nervous system has learned that more active defenses do not work under conditions of inescapable threat. You explain to her that this happens below the level of conscious awareness, and is not under conscious control, but that working in therapy to separate the past from the present and heal the impact of trauma on her nervous system can help her defend herself more effectively in the present.

The chronic activation of immobilizing defenses underlies some of the symptomatology of TRD. As we will further discuss below, the nature of these defenses and how they impact people is becoming increasingly understood. This process includes elements of all three subsystems of the triune brain as well as multiple brain chemicals, including the endogenous opioids (internally produced substances similar to morphine), which appear to be involved in dissociative experiences and passive defenses, and the endocannabinoids (internally produced substances similar to those found in cannabis), which appear to be involved in active defensive responses (Lanius et al., 2018) (Figure 3.1).

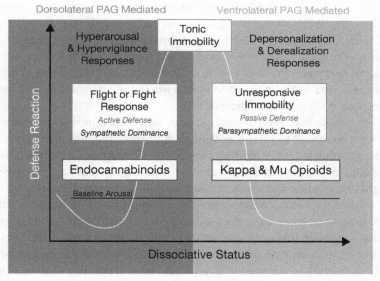

Figure 3.1. This defense cascade figure illustrates the brain areas involved in coordinating defenses, including the dorsolateral periaqueductal gray matter (PAG) in active defenses versus the ventrolateral PAG in passive defenses. It also illustrates the differential involvement of the sympathetic and parasympathetic nervous system in active and passive defenses, respectively, and their generally opposite effects on the person's embodied experience.
Used with permission: Lanius, R. A., Boyd, J. E., McKinnon, M. C., Nicholson, A. A., Frewen, P., Vermetten, E., . . . & Spiegel, D. (2018). A review of the neurobiological basis of trauma-related dissociation and its relation to cannabinoid- and opioid-mediated stress response: a transdiagnostic, translational approach. *Current Psychiatry Reports*, *20*(12), 118. doi.org/10.1007/s11920-018-0983-y. Original figure adapted with permission from *Zeitschrift fer Psychologie/Journal of Psychology* 2010; Vol. 218(2):109–127., p. 111 ©2010 Hogrefe Publishing, www.hogrefe.com.

KEY POINTS

The defense cascade model (Schauer & Elbert, 2010) postulates that there is a set pattern to how people and animals respond to danger. These reactions are innate and reflexive—they are not under conscious control. When something that might be dangerous, like a sudden movement or noise, occurs, the person stays still for a brief period to find out what it is. You can think about how a mouse or other animal goes still when it first hears a footstep. If, after momentary orienting, the situation seems dangerous, the person will first try to escape or interrupt the situation if they can, because getting out of a bad situation entirely is usually the best solution if it is possible. We call these reactions "mobilizing defenses" because they involve being able to move and actively respond. If there is no way to physically escape or successfully defend themselves, the person will go still again. Initially, they will be very tense and still (like a deer in headlights), but eventually, if the danger continues, they will become numb and collapsed, and enter a state in which they no longer feel fear or pain. We call these "immobilizing responses" because they involve staying still. This is an important way of trying to survive an inescapable danger when everything else has failed and resisting would make things worse. A predator will sometimes become disinterested in prey that appears dead; if it does not, and the threat continues, a state of anesthesia and dissociative detachment provides some protection in the moment from overwhelming fear and pain even when the physical body cannot be protected.

When people have been through trauma, especially repeated traumas when they were too small to escape or fight back, their nervous system learns that neither running away nor fighting back is a good solution. Therefore, if something difficult happens in the present, their nervous system can reflexively go straight to collapsing and shutting down because that is the only thing that has ever worked for them. For some people, this shutting down happens almost all the time, even when there does not seem to be an objective life-threatening trauma occurring; this can cause many problems in day-to-day life. This can look like chronic emotional numbness and detachment, chronic fatigue, or difficulty mobilizing to accomplish day-to-day tasks. This is one of the reactions to trauma that therapy can help to heal.

THE REPTILIAN COMPLEX AND DYSREGULATED AROUSAL

The defense cascade model, which we introduced above, divides defensive responses into mobilizing (flight and fight) and immobilizing (tonic immobility and emotional shutdown/collapse) strategies. People who have experienced a one-time trauma in adulthood more typically present to therapy with nondissociative posttraumatic stress disorder (PTSD) and usually struggle largely with hyperarousal (i.e., difficulty turning down their level of activation or being stuck in "flight or fight" mode). Their tendency to experience hyperarousal is a reflection of chronic activation of mobilizing defenses when exposed to reminders of trauma. In contrast, patients who have experienced repetitive, early, and longstanding trauma may also struggle with activated, hyperaroused patterns, but they will often alternate between these hyperaroused states and chronic states of immobilization, also known as hypoarousal (a collapsed, numb state associated with the immobilizing defenses). (For further discussion of animal defenses and dysregulated arousal in the context of trauma, see Nijenhuis et al., 1998b, 2004). These defensive responses are complex and involve thoughts, emotions, and sensations in the body, which will be discussed below. In particular, we will underscore the importance of these reactions being experienced in the body and the importance of addressing the body in treatment so these somatic reactions can be fully healed (see also Ogden et al., 2006a; van der Kolk, 2014). Because these reactions are so complex and widespread, involving the body as well as the mind, understanding the underlying neurobiology is vital to creating and communicating a coherent model of these symptoms that patients can understand.

As we previously discussed, the physical feelings that are associated with both mobilizing and immobilizing defenses are translated from the brain into the body by the autonomic nervous system, which regulates basic bodily functions such as breathing, heart rate, and muscle tension. It is clear from research that in highly dissociative patients, the embodied experience of the defensive response to trauma-related cues is very different from that seen in less dissociative traumatized patients (e.g., those with nondissociative PTSD). For example, in one early study pointing to the existence of the dissociative subtype of PTSD, 70% of patients with PTSD responded to trauma-related cues with an increase in heart rate, while 30% subjectively experienced dissociative symptoms and did not demonstrate any increase in heart rate; this suggested that rather than a sympathetically mediated hyperaroused state, the patients with the dissociative response were likely experiencing a parasympathetically mediated state of hypoarousal associated with immobilizing defenses (Lanius et al., 2006).

Clinical Example: A patient with no previous trauma history is hit by a car and is seriously injured. After the accident, she is unable to go outside by herself. If a car passes her on the sidewalk, she becomes sweaty, her hands start to shake, and she runs home and does not leave the house again for several days. In contrast, a patient who has a history of protracted childhood abuse has a similar accident. When she walks down the street and sees a car, she begins to feel numb, unable to move, and "spaced out," as if nothing around her is real, and her heart rate and breathing slow down. Both patients are reacting to the same trauma-related cue but have very different somatic/embodied experiences of the trauma response. These reactions are often sources of significant shame. It is important to highlight to both patients that whichever defense mechanisms were triggered at the time of the trauma, this was not under conscious control and is therefore not a reflection of their personality or character, but rather a patterned response based on past learning and rapid (but potentially fallible) threat assessment by primitive areas of the brain.

The physical experiences described above are an essential part of the nervous system's response to trauma and are not separate from the changes in thoughts and feelings that go along with trauma. Therefore, while they are ultimately controlled by the peripheral nervous system, they must also be directed by the central nervous system (i.e., the brain and spinal cord). The innate alarm system is one network in the brain that helps to coordinate these defensive responses. The innate alarm system is a network of cortical and subcortical areas (including the superior colliculus, periaqueductal gray matter, amygdala, and prefrontal regions) that are involved in rapidly noticing potential danger, initially before the person is even consciously aware of what has happened. There is evidence that the innate alarm system is overactive in patients with PTSD even when they are resting and not actively engaged in any task, suggesting activation of defensive responses even when there is no overt objective threat (Lanius et al., 2017). Instead, there is a chronic experience of threat and danger that is held in the body as well as in the mind. In other words, the brain and body are never at rest.

Clinical Example: A patient feels constantly on edge when he is outside of his home. He startles in response to any noise and feels edgy if there are people close to him or if there is any unexpected movement, even if he is in a familiar environment. He does not understand why he cannot "just calm down." He tells himself that he is relatively safe and that there is no reason to be anxious, but no matter what he tells himself, he continues to experience high arousal in his body and intense reactivity to any sensory stimuli. You talk to him about the innate alarm system and explain to him that in people with TRD, the brain is excessively alert to any possible threat even when someone is in a situation that they intellectually know to be safe. You explain to him that part of the work of the therapy is to learn new strategies to calm his nervous system in more effective ways than just telling himself to calm down, which implicitly involves some degree of shaming himself for having a reaction that is understandable based on his history.

One critical area for coordinating defensive responses is the periaqueductal gray matter (PAG), which is a brain region that provides a bridge between the brain and the body (Figure 3.2). The PAG is an area in the midbrain that coordinates defensive reactions (including autonomic nervous system activation leading to changes in heart rate, breathing, and other physical responses) in response to perceived danger. The PAG is involved in both mobilizing and immobilizing responses, with different parts of the PAG activated in each type of response. The lateral PAG and the dorsolateral PAG activate the sympathetic nervous system as a part of active defensive responses, whereas the ventrolateral PAG coordinates

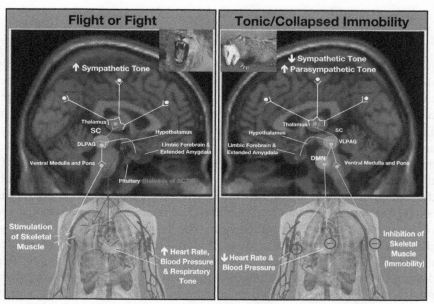

Figure 3.2. Areas of the brain involved in active and passive defenses and related physiological activation and inhibition. ACTH, adrenocorticotropic hormone; DLPAG, dorsolateral periaqueductal gray matter; DMN, default mode network; SC, superior colliculus; VLPAG, ventrolateral periaqueductal gray matter.
This figure is based on ideas presented in Kozlowska et al., 2015. Figure is adapted and used with permission from McKinnon, M. C., Boyd, J. E., Frewen, P. A., Lanius, U. F., Jetly, R., Richardson, J. D., & Lanius, R. A. (2016). A review of the relation between dissociation, memory, executive functioning and social cognition in military members and civilians with neuropsychiatric conditions. *Neuropsychologia, 90*, 210–234. doi:10.1016/j.neuropsychologia.2016.07.017

parasympathetic activation and hypoarousal symptoms (Kozlowska et al., 2015; Terpou et al., 2019). As one of the more primitive areas of the brain, the PAG co-ordinates defensive responding below the level of conscious awareness. Patients with TRD often experience confusion and shame related to reactions to stress that they may intellectually "know" are not serving them well. An understanding of the function of the PAG in this kind of responding is vital in helping patients to understand why they behave in ways that feel inexplicable, or why they have reactions for which they have no words.

Clinical Example: A patient has done significant work on reframing her thoughts about an assault that she experienced. She reports that she no longer cognitively believes that she was to blame, and can explain in detail why this is the case, but when she speaks about it, her body continues to react with hypoarousal and she says that she still "feels" somewhere inside that it must have been her fault. You talk to her about the PAG and explain how the "felt sense" of responsibility is held in her body even after her cognitions have changed, and that other strategies may be a useful complement to cognitive restructuring in changing this felt sense.

Functional connectivity is the extent to which two brain areas are active at the same time, either at rest or during a specific task or state. Increased functional connectivity suggests increased communication and coordinated functioning between two brain areas. Recent literature on functional connectivity of the PAG in TRD offers insight into defensive responses in patients with TRD. For example, in one study all patients with PTSD demonstrated increased connectivity between the dorsolateral PAG and areas involved in mobilizing responses to threat: in contrast, patients with the dissociative subtype of PTSD, which is associated with the immobilizing defenses, showed increased connectivity between brain areas involved in threat detection (e.g., the dorsal anterior cingulate cortex) and the ventrolateral PAG. The PAG is thought to coordinate the somatic responses that characterize the immobilizing defenses. This provides further support for the idea that highly dissociative patients with TRD preferentially activate immobilizing defenses in the face of threat (Harricharan et al., 2016). In addition, in these patients, the ventrolateral PAG demonstrates increased functional connectivity with parts of the brain that are involved in out-of-body experiences, including the left temporoparietal junction, which is implicated in creating detachment from the self, body, and surroundings (including to the point of perceiving these as unreal or belonging to someone else) (Harricharan et al., 2016). These sensory experiences frequently occur in tandem with activation of immobilizing defenses, and this literature on PAG connectivity provides a neurobiological connection between the immobilizing defenses and the subjective experience of dissociation.

The essential role of somatic experience (i.e., physical feelings in the body) in generating and maintaining trauma-related symptoms can be overlooked in favor of symptoms related to feelings and thoughts, although some more recent psychotherapeutic approaches and theories do focus on the role of the body (Ogden et al., 2006a; van der Kolk, 2014). It is clear from recent research that these physical sensations are an integral part of the defensive responses that are often chronically activated in traumatized patients. Recent research highlighting the role of the PAG in bridging from the brain to the body clarifies how crucial the brain is in contributing to trauma-based reactions and their treatment.

KEY POINTS

As we talked about earlier, people's nervous systems respond differently to feeling threatened. People might respond with mobilizing defenses ("flight or fight" mode) or immobilizing defenses (tonic immobility/"freezing" or emotional collapse/shutdown). Many people who have been through trauma flip back and forth between these different reactions. These reactions are associated with physical changes and experiences in the body, such as tension, breathing, heart rate, and others, that are caused by the peripheral nervous system but are controlled by the brain and spinal cord.

One system in the brain, called the innate alarm system, is responsible for being alert for any signs of danger. We do not realize that this is happening, and if the innate alarm system notices something that might be dangerous, we often do not even consciously recognize what it is until our body has already started to respond. Even when people who have been through trauma are not in danger, or not doing anything at all, this brain network is unusually active as compared to people who have not experienced trauma. The periaqueductal gray matter (PAG) is one part of the brain that coordinates either mobilizing or immobilizing defenses in the body, through the peripheral nervous system. The PAG creates a bridge between the brain and the body. In people who are highly dissociative, the innate alarm system seems to be more connected to the part of the PAG that brings about immobilizing defenses. This supports the idea that these immobilizing defenses are more easily triggered in people who are highly dissociative.

THE PALEOMAMMALIAN COMPLEX AND EMOTION REGULATION

Managing emotions is a frequent area of difficulty for patients with TRD. Insecure attachment and relational trauma have a profound impact on a wide range of processes related to emotion regulation (see Schore, 2003, and Siegel, 2015). Many people believe this means trauma survivors are unable to turn down the limbic system (including the amygdala), which they think results in intense and chronic fear and terror. It is increasingly understood, however, that in patients with TRD, many emotions in addition to fear and terror can become difficult to manage, and areas of the brain beyond the limbic system are involved. Other emotions can become problematic and even more prominent than fear, including shame, rage, and sadness. Furthermore, while some patients struggle primarily with difficulty turning down intense emotions, many, particularly those who are highly dissociative, struggle with experiences of emotional numbness and detachment that are due to excessively inhibiting (turning down or entirely turning off) emotions. As we will explore below, a neurobiological explanation for these experiences must go beyond the amygdala and incorporate multiple other brain areas.

The corticolimbic inhibition model, when extended to include not just the amygdala but also an array of other relevant brain areas, provides a framework for understanding some of the changes in emotional experience seen in TRD. This model addresses the excessive inhibition of emotions ("emotion overmodulation") that is typically seen in the dissociative subtype of PTSD (Fenster et al., 2018; Lanius et al., 2010). The dissociative subtype, which is associated with early life trauma and more extensive trauma, is characterized by abnormally strong inhibition of the amygdala, which is involved in fear and fear-based learning, by

higher brain areas, particularly the medial prefrontal cortex. This excessive inhibition of the limbic system, particularly in response to reminders of trauma,
is likely responsible for the feelings of being detached or numb that highly dissociative patients describe when they are exposed to such reminders. Of note,
the bed nucleus of the stria terminalis (BNST) of the brainstem is recognized
as part of the "extended amygdala" and is particularly involved in anticipation
of, and sustained response to, threat. In individuals with the dissociative subtype
of PTSD, there is increased communication between the BNST and the vermis,
an area of the cerebellum that is thought to be involved in regulating emotions
(Rabellino et al., 2018). Similarly, in the dissociative subtype of PTSD, there is
increased communication between the posterior cerebellum, which is also involved in emotion regulation, and the same prefrontal areas that are implicated
in the corticolimbic model (Rabellino et al., 2018). In addition, there is evidence
to support inhibition of the right anterior insular cortex, which is involved in
awareness of one's own body; this likely contributes to the perceptual experience
of being detached from one's body that is often also associated with the emotional numbing reported by highly dissociative patients (Hopper et al., 2007; Shin
et al., 2004). Overmodulation of the PAG, an area involved in coordinating defensive responding, and alterations in connectivity between the PAG and the amygdala have both been shown to occur in the dissociative subtype of PTSD as well
(Brandão & Lovick, 2019; Nicholson et al., 2017). While research on TRD other
than PTSD has been more limited, some changes similar to those described above
have been reported in depersonalization disorder, a dissociative disorder that has
been associated with emotional trauma (see Chapter 1) (Hollander et al., 1992;
Lemche et al., 2007). Taken together, these findings suggest that the corticolimbic
inhibition model, including not just the amygdala but also the extended amygdala, PAG, insular cortex, and some areas of the cerebellum involved in emotion
regulation, may explain some of the difficulties in emotion regulation seen in this
population, and may have broader applicability to TRD and to highly dissociative,
traumatized patients whether or not their primary diagnosis is PTSD.

   Some of the areas implicated in this model also suggest a role for the opioid
neuromodulatory system in producing the chronic dysphoria and numbness that
patients with TRD often experience. There is evidence of increased communication between the BNST and the claustrum, which is involved in consciousness.
The claustrum (a subcortical structure) contains a high concentration of kappa-
opioid receptors, which are bound by dynorphins. Dynorphins are opioid peptides
(naturally produced versions of medications like morphine) that are increasingly
thought to be linked to dysphoria, numbing, and dissociative-like symptoms in
response to chronic stress (Addy et al., 2015; Land et al., 2008; Pietrzak et al.,
2014). These findings support the key role of perceived life-threatening danger in
triggering emotional numbing in these patients, and also provide a neurobiological link between the emotional experience (numbing) and the sensory experience
(unreality) of dissociative responses to perceived threat (i.e., immobilizing defensive responses). These findings also suggest a potential explanation for the experience not just of chronic numbing, but also of chronic dysphoria and negative

affectivity. The potential role of the opioid neuromodulatory system also helps to provide a basis for understanding TRD patients' chronic dysphoria, the mood symptom that is frequently seen alongside numbing and dissociation.

> *Clinical Example*: A patient reports that much of the time, she doesn't feel anything at all—she feels emotionally dead. When she is exposed to reminders of her trauma, she reports that she feels completely numb and has the sense that she is levitating out of her body and watching herself from the outside. When she graduates from university, she attends the graduation ceremony but feels detached and says that even though she knows this is a major accomplishment, she feels blank and numb inside. She does not understand why she is unable to feel happy, even when there are no reminders of trauma and she is in a safe environment. You explain to her that there are many mechanisms to explain chronic numbness in people with TRD, including the presence of opioid-like substances as well as sustained activation of brain areas involved in dissociation and altered states of consciousness. Knowing that there are "real" reasons for these kinds of feelings and experiences that can be studied using neuroimaging decreased her feelings of shame and being "broken." Because people are often familiar with the concept of opioids and their effects, the idea of endogenous opioids is a concept that makes sense to people.

KEY POINTS

People often think that fear is the biggest problem that occurs after trauma, and they might have heard about parts of the brain like the limbic system or the amygdala and how these are involved in TRD. We know, however, that people who have been through trauma often have just as many problems with many other emotions like shame, sadness, or anger. We also know that trauma is not just about feeling too much; many people who have been through trauma have difficulties with feeling too little, or being numb most of the time.

One way of understanding this is through the corticolimbic inhibition model. This model suggests that one part of the brain (the cerebral cortex) excessively "turns down the volume" (i.e., activation) on the parts of the brain that experience emotions, including the limbic system and the periaqueductal gray, as well as other areas that are involved in emotions. This can be triggered by trauma-related cues. Therefore, instead of feeling fear, there is numbness and absence of emotion, including pleasant emotions. The cerebral cortex seems to turn down the volume on other parts of the brain, too, including parts of the brain like the insula that are involved in how we perceive our bodies and surroundings. This can explain why, along with the feeling of numbness, there might be feelings that one's own body or surroundings are unfamiliar or strange. Chronic numbness is also related to chemicals produced in the body, including opioid-like substances.

PERCEPTUAL ABNORMALITIES IN TRD

As discussed above, numbing and disconnection from thoughts, emotions, and physical sensations are a key component of the immobilizing defensive responses and are a part of the day-to-day experience of patients with TRD. As we have explored in previous chapters, dissociative experiences (e.g., depersonalization or derealization), which represent an altered perception of self or surroundings, are a feature of TRD both in response to trauma-related cues and spontaneously.

Psychotic-like symptoms are a lesser-known but also frequent occurrence in TRD. Some of these symptoms are almost identical to those experienced by people with schizophrenia (e.g., auditory verbal hallucinations or "hearing voices") and are frequently misdiagnosed as true psychosis. Some are considered unusual or unlikely (e.g., olfactory or visual hallucinations) in the context of what is known about psychotic disorders and are therefore often misidentified as malingering (Schiavone et al., 2018a). While on the surface psychotic-like and dissociative symptoms may not seem connected, and psychotic-like symptoms may not seem dissociative in nature, both are reflections of impaired handling of sensory information in the brain, leading to misperception of self and surroundings (e.g., failure to recognize one's own body, familiar surroundings, or other stimuli) as well as perceiving things that are not there (i.e., hallucinations). The neurological basis for these symptoms is complex and is related to a variety of areas in the brain that process sensory information from inside and outside the body. This includes areas like the cerebral cortex, particularly the parietal lobe and the temporal lobe, as well as lower areas such as the cerebellum, and the vestibular system. Strikingly, as we will now review, all of these areas have been found to be abnormal in structure and/or function in those with TRD, providing a neurobiological explanation that unites a seemingly unconnected and difficult-to-understand set of symptoms.

The cerebellum and the vestibular system gather information related to all five senses and pass this information on to areas of the cerebral cortex involved in putting the information together and, particularly, putting the information together with respect to one's own body, as well as one's location with respect to the environment. Therefore, it is logical that both of these areas may be involved in dissociative experiences such as depersonalization and derealization. While the cerebellum is stereotypically associated with movement and balance, there is increasing research indicating that the cerebellum also has important functions in processing and putting together information from the five senses. Compared to people with PTSD without dissociation as well as to people without PTSD, people with the dissociative subtype of PTSD show decreased communication between the anterior cerebellum and brain areas involved in putting together sensory information, such as the temporoparietal junction, the right postcentral gyrus, and the right superior parietal lobule. These areas are involved in bodily self-consciousness, including integrating five sense information about the body and experiencing the body as a single whole (Rabellino et al., 2018a).

Similarly, the vestibular system, which obtains five sense information about the location of the body in space, has altered communication in patients with the dissociative subtype of PTSD compared to healthy individuals and to patients with PTSD. In one study, the dissociative subtype was associated with a lack of communication between the vestibular nuclei (in the brainstem) and the right posterior insula, which is involved in awareness of sensations inside the body. There was also a lack of communication with the right temporoparietal junction, which could result in difficulty assessing one's own position in space, as well as feeling outside of or detached from the body (Harricharan, 2016). In dissociative PTSD, elements of the innate alarm system (e.g., the superior colliculus) have also been found to communicate with the temporoparietal junction (Olivé et al., 2018).

The temporal lobe, which receives information from the cerebellum and the vestibular nuclei, among other areas, is critical for complex sensory integration (putting together five sense information), particularly object recognition and self-recognition. Across a range of TRD, including PTSD (particularly the dissociative subtype), borderline personality disorder, and dissociative identity disorder, there are strikingly similar changes in temporal lobe structure and function, including volume loss in the right temporal lobe and increased temporal lobe activation in those who dissociate in the presence of trauma-related cues. Notably, there is a significant overlap between the dissociative and psychotic-like symptoms experienced by these patients and those experienced by patients with temporal lobe epilepsy, which is characterized by abnormal electrical discharges in the temporal lobe (Schiavone et al., 2018a). Specifically in patients with complex dissociative disorders (dissociative identity disorder and Other Specified Dissociative Disorder-1 [OSDD-1]), there is literature suggesting temporal lobe involvement in the process of switching between dissociative self-states as well as differences in temporal lobe activation patterns between dissociative self-states (Dorahy et al., 2014; Schiavone et al., 2018a). Taken together, these findings suggest a critical role for sensory integration areas, particularly the temporal lobe, in both dissociative and psychotic-like symptoms in patients with TRD.

Clinical Example: A patient reports that she hears voices. She frequently hears the voices of children screaming and crying inside her head. She also sometimes smells something burning when she is home alone. She does not recognize herself in the mirror and frequently feels like she is floating outside of her body when she is under stress. She has been told that she has schizophrenia, but her symptoms have not responded to multiple antipsychotic medications. She is confused about why she has these experiences, feels "crazy," and worries that it will be impossible for her to ever get better since so many medications have failed to help her. Psychotic-like experiences can be frightening to patients, particularly given societal stigma around psychotic disorders like schizophrenia, and many patients with TRD have had experiences of unsuccessful treatment for "psychosis" that leave them feeling hopeless. By normalizing these symptoms as understandable and expected in some forms of TRD, and as neurobiologically different from those seen in schizophrenia, patients can be helped to understand their symptoms in a new way and develop a sense of hope that they can recover.

As we reviewed in the chapter on assessment, psychotic-like and dissociative symptoms often go together and are frequently misunderstood. It is vital for clinicians to situate these symptoms in a neurobiological context in order to recognize that in many patients, psychotic-like symptoms are an expected part of the TRDs and may in fact be related to dissociation, rather than occurring because the person has an additional diagnosis of a psychotic disorder. While there are no formal treatment guidelines for psychotic-like symptoms in the setting of complex trauma, and while true psychosis can in some cases coexist with TRD, it is important to be aware of the need for careful assessment before diagnosing a comorbid primary psychotic disorder (e.g., schizophrenia or delusional disorder), and clinicians should recognize that in the absence of a primary psychotic disorder, the foundation of treatment should be treatment of the underlying TRD.

KEY POINTS

Many people with TRD have symptoms that seem unusual or psychotic, such as hallucinations (including not just hearing voices, but also abnormal smells, tastes, visions, and sensations on the skin). Some of these symptoms can look very similar to those seen in psychotic disorders like schizophrenia. There is evidence, however, that suggests that these symptoms are actually more similar to dissociative symptoms like "spacing out" or feeling outside of your body. Both psychotic-like (e.g., hallucinations) and some dissociative symptoms (e.g., depersonalization and derealization) are examples of abnormal processing by the brain of information coming from the five senses. When we are out in the world, we see, hear, smell, touch, and taste many things simultaneously, and the brain needs to be able to interpret and organize this information to help us decide what is happening around us. In particular, areas of the brain like the cerebellum and the vestibular system collect and put together information from all of the five senses, but, in people with TRD, they seem to have less ability to communicate with other areas that do this, such as the temporal and parietal lobes. There is also evidence that the structure and the function of the temporal lobe itself are abnormal in TRD. These changes lead to difficulties with things like recognizing your own body, recognizing whether your environment is familiar or not, and figuring out how to interpret incoming five sense information (e.g., what it is and where it is coming from). For that reason, it makes sense that in people with TRD, sometimes information is missed, added, or incorrectly interpreted. This is not the same thing as being psychotic, which is why people often do not get better when they take medications that are designed to help with psychosis. As far as we know, the best way to work on these problems is to work on treating the TRD.

MEMORY, ATTENTION, AND COGNITION

Difficulties with multiple higher-level cognitive functions (e.g., memory, attention, planning, and organization) have been repeatedly associated with a range of TRD, including PTSD, borderline personality disorder, and dissociative identify disorder, as well as specifically with dissociative symptoms (McKinnon et al., 2016). This makes sense in the context of the definition of dissociation, which includes disturbances in the coherent functioning of consciousness, memory, and sensation (American Psychiatric Association, 2013).

One way of understanding how different areas of the brain work together is the concept of intrinsic connectivity networks, or groups of brain regions that are functionally interconnected (communicate with and influence each other). It has been proposed that there are three key intrinsic connectivity networks that may be related to a variety of PTSD symptoms, including cognitive symptoms (Akiki et al., 2017; Lanius et al., 2015; Yehuda et al., 2015). These three networks are the *central executive network*, which is involved in working memory and executive functioning (including top-down regulation of emotions); the *salience network*, which filters and integrates internal and external stimuli (including threat detection); and the *default mode network*, which is involved in self-referential mental processes (e.g., self-reflection) (Menon, 2011). Typically, the default mode network is active when the mind is not doing anything in particular, and inactive when the salience network and the central executive network are activated (during times of active thinking and execution of cognitive tasks).

In this section, we will look particularly at the role of intrinsic connectivity networks in understanding cognitive symptoms of TRD. These abnormalities can include changes in communication within these networks and in the brain's ability to appropriately shift between networks when needed (i.e., to move from doing nothing in particular to completing a cognitive task). The central executive network is potentially particularly implicated in cognitive symptoms associated with TRD. There is some evidence that PTSD is associated with an impaired ability to successfully switch between the default mode network and the central executive network, including failure to suppress default mode network activity when switching to a cognitive task, and incorporation of parts of the salience network and default mode network into the central executive network when exposed to threatening stimuli (Daniels et al., 2010; Rabellino et al., 2018a). In one study, high levels of dissociative symptoms in women with PTSD were associated with greater resting connectivity between a brain region that is typically part of the central executive network (the dorsolateral prefrontal cortex) and elements of the default mode network (Bluhm et al., 2009). Furthermore, in a study of healthy adults with a history of childhood trauma, executive functioning deficits were also associated with diminished connectivity within the default mode network (Lu et al., 2017). Taken together, these findings suggest in TRD, when completing a cognitive task, the brain remains overly involved in mental processes that are not relevant to the task at hand, and that there may be specific changes that are seen in highly dissociative TRD. This may underpin some of the executive functioning deficits (e.g., difficulties with planning ahead and switching tasks) that are seen in TRD patients.

KEY POINTS

Intrinsic connectivity networks are groups of brain regions that communicate with and influence each other. Thinking about intrinsic connectivity networks is one way of understanding how different parts of the brain work together to carry out day-to-day mental operations. The default mode network is involved in self-reflection and is typically active when the mind is doing nothing else (when the other two networks are not active). The central executive network is involved in complex thinking tasks. The salience network puts together internal and external information and decides what is relevant. In TRD, there is difficulty switching between these networks when it is necessary to complete cognitive tasks and, in particular, in appropriately and primarily activating the central executive network to complete a cognitive task rather than continuing to engage in mental processes that are not related to the task at hand. This may help explain why people with TRD sometimes struggle with thinking and executive functioning.

CONCLUSION

As we have detailed in this chapter, the complex array of symptoms that characterize complex trauma is increasingly being explained by neurobiological research on TRD. Even therapists without extensive background in neuroscience can (and should) provide basic psychoeducation on the neurobiology of trauma to their patients as an important aspect of their treatment. Many patients welcome this education and find that it reduces shame and their feeling of stigma. This information can be particularly beneficial for TRD patients who may have difficulty functioning at school or at work due to problems with memory, organization, and planning. Patients who learn about the impact of trauma on the brain often report feeling less ashamed and self-blaming about their difficulties with daily functioning. Patients often benefit from being taught strategies to cope with some of these deficits. Furthermore, they are often more motivated to practice these strategies that can help them heal from the impact of trauma when they can link the symptoms they experience to scientifically based findings in the brain.

SUMMARY

- Patients with TRD report a wide range of symptoms, including problems with emotion regulation, planning, organizing, and remembering; an absence of physical sensations alternating with body sensations related to past traumas; chronic alternating hypoarousal and hyperarousal; and sensory experiences in the absence of external stimuli. These difficulties may appear unconnected but in fact are linked to neurobiological alterations in the brain related to trauma.

- The triune brain model is a useful way of conceptualizing different levels of functioning and highlights the importance of less advanced, subcortical structures (i.e., the reptilian brain) in producing and maintaining symptoms of TRD, and the degree to which these symptoms involve the body (via the peripheral nervous system).

- Patients with TRD frequently struggle with extremes of arousal related to ongoing defensive responses to perceived survival threat. While nontraumatized individuals may initially respond to perceived threat with active defensive responses (flight or fight), chronically traumatized individuals may have learned through conditioning that they cannot escape or fight back. Instead they may default to more passive defenses ("freezing" in tonic immobility/"playing dead" and emotional shutdown/ collapse), even if the present situation is potentially escapable. Because threat is subjective and may be perceived by patients with TRD even in the absence of external threat, these defenses can be frequently and easily activated in a variety of day-to-day situations, leading to significant functional impairment.

- Individuals with TRD often show heightened sensitivity to perceived threat and overactivity of the innate alarm system, leading to activation of defensive responses even in the absence of any threatening stimulus.

- There also appears to be excessive top-down inhibition or underactivity of brain areas involved in sensory processing, recognizing one's own body, and emotional responses. These alterations involve the amygdala, the periaqueductal gray matter, as well as the insula, cerebellum, and areas in the temporal lobe. This leads to chronic numbness, dissociation, dysphoria, and psychotic-like symptoms, both in response to trauma-related cues and in the resting state.

- Literature on intrinsic connectivity networks, or sets of brain regions that are functionally connected and are differentially active during certain tasks versus at rest, suggests that there are alterations in TRD that may help explain the pervasive difficulties with executive functioning that are often reported.

4

An Overview of Complex Trauma-Related Disorder Treatment and the Treatment of Patients with Dissociative Disorders (TOP DD) Studies' Research Findings

In this chapter, we provide an overview of how to help patients with complex trauma-related reactions and discuss the staged treatment model for complex trauma-related disorders (TRD) and treatment-related research, including studies conducted by the Treatment of Patients with Dissociative Disorders (TOP DD) research team.

OVERVIEW OF THE STABILIZATION PHASE OF TREATMENT FOR COMPLEX TRD

Treatment for complex trauma, including TRD, is conceptualized as occurring in three phases or stages (Courtois & Ford, 2013; Herman, 1997; Kluft, 1993a, 1993c):

1. The first phase of treatment is the *symptom management and stabilization* phase, in which patients learn healthy ways to manage trauma-related dysregulation and symptoms. This foundational work is the primary focus of this book and must be completed carefully and comprehensively in order to help patients get and feel safer before engaging in the otherwise overwhelming work of trauma processing in

the second phase of treatment. In addition, the therapeutic relationship must be well established before discussing relational trauma, which can activate attachment-related disorganization.

2. The aim of *processing*, the second phase of treatment, is to allow the person to examine and work through the impacts of their trauma. This work can be done through bottom-up (i.e., driven by somatic pattern awareness), top-down (cognitive-driven), exposure-focused, and/or combination approaches.

3. The third phase, *reconnection*, is more individualized and typically focuses on reconnecting with oneself and others in new ways with the benefit of having resolved traumatic experiences into painful memories rather than disruptive flashbacks, nightmares, and other intrusive symptoms (Brand et al., 2014a; International Society for the Study of Dissociation, 2011).

These phases are heuristic in the sense that safety and trauma-related issues are addressed throughout treatment.

Early in treatment, traumatic experiences are generally addressed from a cognitive perspective (e.g., discussing how traumatic experiences may impact the individual's self-image, relationships, and struggles with safety) rather than being discussed in detail with attention to somatic sensations and emotional feelings. The overarching goal of trauma therapy is assisting the individual to develop a life that is adaptive and fulfilling (Brand et al., 2014a).

STABILIZING SAFETY

Early in treatment, most individuals with TRD have considerable difficulty with safely tolerating emotions and managing trauma-related symptoms, and often engage in risky and unhealthy behaviors, including substance abuse, medication misuse, disordered eating, self-injurious behavior, suicide attempts, and other risky and dangerous behaviors (Brand et al., 2009b, 2019b). Therefore, treatment guidelines for complex trauma emphasize present-centered work, including improving emotion regulation and stabilizing safety, early before focusing in detail on past traumas (Cloitre et al., 2012a; International Society for the Study of Dissociation, 2011; Kezelman & Stavropoulos, 2012; McFetridge et al., 2017). Specific expert consensus treatment guidelines are available for adults diagnosed with dissociative identity disorder (DID) (International Society for the Study of Dissociation, 2011) as well as for children and adolescents with dissociative disorders (DD) (International Society for the Study of Trauma and Dissociation, 2004).

The goals for this early phase of treatment are improving safety; stabilizing symptoms; developing symptom management and affect regulation skills; building and maintaining a therapeutic framework, including a therapeutic alliance between the patient and therapist; increasing the individual's understanding and compassion toward themselves; and, when applicable, increasing awareness and acceptance of dissociative self-states (Brand et al., 2012b; Myrick et al., 2015).

Understanding why people engage in risky and unhealthy behaviors

The phasic model of treating patients with complex TRD, including those with DD, conceptualizes high-risk/unhealthy behaviors as attempts at self-regulation. While some individuals with TRD may understand some of these behaviors as "unsafe," for others these behaviors seem "normal." People with trauma histories are at risk for engaging in a wide range of risky and unhealthy behaviors, including suicide attempts; failing to take essential medications as prescribed; substance use; eating too little or too much; gambling; shoplifting; driving dangerously; non-suicidal self-injury (NSSI); failing to maintain boundaries with strangers; being involved in emotionally, physically, and sexually exploitive and abusive relationships (as victim, abuser, or both); engaging as a sex worker; and so on.

Unfortunately, these behaviors are particularly prevalent in patients with DD. For example, studies of patients involved in treatment indicate that most DD patients will attempt suicide at least once and approximately half of DD patients engage in NSSI (Coons & Milstein, 1990; Foote et al., 2008; Putnam et al., 1986a; Ross & Norton, 1989). The risk of multiple suicide attempts is higher for individuals with DD than it is for other psychiatric disorders, even borderline personality disorder (BPD) and posttraumatic stress disorder (PTSD) (Foote et al., 2008). Specifically, the risk for multiple suicide attempts among individuals with DD is more than *15 times* that of other psychiatric patients.

Revictimization is also alarmingly high among patients with DD. For example, the TOP DD therapists reported that approximately 7% of their patients had experienced sexual revictimization and/or physical revictimization, and approximately 36% had experienced emotional revictimization *in the last 6 months* (Myrick et al., 2013). Revictimization is linked to patients' symptoms suddenly worsening, rather than improving, despite being engaged in psychotherapy. Therefore, the establishment of safety in relationships must be a critical focus in treatment, which is why we made improving safety, including safety in relationships, one of the key issues addressed in the TOP DD Network study (Myrick et al., 2013).

Revictimization and unsafe behaviors are viewed through a lens informed by trauma and attachment issues: Unhealthy relationship patterns and other unsafe behaviors are often strongly shaped by unhealthy and abusive early relationships. When caretakers and other adults do not protect a child, and instead neglect or emotionally, sexually, and/or physically abuse the child, the child develops a sense of self and others that is rooted in neglectful and abusive treatment of themselves. Thus, later revictimization and unsafe behaviors may be reenactments of trauma-based dynamics (Brand, 2001; Brand et al., 2014a). Viewing these problems through this lens clarifies why changing these ingrained patterns is so difficult.

Having repeated relapses into unsafe behaviors and experiencing tremendous ambivalence and difficulty disengaging from abusive relationship patterns are common among individuals with TRD. Unsafe behaviors and abusive relationships can be powerfully reinforcing. Imagine how essential it may feel to a person who has been chronically helpless and self-loathing to have a proven and reliable method for numbing emotional pain and regaining some semblance of control over their bodies, emotions, and symptoms by engaging in NSSI or drinking, to name just a few methods used by traumatized individuals to self-regulate. Ceasing to use these ingrained methods is terrifying and may feel dangerous. The notion of "getting safe" can feel entirely unconceivable because they may have never known safety. What is unknown is unpredictable to trauma survivors and therefore is a trigger signaling danger. Getting safer can seem like a trick, a way the therapist or other supportive people may be attempting to reduce the patient's defenses in order to humiliate or harm them. Getting safer can feel as impossible as "getting sober"; indeed, these behaviors and relationships can feel as powerful as addictions to some patients.

Despite this tremendous challenge, individuals with TRD *must* begin to get safe from ongoing victimization in order to truly stabilize and benefit from treatment, so addressing any ongoing abusive relationships is an urgent safety issue. Similarly, ongoing, repetitive NSSI, suicide attempts, and other unsafe behaviors can be life-threatening, sometimes requiring repeated inpatient hospitalizations, and are disruptive to treatment. Chronic safety problems impair an individual's ability to function on a daily basis, including potentially interfering with their academic or occupational functioning, their ability to parent, and their ability to have healthy relationships. The chronicity and severity of safety problems among TRD individuals makes it imperative for research to address methods to improve patients' safety. Furthermore, clinicians who treat these individuals must be aware of, and prepared to, guide patients toward establishing safety.

Thus, "safety" is essential—even though it may feel impossible and/or dangerous. This paradox presents a challenge to patients, clinicians, and researchers. Indeed, it was challenging to design a program to educate patients about stabilizing safety, among other outcomes, because we understood that simply talking about safety would be a trigger for some participants.

EMOTION REGULATION

Dissociation serves a protective function in the face of overwhelming stress such as during childhood trauma (Putnam, 1985, 1997). Thus, trauma-related dissociation can be seen as an emotion regulation strategy. When overwhelmed with emotion, individuals with TRD may dissociate to avoid feeling emotion, or they may engage in unsafe behavior as a means of managing emotion or, in many cases, avoiding emotion. Even though dissociation enabled them to survive during trauma, over time, if dissociation continues to be frequently used to manage daily stress and emotions, it becomes maladaptive because the individual does not learn how to deal with emotions in healthy ways.

Difficulties with emotion regulation contribute to these chronic safety struggles. Individuals with TRD often experience intensely painful emotions due to intrusions related to trauma (e.g., trauma-related thoughts, images, smells, sensations, emotions); a profoundly negative self-image; frequent crises and revictimization; difficult family and social relationships; a variety of comorbid and often severe psychiatric and medical disorders; and internal conflict among self-states (among those with complex DDs).

The complex trauma literature (e.g., Allen, 2005; Boon et al., 2011; Brand, 2001; Brand & Lanius, 2014; Brand et al., 2012b; Chu, 2011; Courtois et al., 2009; Dorrepaal et al., 2012; Ford & Courtois, 2009; Frewen & Lanius, 2015; Kluft, 1993c; Lanius et al., 2011; Najavits & Hien, 2013; Putnam, 1989; van der Hart et al., 2006) indicates that becoming overwhelmed with emotions including shame, despair, self-hatred, anger, and terror; unmanageable symptoms of PTSD and dissociation; revictimization; and internal conflicts among self-states for patients with dissociative self-states contribute to difficulties maintaining safety. Researchers examining dissociation with traumatized individuals have concluded that emotion regulation skills are important in the treatment of trauma and are crucial in stabilizing safety and interrupting the intergenerational transmission of trauma (e.g., Narang & Contreras, 2005).

Neurobiological studies about PTSD, particularly when it is associated with high levels of dissociation, show that individuals with TRD have biologically driven emotion regulation difficulties. For example, they have altered brain activation patterns vacillating between emotion underregulation and overregulation, which means they tend to feel too much or too little (see more in Chapter 3; Lanius et al., 2010; Reinders et al., 2006; Schlumpf et al., 2013, 2019). Difficulties with emotion regulation contribute to the severity and persistence of PTSD symptoms in adult survivors of child abuse (Lilly et al., 2014; Stevens et al., 2013). In adults with PTSD, difficulties with emotion regulation are associated with risk for sexual revictimization in adulthood (Weiss et al., 2019) and unsafe behaviors, including NSSI and drug use (Dixon-Gordon et al., 2014).

Thus, difficulties with emotion regulation are one of the core vulnerabilities that contribute to overall instability in TRD, just as they are among individuals with BPD, who engage in frequent NSSI and other unsafe behavior (Linehan, 1993). Cognitive-behavioral treatments such as dialectical behavior therapy (DBT) that teach emotion regulation skills result in reductions in NSSI in patients with BPD (DeCou et al., 2019), even when the disorder occurs along with PTSD (Harned et al., 2014; Wagner et al., 2007). However, dissociation hinders BPD patients' response to DBT (Kleindienst et al., 2011, 2016), leading the researchers who conducted the DBT study to conclude that specific interventions need to be developed to help patients manage dissociation so they can benefit from DBT.

There are some similarities between patients with DD and BPD; for example, both groups of patients often struggle with high rates of trauma exposure, dissociation, NSSI, suicide attempts, and difficulties with emotion regulation. These similarities, as well as the importance of providing staged treatment focusing initially on stabilizing symptoms, emotions, and safety, suggest that these disorders may be conceptualized, at least in part, as disorders of emotion regulation (Brand & Lanius, 2014). Preliminary case studies suggest that staged treatment approaches, including adaptations of DBT, can be beneficial to DID patients, including improved emotion regulation and management of dissociation over time (Foote & Orden, 2016; Pollock et al., 2017).

Taken together, this body of research suggests that individuals with TRD struggle with emotion dysregulation and that it may be beneficial to target emotion regulation in trauma treatment. Importantly, individuals with complex trauma and high levels of dissociation show improvements in dissociation following staged treatment that teaches emotion regulation (Cloitre et al., 2012b; Schlumpf et al., 2019). There is preliminary evidence that inpatient trauma treatment may be associated with beneficial changes in brain network functioning that reflect improved emotion regulation (Schlumpf et al., 2019).

Consistent with these clinical observations, expert consensus guidelines for DID suggest that in the first stage of treatment, patients need to learn skills to manage emotions and symptoms so that they can establish and maintain safety and self-regulation, and so they can gradually become safer (International Society for the Study of Dissociation, 2011). TRD patients also need to improve self-care, impulse control, interpersonal skills, and self-understanding and self-compassion (including starting to develop at least some degree of tolerance for dissociative self-states, if applicable) (International Society for the Study of Dissociation, 2011).

USEFUL SKILLS FOR TRAUMA SURVIVORS

Specific skills that need to be taught, practiced, and used during therapy sessions as well as outside of sessions include the following (Brand et al., 2019b):

- *Grounding* when first beginning to feel too much or too little to prevent emotional overwhelm and/or dissociation
- *Separating past from present*, including containment of intrusive imagery, recollections, bodily sensations, and interrupting cognitive and behavioral reenactments related to trauma (e.g., trauma-based beliefs and behavioral "scripts")
- *Emotion regulation* (including self-compassionate use of grounding and other recovery-focused skills) as alternatives to unhealthy, risky, or unsafe behaviors; dissociation; no-longer-necessary trauma-related reactions; and/or habitual avoidance of emotions
- *Getting healthy needs met safely*, including through the use of healing-focused recovery skills and the development of distress management

plans to help patients recognize and interrupt no-longer-adaptive patterns of risky, unhealthy, or unsafe behavior.

Although these skills are separated into four domains, they are interrelated. For example, individuals who are working on grounding may be able to break a cycle of unhealthy behavior by regulating their emotions. This may help them get healthy needs met more safely, and they may experience some emotions that they have previously dissociated.

Individuals with TRD need to gradually develop understanding of what contributes to their risky behaviors and learn, as well as actually use, alternative, healthier ways of emotion and symptom regulation, and managing relationships, dissociative self-states, and stressors. It is common for these individuals to be reluctant to use these skills even when they have learned them, for a variety of reasons (see Topic 14 in the Workbook for a list of many of these reasons). Improving TRD patients' capacity for emotion regulation is of critical importance for their recovery. Increased capacity for emotion regulation enables TRD patients to tolerate painful emotions, thereby reducing their reliance on NSSI, dissociation, drugs, and other unhealthy coping strategies to manage traumatic intrusions, overwhelming emotions, and compartmentalized self-states.

An important reason to reduce patients' reliance on dissociation is that dissociation can interfere with treatment response. Specifically, the *timing* of dissociation has been shown to be a predictor of treatment outcome. Dissociation occurring *during* treatment sessions can interfere with the inhibitory learning that takes place while processing trauma; thus, dissociation could interfere with trauma-based fears and shame being unlearned (Lanius et al., 2012). Research supports this possibility. Dissociation at the onset of treatment was the only variable that predicted treatment outcome among people presenting to an emergency room for care following a trauma (Price et al., 2014). In fact, dissociation at the start of treatment accounted for a surprisingly high level of PTSD following treatment (i.e., 51%), indicating just how serious an impediment to treatment dissociation can be. A great deal more needs to be learned about dissociation's impact on treatment outcome, including about the timing (i.e., dissociation at intake into a study versus at the start of treatment versus during therapy sessions), chronicity (i.e., peritraumatic dissociation versus chronic trait-like dissociation), severity, and type of dissociation experienced (e.g., emotional numbing versus depersonalization/derealization versus identity fragmentation versus amnesia).

EXPERTS' RECOMMENDATIONS FOR TREATING COMPLEX DD

Although additional research is necessary, available research does provide a window into what experts have found most effective. Recommendations from experts can provide important guidance for TRD treatment.

DD expert survey

The TOP DD research team surveyed 36 international DD experts to identify interventions that they recommended using across the stages of treatment for DID (Brand et al., 2012b). The experts rated the frequency with which they recommended the use of 28 interventions in treating DID. The "top 10" most recommended interventions across the stages of treatment were reported. Due to the high level of chronic unsafe behaviors, the DD experts advocated that clinicians continually address safety as a "top 10" most frequently recommended intervention throughout DD treatment until the last stage of treatment. During the stabilization as well as the trauma processing stage, experts recommended interventions related to stabilizing clients, helping them manage dissociation via grounding techniques and PTSD symptoms via containment techniques, as well as improving tolerance of emotions and impulse control.

DD experts' treatment recommendations compared to clinicians' interventions

The TOP DD team compared treatment interventions reported by the clinicians who participated in the TOP DD naturalistic treatment study to those recommended by DD experts (Myrick et al., 2015). Our goal was to determine if community clinicians provided treatment that was generally consistent with experts' recommendations. The community clinicians and the DD experts reported on the treatment interventions they used with their DD patients using the same interventions assessment measure, the Dissociative Disorders Treatment Activities Questionnaire (Brand et al., 2012b; Myrick et al., 2015). Here we review only the comparison for the stabilization phase because this phase is the most crucial for the treatment of TRD and is the focus of the TOP DD Network study.

The comparison between clinicians and experts indicated that the community therapists generally reported using treatment interventions that were consistent with those recommended by DD experts in the stabilization stage. However, clinicians reported less use of some of the important stabilizing techniques, including improving safety and teaching patients about symptom management techniques (e.g., grounding and containment). These results suggested that therapists might benefit from additional training about stabilizing complex dissociative patients.

Figure 4.1 shows the comparison of the interventions recommended by the experts versus the community clinicians. The experts and therapists agreed about the frequency of working with dissociative self-states beginning in the first stage of treatment, as well as teaching cognitive-behavioral techniques, stabilizing the patient during crises, and refraining from detailed processing of specific traumatic events.

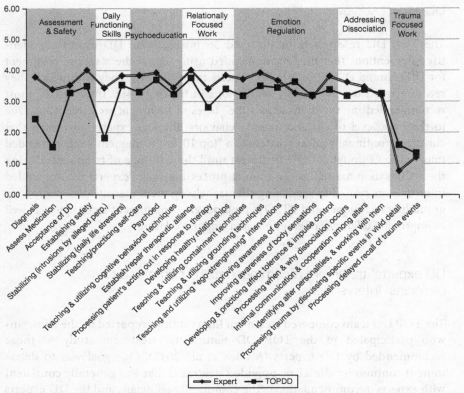

Figure 4.1. A comparison of the interventions recommended by dissociative disorder experts compared to the community clinicians in the TOP DD study.
Used with permission from Myrick, A.C., Chasson, G.S., Lanius, R., Leventhal, B. & Brand, B.L. (2015). Treatment of complex dissociative disorders: A comparison of interventions reported by community therapists versus those recommended by experts. *Journal of Trauma & Dissociation, 16*:1, 51–67. doi:10.1080/15299732.2014.949020

Despite the similarities between the experts' and clinicians' interventions, there were some significant differences between the groups. In general, the experts advised doing more assessment (i.e., diagnosing psychiatric illnesses and response to medications), more focus on emotion and symptom regulation (i.e., teaching and practicing containment and grounding, as well as working with patients to develop affect tolerance and impulse control), and more relationally focused work (i.e., establishing/repairing the alliance; processing the patient's reaction to therapy; developing healthy relationships). Community clinicians were less likely to emphasize affect tolerance, impulse control, containment, and grounding; this indicates the need for training about the importance of these stabilizing interventions, particularly because the clinicians also reported less focus on establishing safety and more frequent use of "exposure" (in-depth emotional processing of trauma) techniques than did the DD experts.

These important findings guided the development of the TOP DD Network study and program, as well as writing this book and the companion workbook. The main goals of the TOP DD Network study and this book are increasing clinicians' and TRD individuals' awareness of, and skill using, the interventions that are essential to the stabilization and safety of TRD individuals. Clinicians and individuals with TRD who know the importance of these crucial stabilization skills can work together to build a solid treatment foundation. The success of a dissociative individual's progress in treatment depends on having a solid foundation in these areas (International Society for the Study of Dissociation, 2011; Kluft, 1993c).

THE TOP DD TREATMENT STUDIES

The TOP DD naturalistic study

Research indicates that DD treatment that is generally consistent with the stage model is associated with a range of improvements for DD patients. For a review and meta-analysis of early DD treatment studies that were conducted, see Brand et al. (2009b). The TOP DD naturalistic study and TOP DD Network results are consistent with the findings from the earlier, mostly inpatient, DD treatment studies. In general, these studies show that if trauma treatment is provided that is consistent with expert guidelines about complex trauma-related dissociation, highly dissociative patients show improvements in many areas (Brand et al., 2009b; International Society for the Study of Dissociation, 2011; Jepsen et al., 2014). Taken together, the treatment studies suggest that DD patients benefit from a trauma- and dissociation-focused treatment that follows a staged, carefully paced approach in which their safety and severe symptoms, including dissociation, are addressed and stabilized.

The first study examining how DD patients did in treatment conducted by the TOP DD research team was called the *naturalistic* TOP DD study (Brand et al., 2009b, 2013) because the researchers did not alter the treatment or offer any additional intervention to the participants; rather, they studied how patients fared "naturally" over time in individual psychotherapy treatment. The study was "prospective," meaning that information about the patients' symptoms and functioning was collected longitudinally throughout 2.5 years of treatment. It was the first international treatment study of DD patients, with input from 280 individuals diagnosed with DID or DD not otherwise specified (DDNOS) and 292 therapists. We asked patients and therapists to share information about how the patient was doing four times over 30 months.

Therapists participating in the TOP DD naturalistic study indicated which treatment stage their patient was in during the previous 6 months of treatment. A comparison of the patients at different stages—that is, the "cross-sectional" comparisons—found that patients in the first stage of treatment had higher levels of dissociation, PTSD, self-injurious behaviors, and general psychiatric symptoms;

more hospitalizations; and less healthy daily functioning than patients in the last stage of treatment (Brand et al., 2009b).

The "longitudinal" naturalistic TOP DD results (i.e., the analyses that compared patients at the beginning of the study to how they were doing at the 30-month follow-up) indicated patients had decreased levels of dissociation, PTSD, depression, suicide attempts, self-harm, dangerous behaviors, drug use, physical pain, and psychiatric hospitalizations, as well as improved functioning and adaptive skills (Brand et al., 2013). Moreover, DD patients reported they were more often volunteering and/or attending school, socializing, and feeling good. Furthermore, more patients progressed from the early stage of treatment to a more advanced stage than regressed from an advanced to an early treatment stage.

Indeed, even the TOP DD patients with the highest levels of dissociation, as well as those with the most severe depression, showed significant improvements in these symptoms over 30 months (Engelberg & Brand, 2012). In many studies, the patients with the worst symptoms are the ones who do not improve, so it is crucial to find that treatment is associated with improvement even among the most symptomatic individuals.

Therapists reported an alarming level of revictimizations in the prior 6 months: Between 3.5% and 7% of patients experienced either sexual or physical revictimization and 2.9% to 6% experienced emotional abuse in a relationship (Myrick et al., 2013). Crucially, treatment may have helped patients get safer in relationships because the number of patients who were revictimized showed a trend toward declining over the course of the study.

Furthermore, more patients showed "sudden improvement" compared to "sudden worsening" (i.e., 20% increase or decrease in symptoms) at one or more time points. Therapists reported fewer episodes of revictimization and revictimization-related stressors among the "sudden improvement" group compared to the group who suddenly worsened, suggesting that revictimization and/or stressors may have contributed to worsening in treatment. Worsening over more than one data collection point occurred in only a small minority (1.1%) of the patients.

Unfortunately, it is a sad reality that there are individuals who do not respond, or who even worsen, in psychotherapy (Leichsenring et al., 2019). Few researchers have been willing to study and report rates of worsening; it is an area about which the mental health field needs to learn a great deal. The rate of 1.1% sustained worsening in the TOP DD longitudinal study compares favorably to the 5% to 10% of psychiatric patients who show worsening symptoms during treatment in general (Hansen et al., 2002).

Consistent with other research, the DD participants in the TOP DD longitudinal study required frequent hospitalization due to their high rate of unsafe behaviors. Therapists reported that 56% of the patients in the stabilization phase had engaged in NSSI in the 6 months prior to the start of the study and an alarming 38% had attempted suicide in the last 6 months (Brand et al., 2009b). Given this exceedingly high level of unsafe behavior, it is not surprising that almost a quarter (23%) of the patients had *required between one and three hospitalizations in the last 6 months* prior to enrolling in the study (Brand et al., 2013). It is particularly noteworthy that even with such high rates of NSSI, suicide attempts, and hospitalization, the patients showed a reduction in all three of these serious problems after 30 months of individual therapy. This is striking, given that a recent meta-analysis of 32 randomized controlled trials found that across studies examining NSSI, psychotherapy was not found to be effective in reducing NSSI, although it was effective in reducing suicide attempts (Calati & Courtet, 2016).

The study found several other encouraging results. A comparison of the younger to older TOP DD participants illustrated that the young adult patients stabilized self-injurious behaviors and suicide attempts more rapidly than did the older adults (Myrick et al., 2012). This is a very important finding because it suggests that early diagnosis and DD treatment could result in more rapid stabilization of potentially life-threatening symptoms. These results bring up the hopeful possibility that early identification of TRD could lead to early intervention that might reduce the demoralization and the pathway that leads to some individuals with TRD becoming chronically disabled due to the severity of their symptoms and the need for repeated hospitalizations. Research in this area is desperately needed.

Another promising and crucial finding from the naturalistic TOP DD study related to the economic burden associated with DD. Research has only recently begun to investigate the economic costs of TRD. However, recent data about the staggering costs of child abuse likely generalize to those with TRD. Child abuse and neglect is estimated to cost the United States over $100 billion each year due to the myriad psychological, medical, academic, social services, occupational, criminal justice, and other enduring impacts (Wang & Holton, 2007). The severe trauma histories and levels of disability associated with DD make it likely that there are very high costs associated with these disorders.

In one of the first studies of the economic costs of DD treatment, the TOP DD team estimated the costs of outpatient treatment sessions and inpatient hospitalization for each patient in the study. These costs were analyzed for patients in early- versus late-stage treatment (i.e., cross-sectional) as well as over time (i.e., longitudinal). According to patients' reports of days hospitalized, the cost of hospitalization was lower at later stages of treatment compared to earlier stages. Similarly, cost estimates decreased over time in the longitudinal comparisons. Cost estimates using therapists' reports of days hospitalized showed declines over time. Therapists were also asked about the number of psychotherapy sessions that the patient received in the prior 6 months. Using cost estimates for outpatient sessions, the estimated costs of outpatient treatment decreased over time. It seems likely that reductions in NSSI and suicide attempts over time in treatment contributed to the decreased costs of inpatient and outpatient treatment over time, although the design of the study does not allow us to conclude definitively that the treatment caused the improvements that were linked to decreasing costs.

As noted above, the 30-month longitudinal results were quite encouraging. The TOP DD research team decided to see if the improvements endured, increased, or perhaps lessened after the study ended. We attempted to locate the therapists several years after the study concluded to determine patients' long-term outcome. We were able to locate and obtain long-term follow-up data from 61 of the original

TOP DD therapists in a brief follow-up survey (Myrick et al., 2017b). On average, therapists were contacted 6 years after they had been recruited into the TOP DD study. According to therapists' reports, the patients still in treatment continued to show improvements: They had fewer overall stressors, psychiatric hospitalizations, and sexual revictimizations over the 6 years. TOP DD patients were 60 times more likely to be sexually revictimized at 6 months into the study than they were at the 6-year follow-up, indicating that this is a very important area of improved safety related to treatment. Only 1.6% of the patients required hospitalization in the 6 months prior to the 6-year follow up. Furthermore, their daily functioning had significantly improved, according to therapists' reports. There was less conflict among dissociative self-states over time, which is crucial because entrenched conflict among dissociative self-states is associated with poor prognosis for DD individuals (Kluft, 1994b).

However, there were still areas of marked difficulty at the 6-year follow-up: 46% of patients had very poor, unstable, or no romantic relationships, 37.7% were unable to hold a job or were receiving disability benefits, 40% had considerable health-related stressors, and 32.2% struggled with stress related to their family of origin (Myrick et al., 2017b). More than a fourth of the patients (38.2%) were no longer in treatment with the TOP DD therapist. Therapists reported a variety of reasons for the discontinuation of treatment: 12.8% ended successfully without full integration of dissociated self-states, but functioning well, and another 12.8% had successfully ended treatment after full integration of dissociated self-states. A large group (38.5%) ended primarily due to external reasons (e.g., relocation, financial constraints, medical illness). Almost a fourth (23.1%) of those who ended working with the TOP DD therapist had discontinued treatment for primarily personal reasons, which could include lack of motivation and not finding treatment helpful. Unfortunately, some patients (2.6%) had died due to medical problems the therapist believed were exacerbated by poor self-care.

These longitudinal results are encouraging and sobering, depending on the patient. They illuminate the difficult reality of the long-term treatment and recovery for DD patients. That is, despite years of treatment, and alongside considerable improvements in symptoms, functioning, and treatment costs, a sizeable minority nonetheless generally struggle for years with difficulties related to relationships, health problems, family of origin, and occupational functioning.

In summary, the TOP DD naturalistic study documented that, with appropriate DD treatment, a wide range of symptoms and adaptive functioning improve while utilization of higher levels of care decreased. The consistency of this pattern across a breadth of outcome variables, corroborated by data from both therapists and patients, strongly suggests that treatment contributed to the improvements.

The TOP DD Network study

No systematic intervention targeting safety and emotion regulation difficulties had been published for DD patients, and no online educational program had been developed or studied for either DDs or TRD patients when the TOP DD team began to consider developing such a program. We developed the Finding Solid Ground program to specifically test whether providing an online psychoeducation program to TRD/DD patients and therapists would be associated with stabilizing a wide range of unsafe behaviors and trauma-related symptoms and improving emotion regulation.

It seemed that one potential method for improving patients' safety could be providing psychoeducation to both members of the treatment dyad about healthy methods of emotion regulation and symptom management techniques, including adaptive methods of managing unsafe urges. Developing skill in emotion regulation and symptom management may allow patients to function better and be better able to tolerate the emotions that arise in and outside of treatment. Enhancing emotion regulation skills could allow patients to participate more comfortably and meaningfully in treatment rather than repeatedly dissociating in response to feeling emotions during session. Dissociation during therapy interferes with productively working during the session.

DEVELOPMENT AND DESIGN OF THE TPO DD NETWORK STUDY

At about the time the TOP DD naturalistic study was nearing completion, researchers were beginning to show that online treatments and educational programs could be quite helpful for a variety of psychological disorders, but an online intervention had not been attempted with DD patients prior to the TOP DD Network study. Research was emerging showing that participants with problems such as depression and anxiety found these online programs beneficial (Catrin Lewis et al., 2012). These programs were accessible, affordable, and convenient and did not require travel nor finding a therapist with skill and availability to provide treatment. Research was beginning to show that a collaborative relationship could be developed with the online therapist or trainer (Klein et al., 2010; Knaevelsrud & Maercker, 2007). The decades-old standard of needing to be face to face in an office to provide services was being challenged by these innovative online programs (Morland et al., 2014). Critically, participation in online educational and treatment programs is associated with improved symptoms for a variety of disorders, including PTSD (Lewis et al., 2019; Sijbrandij et al., 2016), and these programs have proven acceptable to patients (Simon et al., 2019). These promising online mental health programs were gaining credibility and therefore becoming popular just as the TOP DD team began to consider the daunting unmet need for treatment for DD patients.

The TOP DD team was aware of trauma experts who were conducting workshops worldwide to meet the tremendous need for training therapists. This was a wonderful way of providing training, yet not all therapists could attend these workshops. Furthermore, there were limited numbers of clinicians who had the expertise and who could travel internationally to provide these courses. A couple of pioneering professional organizations began to develop and sponsor online training workshops for therapists (e.g., the International Society for the Study of Trauma & Dissociation; the European Society for Trauma & Dissociation).

Online webinars began to be a popular and accessible means of reaching a wide audience of therapists.

This was the context in which the TOP DD team discussed the next step that was needed in DD treatment research. How could we respond to the daunting need for treatment research and training when there was so little funding and so few clinicians who could provide training to therapists, and yet so many people who needed treatment? It was clear that DD patients around the world desperately needed treatment, and the mental health field had to find ways to provide easily accessible and affordable training to a large number of therapists so they could competently provide that treatment. The TOP DD team brainstormed ways to address the unmet need for DD treatment around the world. The result that emerged was the TOP DD Network study, which is the mental health field's first standardized intervention for DD outpatients. It is considered groundbreaking because it was the first study that delivered a standardized online educational program to patients and therapists aimed at stabilizing DD patients' symptoms and providing basic training to therapists about methods for stabilizing patients' symptoms, while at the same time studying the treatment outcomes for patients.

We developed the Finding Solid Ground program informed by the clinical problems and related research and expert guidelines reviewed above. We recognized that most clinicians do not receive systematic training in complex trauma and dissociation and often do not feel prepared to treat individuals with complex dissociation. Based on the findings from our research, additional training about stabilizing interventions appeared to be needed by both the patients and their treating clinicians. Our goal was to create a program that could help both patients and therapists learn to improve patients' safety, symptoms, and ability to tolerate and safety manage their feelings and dissociated parts of self. We also sought to increase patients' self-understanding and self-compassion.

Along with our wonderful team of collaborating researchers and expert trauma clinicians,[1] we developed the TOP DD program as an online program so it was easily accessible and feasible to deliver on a large scale. The program provides education through a series of videos and written materials that aim to help patients stabilize their safety by increasing their awareness of what contributes to urges to be "unsafe," with safety being broadly defined. We provide education about trauma-related symptoms and early warning signs that might indicate that the patient is becoming overwhelmed and distressed. Recognizing early warning signs is crucial because they are signals to use symptom management and self-soothing techniques before the patient is overwhelmed and less capable of remaining safe.

The program teaches patients a variety of ways to manage symptoms, unsafe urges, trauma-based triggers, and emotions. In order to maintain safety and manage trauma-related symptoms, patients need to be able to identify, regulate,

---

1. List of TOP DD collaborators: Bethany L. Brand, Hugo J. Schielke, Frank W. Putnam, Richard J. Loewenstein, Amie Myrick, Karen Putnam, Ellen K. K. Jepsen, Willemien Langeland, Clare Pain, Kathy Steele, Catherine Classen, Suzette Boon, Paul A. Frewen, and Ruth A. Lanius.

and make healthy use of emotion. We developed the Finding Solid Ground program so that it would enhance patients' emotion regulation skills, as well as reduce the shame and harsh self-criticism that often contribute to unsafe behaviors and may increase the risk for depression and suicide. To support the goals of easing shame and self-criticism, as well as to enhance their ability to have healthy relationships, we also focused on identifying and challenging trauma-based distorted beliefs, particularly the beliefs that might contribute to safety problems.

The TOP DD Network's program content and interventions are primarily aimed at the stabilization stage of treatment for complex dissociative patients, although problems with safety, dissociation, and emotion dysregulation occur throughout the stages of treatment. Consistent with the need for these skills across the course of treatment, a number of participants who had already worked to stabilize their symptoms and safety participated in the TOP DD Network study; some of these more advanced patients informed us that the program helped them learn to more broadly understand what safety entails and to deepen their self-care to include this enhanced awareness of safety. They reported learning to take care of themselves in new ways such as setting self-protective boundaries in unhealthy relationships, reducing excessive computer gaming and/or media use, and eating healthier, to name just a few.

The TOP DD Network was designed as an adjunctive intervention intended to provide the knowledge and skills needed for symptom management and stabilization. The educational materials targeted unsafe behaviors as well as the symptoms and emotions that contribute to them. Therefore, the primary goals were to (1) educate patients and their therapists about trauma-related symptoms; (2) support patients in developing healthy methods for managing the emotions and symptoms that contribute to unsafe urges; and (3) enhance patients' self-compassion and quality of life (Boon et al., 2011; Kluft, 1993a; 1993c, 2007; Loewenstein, 1991, 1993, 2006; Mendelsohn et al., 2011). We also hoped to provide clinicians with knowledge about TRD and the steps that can be used to stabilize NSSI, suicidal urges, and symptoms in early treatment with traumatized patients.

Due to the ethical imperative to support these individuals, most of whom struggled with NSSI, suicidal thoughts, and/or unsafe behaviors and other severe symptoms, they were required to be in treatment with a therapist. The team understood that learning and thinking about topics such as dissociation, emotions, trauma, and safety might be quite challenging for many participants. Although patients in the early phase of treatment needed to work on these issues, it was possible that some participants would become briefly filled with emotions that might lead to more dissociation or even urges to be unsafe. As a safeguard, the patient's therapist also had to be willing to participate in the study so they could be aware of and potentially benefit from the information provided, helping the therapist understand the patient's difficulties and be better equipped to support the patient.

There were many sources of knowledge, expertise, and research that guided the development of the Finding Solid Ground program. Clinical theory about complex trauma, trauma treatment research, and expert guidelines and treatment recommendations for DDs were highly influential in the program's development (including but not limited to Boon et al., 2011; Brand et al., 2012b; Briere & Scott, 2006, 2015; Chefetz, 2015; Chu, 1988, 2011; Cloitre et al., 2009; 2012a; Courtois & Ford, 2009; Ford & Courtois, 2009; Frewen & Lanius, 2015; Herman, 1992, 1997; Howell, 2011; International Society for the Study of Dissociation, 2011; Kluft, 1993a, 1993c, 2006, 2007; Kluft & Fine, 1993; Loewenstein, 1993, 1994, 2005, 2006; Putnam, 1989, 1997, 2016; Steele et al., 2017; van der Hart et al., 2006). The structure and content of the program was also informed by patient and therapist participants' feedback from the naturalistic TOP DD study (Brand et al., 2009b, 2013) and by the differences noted between the interventions clinicians reported using and the interventions recommended by DD experts. We were also guided by our own decades of learning from our clinical work. Finally, we had a consumer panel of individuals with TRD who reviewed our educational materials to improve the acceptability of our educational explanations and exercises. The Finding Solid Ground program can be seen as a "group sourced" compilation of experts', clinicians', and patients' wisdom and feedback, and informed by research. The program epitomizes the TOP DD logo: "Work together, learn together, heal together!"

This approach to our work is also evident in our response to feedback we received during the study. Initially, we planned to give participants access to the psychoeducational materials for only 1 year, which would enable us to have a 1-year follow-up period. However, feedback from patients and therapists indicated that they needed more time in between the videos to complete the written and practice exercises, and to feel ready to move to the next topic. Based on this feedback, we decided to allow participants access to the materials for the full 2-year time period.

PROCEDURE FOR THE TOP DD NETWORK STUDY
Of critical importance, patients were *not* excluded from participating in the TOP DD Network study due to any comorbid disorders, self-harm, suicidality, ongoing interpersonal traumatization, homicidality, type of trauma, or recent hospitalization(s). Said differently, there were no exclusion criteria based on psychiatric status or severity or type of trauma. We know of no other intervention for traumatized patients, or any psychiatric diagnosis, that has not excluded patients for one or more of these reasons.

Due to concerns about patient safety and the importance of pacing and practicing new skills, we gave access to the next set of materials no sooner than a week had passed, and only after both therapist and patient had reviewed the materials. We received several requests to change this pacing restriction. Some patients described being frustrated at their therapist's relatively slower pace, and some therapists were faster than their patients. However, we felt it was important that therapists were aware of the skills and approach their patients were working on, so we did not alter this aspect of the study.

RESULTS OF THE TOP DD NETWORK STUDY
The large amount of data from the TOP DD Network study will continue to be analyzed for several years. What follows are the results to date. The patient

participants in the program were mostly female (88.3%) and Caucasian (86.5%). The analyses that we present here are based on 111 patients who completed surveys at intake into the study and again at either the 12-month or 24-month time points (Brand et al., 2019b). (Note: Comparisons of the demographics and baseline symptoms of the participants who did not opt to complete the 12- or 24-month surveys indicated that they were not different in terms of any demographics such as age or severity of symptoms.)

The DD patients showed many exciting improvements over the course of the study. The emphasis on improving safety and ability to manage emotions in healthy ways appears to have been quite helpful, in combination with individual therapy. (However, it is important to note that we cannot be certain that the TOP DD Network intervention and/or individual psychotherapy caused the following improvements, due to the lack of random assignment to a control group. At the time of writing this book, we are developing an online randomized controlled trial of the TOP DD Network study that will be able to determine if this program causes improvements.)

Symptoms of dissociation and PTSD became less severe and debilitating over the 2 years. The patients improved their adaptive capacities, such as their ability to tolerate and manage emotions, impulses, and trauma-related symptoms; ability to have healthy relationships; better self-care; and emotion and symptom management techniques, among other abilities. Adaptive capacities were assessed by the Progress in Treatment Questionnaire (Schielke et al., 2017) for patients and therapists; see Chapter 2 and Appendix A for information about, and copies of, these questionnaires. (For readers who appreciate knowing how large research findings are, the improvements in dissociation and PTSD symptoms, emotion regulation, and adaptive capacities were in the moderate to large range, with effect sizes [ES] $|d| = 0.44$–0.90.)

As reviewed above, typically in treatment studies the individuals with the most severe symptoms are least likely to improve. However, we specifically developed the Finding Solid Ground program to benefit individuals with severe DD. We hoped to be able to teach patients with dissociative self-states the steps that would enable them to improve their ability to manage their emotions, symptoms, and safety. The TOP DD Network study results suggest that those in the study seem to "buck the trend" of primarily helping the least impaired individuals. Specifically, we compared the participants with the highest level of dissociative symptoms to those with those with lower levels of dissociative symptoms (i.e., those above and below the cutoff of 30 on the Dissociative Experiences Scale) to see if both groups showed improvements. We found promising results: Although both groups showed significant improvements, participants with higher dissociation *showed even greater and faster improvement than* did those who were lower in dissociation (moderate to large effect sizes depending on the outcome being compared, ES $|d| = 0.54$–1.04 versus $|d| = 0.24$–0.75, respectively) (Brand et al., 2019b).

More than two thirds (69%) of the individuals who engaged in NSSI in the 6 months before the study began decreased NSSI over the 2 years (Brand et al., 2019b). The most dissociative patients showed the most significant improvement in safety. The patients who most often engaged in NSSI showed impressive stabilization. Specifically, the therapists of the three patients who had the highest NSSI, self-harming approximately 100, 125, and 150 times in the 6 months before the study began, reported their patients had self-harmed 0, 10, and 10 times, respectively, in the final 6 months of the study. This is a particularly compelling finding. Even though these individuals would have been excluded from other trauma treatment studies, they were nonetheless able to benefit from this program, combined with individual therapy that addressed their DD.

There were additional promising findings related to safety. At the beginning of the study, patients required almost 23 days of hospitalization on average in the prior 6 months, compared to 11.5 days of hospitalization 2 years later (Brand et al., 2019b). This change in days hospitalized was not statistically significant, although it was in the direction suggesting that hospitalizations were trending toward declining. Suicide attempts in the prior 6 months at the end of the study were lower (average = 0.17 attempts in the last 6 months, SD = 0.80) than they were at the beginning of the study (average = 0.39 attempts in the last 6 months, SD = 1.54), although this was not a statistically significant decline. Nonetheless, these important shifts were in the direction of stabilization, suggesting that the TOP DD program, combined with individual therapy, was associated with widespread improvements in the patients' safety and symptoms, possibly due to their enhanced adaptive capacities, including improved emotion regulation.

The results of the Network study and other DD treatment studies show that although DDs are challenging to treat and recover from, when provided with individual therapy and psychoeducation about trauma and dissociation, *patients with DDs can be helped to heal and grow* (Brand, 2001). Treatment that enables severely dissociative individuals to healthfully manage their trauma-related symptoms and emotions guides these individuals to *find solid ground*.

Summary and implications of the TOP DD studies

The TOP DD studies have important implications for individuals with DD and their loved ones, the mental health field, and health care systems.

First, DD patients' complex and chronic symptoms contribute to an incredible degree of suffering and an alarming level of suicidality that necessitate high levels of restrictive and expensive care.

Second, frequent hospitalizations are common among these individuals. Hospitalizations are necessary to save the lives of suicidal patients. Nonetheless, hospitalizations and the tremendous pain that necessitates them seriously impair the quality of life for DD patients. Crucially, when they are being treated by a trauma-trained clinician who recognizes and attends to their DD diagnosis, according to the TOP DD studies, patients' safety improves and hospitalizations become less frequent over time.

Third, hospitalizations are expensive for the patients and the health care system, but the costs of treatment decrease over time in treatment for DD (Myrick et al.,

2017a). Most of these patients would have been excluded from treatment studies due to the severity of their symptoms. The result is a concerning gap in the evidence base needed to guide and inform clinicians about the best treatments for these highly symptomatic individuals.

These underrecognized patients are also underserved (see Chapter 1). The findings from the TOP DD studies indicate that education about safety, emotion regulation, and symptom management, combined with individual therapy that addresses their TRD, is associated with a wide range of improvements for TRD individuals. Simply put, education and treatment seem to help highly dissociative patients find solid ground in healing from trauma.

5

Understanding and Addressing the Impact of Trauma on Relational Functioning

The relational history of patients with trauma-related disorders (TRDs) is typically marked by serious and frequent boundary violations in their close relationships, including violations or blurred boundaries in relationships with caretakers and authority figures. This frequently includes experiences of physical, sexual, and emotional abuse and/or neglect in childhood as well as intimate partner violence and physical and sexual assault in adulthood. Unfortunately, interpersonal violence frequently continues, often without the therapist's knowledge, during the course of the therapy (see Chapter 8). Their relational history may also include more subtle boundary violations such as parental intrusiveness, early parentification, and exploitation to meet others' emotional needs. Having not learned about the necessity of having and maintaining healthy boundaries, these individuals may have little awareness of boundaries.

Therefore, it is not surprising that issues around the therapeutic frame frequently and repeatedly emerge in the treatment. Patients often expect the therapist to engage in abusive behavior and boundary violations, because this has been their experience of authority figures throughout their lives. Many of these patients do not have a template for a relationship with an authority figure where they are not abused or exploited. They may not even be able to conceptualize that such healthy relationships could occur. They may intentionally or unintentionally act out their history of relational betrayals by creating reenactments of familiar abusive dynamics, simply because, to them, "this is the way relationships are" and there is no other way to be in relationship.

Patients may also consciously or unconsciously wish for therapists to provide high levels of nurturance and caretaking to compensate for the nurturance and protection they missed in childhood. They may be profoundly ashamed of longing for attachment and care, which likely increases the risk for it being acted out, rather than reflected on and discussed. If the therapist is not attentive to these possibilities, the result may be a reenactment, whereby previous abusive or betrayal dynamics are replayed in the therapeutic relationship without being processed or reflected upon, typically to the detriment of the treatment and the patient (Chefetz, 2015; Kluft, 1994a; Loewenstein, 1993; van der Kolk, 1989). For example, a patient with insulin-dependent diabetes who experienced neglect and abuse in childhood, including not having had regular meals provided by her parents, might repeatedly show up for therapy sessions reporting she does not feel well and has not eaten all day due to a lack of food in her home. The therapist and patient are aware that very low blood sugar levels may be causing her to feel ill and this situation could be a medical emergency. The therapist could easily feel compelled to provide food for the client, acting out the role of rescuer with the patient reenacting the role of starved child victim, rather than naming and exploring the dynamic that is being enacted.

Concurrently, the therapist may react with a confusing mixture of feelings, including deep care, sorrow, guilt, and fear of provoking the patient's disappointment or anger, and may at times feel utterly compelled or coerced into providing greater and greater levels of support and caregiving, particularly when the dynamic revolves around potentially emergent issues such as suicide, risky behavior, or uncontrolled medical illness. Even well-trained therapists can find it confusing to know when and how to set limits so that requests for caretaking do not escalate into blurred boundaries and boundary violations. Excessive caregiving can drain the therapist's compassion and energy and lead to increasing amounts of time spent outside of session worrying about, or dealing with, the patient. This erosion of boundaries results in the therapist working excessively hard in and outside of the sessions, rather than the patient carrying the responsibility for their recovery.

Therapists need to model that life is about much more than just being in, or providing, therapy. If therapists do not help patients learn about, and if necessary insist upon, the maintenance of healthy boundaries, it ultimately shifts the dynamic of the relationship from one that supports growth and increasing levels of self-care and independence to one that inadvertently undermines the patient's ability to manage without the therapist. What may have started out as a well-meaning therapist's attempt to show the patient that he or she is valuable and worth caring about can evolve into a pattern in which the patient is excessively childlike and dependent upon the therapist, and perhaps others, in ways that are damaging. For example, the patient may not be able to tolerate the idea of getting better because it would mean losing the therapist, so the patient may stagnate in treatment and fail to develop, or fail to use, skills and abilities that are necessary to live a full, meaningful life.

If the therapist avoids discussing requests from the patient as they begin to become too frequent, too dependency-forming, or otherwise unhealthy, the therapist can become entangled in an unconscious collusion with the patient to avoid grieving the profoundly painful losses and betrayals of childhood. Although it is entirely understandable why these patients might desperately want to be cared for in warm, intimate ways that are more appropriate for parent–child relationships, attempting to make up for these losses in a therapy relationship creates a level of dependency and regression that undermines the treatment. This ultimately harms, rather than helps, the patient. Therapy must strengthen the patient's ability to know, attend to, withstand, and accept their past experiences and feelings, as well as their current needs and feelings, and encourage them to develop a life that is worth living at a level commensurate with their age. While therapists may at times feel (and the patient may directly assert) that they are asking too much of the patient, or unfairly depriving them, it is important to remember that trauma survivors are incredibly resilient simply by virtue of the fact that they have survived. These patients typically have a number of strengths, and if the therapist can foster these strengths, the patient can begin to thrive.

One model for understanding dynamics that may emerge in treatment is Karpman's triangle (Karpman, 2011), which seeks to map out the ways in which both therapists and patients may be pulled into replays of early life events. This model suggests that in many trauma narratives, there are several roles that tend to occur: the sadistic perpetrator, the helpless victim, the overinvolved rescuer, and/ or the neglectful bystander (for more discussion of this model, see Clark et al., 2015; Karpman, 2011). Even after the trauma is over, patients (and therapists) may find themselves pulled into traumatic reenactments: In a reenactment, these rigid roles are played out without nuance or flexibility, and without the capacity to reflect on the process, to the detriment of both parties (van der Kolk, 1989, 2005).

Some examples of traumatic reenactments in therapy are as follows:

1. A patient who cannot pay her rent insists that there is nothing she can do to solve the problem and that she will end up homeless if the therapist does not solve this crisis for her (victim). The therapist (rescuer) lends the patient money to pay her rent or calls the landlord to negotiate on the patient's behalf even though the patient has the capacity to do this herself. Alternately, the therapist becomes overly frustrated with the patient and berates her for not managing her money properly (perpetrator) or avoids dealing with this topic as much as possible (bystander).
2. A patient yells at the therapist for canceling a session (perpetrator), and the therapist feels helpless and does not set boundaries around the patient's communication style (victim). After a time, the roles may invert: The therapist (perpetrator) may find themselves criticizing the patient for being so unreasonable, to which the patient reacts with passive helplessness (victim).
3. The patient (rescuer) may ask the therapist about the therapist's own life and reassure the therapist about how helpful and good the therapist is. The therapist then becomes overly passive and allows the patient to provide them with emotional support (victim).

Given that most therapists value being helpful to others, and that some TRD patients may present at times as extremely vulnerable and needy, the role of rescuer can be a particularly tempting one for therapists, which is one reason that attention to healthy boundaries and maintaining the therapeutic frame is so important. It is crucial to understand that over the course of the therapy, both the therapist and the patient will likely be repeatedly pulled toward all of these roles, and that even within a few minutes, roles can shift back and forth multiple times. Therapists need to be able to self-monitor: When they notice that they are interacting with a patient in a way that is not characteristic, they must step back and assess whether a reenactment could be occurring. Reflecting on, discussing, and understanding these pulls toward reenactments are wonderful, albeit challenging, opportunities to provide patients with experiences of healthy communication, tolerance of emotions and needs, and establishing and maintaining healthy boundaries. In fact, these interpersonal opportunities are considered by many therapists to be one of the mechanisms by which treatment enables TRD patients to heal their trauma and attachment histories.

Some examples of patient behaviors that may pull for reenactments include the following:

1. Making frequent phone calls or repeatedly emailing or texting between sessions
2. Having frequent crises that require attention from the therapist
3. Asking for, or demanding, increasingly frequent sessions or longer sessions
4. Having difficulty ending or leaving the session
5. Frequently attending sessions late or missing sessions
6. Asking for or initiating physical contact (e.g., hugs, hand holding)
7. Repeatedly asking for personal information about the therapist
8. Attempting to make the relationship overly intimate, romantic, or sexual.

PRAGMATICS OF BOUNDARY MANAGEMENT

Establishing a clear treatment frame at the beginning of the therapy is essential. For some therapists, this may take the form of a written informed consent document that is signed by both parties; for others, it may be a verbal discussion. (For a list of various professional groups' informed consent forms, and other useful resources, see https://kspope.com/consent/.) Whatever form it takes, essential aspects of the frame should be spelled out at the beginning of treatment, and they will likely need to be revisited throughout the treatment as issues arise.

Treatment frame issues to discuss and/or include in informed consent forms are as follows:

1. Duration, location, and frequency of sessions
2. Therapist availability between sessions and methods for communicating with therapist outside of sessions, including which forms of communication are acceptable (email, phone, text, etc.) and for what reasons. Therapists may need to address interactions on social media,

as some patients may try to engage with the therapist through the therapist's personal social media accounts. Therapists should also explicitly explain their policy regarding returning communication (e.g., how quickly do they respond and during what hours) and verify whether they can leave a voicemail if they are unable to reach the patient by phone when returning a call. They should identify alternative crisis resources that patients can use in an emergency.

3. Fees (and insurance information), including fees for missed appointments and other uninsured services if applicable
4. Cancellation policy, including whether fees are charged for canceled or missed appointments
5. Confidentiality and circumstances under which information may be disclosed without the patient's consent (e.g., imminent risk of harm to self or others).

There are a variety of views on aspects of the therapeutic frame (e.g., the role of touch in therapy, amount of personal disclosure, limits around between-session phone calls and emails). This may depend on the therapist's theoretical orientation, the modality that they practice, the ethical code of their profession, and/ or their own personal needs and limits. While there are some absolutes (e.g., the prohibition of sexual contact between therapist and patient), therapists will likely differ in other aspects of their treatment frames. Aside from these absolutes, the specific frame is less important than that whatever frame the therapist sets be consistent and thoughtful and stem from a sound clinical rationale that prioritizes the overall well-being of the client balanced with legal, ethical, and professional constraints of the therapist. The treatment frame provides the patient with a sense of predictability and security, both of which are frequently lacking in the relational history of TRD patients. It also models healthy boundaries and can provide an anchor for the therapist at times in the treatment when there may be a temptation to stray from the frame.

While only some TRD patients meet criteria for dissociative identity disorder, the Guidelines for the Treatment of Dissociative Identity Disorder in Adults, published by the International Society for the Study of Trauma and Dissociation (ISSTD), contains useful guidance about establishing a treatment frame that is beneficial for any severely traumatized and dissociative patients with attachment and relational challenges (ISSTD, 2011). Broadly speaking, the ISSTD guidelines suggest that patients typically need treatment sessions weekly for 45 to 50 minutes, although more frequent sessions (two or three times a week) or longer sessions (up to 90 minutes) may be useful, particularly when working with traumatic memories. Starting and ending times should be communicated to the patient ahead of time, and therapists should do their best to stay within the planned times. If the therapist has policies about payment for nonattendance or late cancellation, these should be observed consistently and applied promptly following the missed session. In other words, patients should not be allowed to accumulate large amounts of debt to the therapist without creating an arrangement for payment, as this can cause the patient to feel insecure and ashamed, and/or the therapist to feel resentful.

The therapeutic frame should be clearly communicated to the patient at the beginning of treatment and should remain generally consistent. When a change in the frame is requested (or demanded) by the patient, it is important to explore the meaning of the request rather than immediately granting or denying it. Even if the request is clinically reasonable, and the therapist does ultimately alter the frame, the act of talking about and exploring such requests provides a useful contrast to the covert boundary violations and secrecy of abuse, and therefore helps to establish a sense of safety and provides practice for negotiating needs in other relationships. It is important to explicitly explore whether such requests reflect a wish for reparenting, as there may be underlying grief or anger about the inability to repair an abusive childhood that needs to be processed.

If, after considered reflection, the therapist believes that it is indicated to change the frame (e.g., offering increased between-session contact or extra sessions during a time of crisis), the meaning of this shift should be carefully discussed with the patient, including any mixed feelings the patient might have, and any impact that this may have on the patient's sense of safety in the relationship. Loosening of boundaries can at times cause the patient to wonder if there is an impending boundary violation and therefore counterintuitively decrease safety, even if the change was made at the patient's request. If the shift in the frame is a temporary arrangement, such as during a time of crisis, it is important to also discuss when the usual frame will resume.

In patients with dissociative self-states, it is important to maintain generally consistent boundaries despite interacting with a range of dissociative self-states. Drastically altering the therapeutic frame, or the manner in which the therapist talks or acts, depending on which self-state is present, can inadvertently reinforce a sense of dividedness among some self-states, or foster a sense that the therapist is more interested in some self-states than others, rather than conveying that the therapist is dedicated to treating the whole patient. This will be discussed further in the chapter on understanding and working with dissociative self-states (Chapter 7).

Therapists should carefully monitor their own reactions to the patient. A wish to alter the frame or treat the patient as "special" in some way can eventually lead to boundary violations that are not in the patient's best interests. These situations can be quite confusing and bring up emotions for the therapist and the patient alike. Thus, frequent informal, and occasional formal, consultations are essential to providing sound treatment. All therapists need to seek advice from colleagues and, at times, from those who are experienced in the management of TRD patients. Therapists are particularly urged to seek consultation with a colleague who has experience with this population if they are feeling confused, conflicted, exhausted, or frustrated; find themselves feeling embarrassed or reluctant to discuss the case with colleagues; or are concerned about the boundaries with a patient. Furthermore, if they find themselves beginning to treat a patient differently from others, or rationalizing why a particular patient needs unusual boundary alterations, this is a signal that consultation would likely be useful.

PHYSICAL TOUCH

It is important to recognize that severely traumatized patients are a particularly vulnerable population and that their trauma histories often involve an association between touch and physical or sexual violation, so even incidental touch can be extremely triggering and evocative of past trauma. Therefore, the use of touch is generally not recommended with these individuals, though there are some special circumstances where touch may be considered. However, discussions about touch should happen prior to engaging in touch with patients, even if it seems minor and "normal" to the therapist, such as shaking hands when greeting each other.

Here are some possible circumstances when brief touch may be permissible:

1. Culturally normative professional touch, such as shaking hands on a first meeting, is typically acceptable, especially if initiated by the patient.
2. Some body awareness–oriented therapies include highly specific therapeutic interventions that involve physical contact. These techniques may require modification for use in this population (i.e., modified to not include direct interpersonal contact).
3. Medical practitioners may need to use touch as part of a physical examination (e.g., for side effects of certain medications).
4. Some treatment modalities, such as neurofeedback, may require incidental touch (e.g., to secure leads on the patient's head).

In the case of the body-oriented therapies, special training is required in the use of touch, and when working with highly traumatized or dissociative patients, it may be advisable, in some cases, to modify these techniques to avoid direct touch. For example, the therapist may place a pillow between the therapist's hand and the patient's body. Further research is required to explore the use of touch in this context with this population.

Medical examinations or treatment modalities requiring even incidental touch should only occur after explicit conversation with the patient and after consent has been obtained. If more extensive or frequent examination is necessary, or if the patient is uncomfortable with the therapist touching them, it may be better to have the examination or procedure performed by another therapist or physician. For example, a psychiatrist who is also prescribing antipsychotics may need to perform a limited physical examination to monitor for extrapyramidal symptoms but may choose to ask the patient's primary care provider to perform the examination if the patient is uncomfortable.

BETWEEN-SESSION CONTACT

We do not recommend extensive between-session contact, as it is important for patients to practice using their own coping skills and natural supports to manage difficult emotions. Some between-session contact can be therapeutic in times of crisis, however. The purpose of such contacts should not be to conduct therapy over the phone but to assist the patient in identifying and using skills to manage the crisis, such as containing emotion and/or traumatic material, until the next session.

The therapist's availability between sessions should be clearly communicated to the patient. To increase the likelihood that any between-session contact is beneficial, we recommend proactive conversations about when to reach out for between-session contact and what to expect in such contacts (e.g., a focus on identifying healthy ways to manage the crisis and speaking only for 10 minutes). For example, the therapist might spend session time helping the patient identify a list of coping techniques to manage an upsurge in feelings or symptoms *prior* to placing a crisis call to the therapist. The therapist should ask at the beginning of subsequent crisis calls what techniques the patient has used and what occurred when they used the techniques. Patients should also be provided with emergency resources, such as crisis lines and local emergency departments. Many therapists find it useful to set limits on the length of calls by making statements such as, "We cannot resolve this over the phone, so we'll need to address this in our next therapy session. Let's discuss what you can do in the meantime to take care of yourself." If patients continue to request frequent calls, additional discussion and limits will be needed.

PATIENTS WHO ARE TRIGGERED BY THE THERAPIST

While many patients have emotional triggers that are overtly related to traumatic content (e.g., the sound of footsteps, the smell of perfume), for patients who have been repeatedly traumatized in the context of interpersonal relationships (particularly caregiving relationships), the therapeutic relationship itself and its inherent vulnerability and power differential can also represent a powerful trigger for trauma-related reactions, including repeated loss of contact with the present moment in response to even basic components of the treatment (e.g., being behind a closed door, or the therapist standing or shifting position) that the therapist may take for granted. This dynamic, expressed either overtly or covertly, can slow down or stall the therapy if not directly and repeatedly addressed by the therapist. We will address in the next section the practical management of ungrounded states in general, but here we will first discuss fear of the therapist, and how the therapist might intervene to increase safety in the relationship. For further discussion of these themes see also Chefetz, 2015; Fisher, 2017; Steele et al., 2017; and van der Hart et al., 2006.

Most therapists are prepared to address some degree of fear or hesitancy at the beginning of treatment, but they may not be prepared for how pervasive and long-lasting this fear may be in TRD, or how far into the therapy the fear may persist. Therapists may also be unprepared for some of the specific fears that patients may have. For example, a therapist may take it for granted that they will not sexually abuse the patient, but the patient, who may have experienced repeated violation by authority figures, may in fact take it for granted that sexual violation is inevitable. No matter how hard the therapist tries to demonstrate that they are well intentioned and that the therapy is safe, patients may experience the therapist as rejecting, uncaring, violent, or even frankly sadistic/malevolent, and may interpret even benign behavior through this lens. They may fear that they will be physically or sexually abused, that they will be rejected, that they will become attached and then lose the therapist, that they will not be helped and will be disappointed, that they will harm or disgust the therapist by discussing their trauma, that the therapist will violate their confidentiality, that the therapist will take pleasure in their suffering, that the therapist will want to control them, that they will experience emotions in an unsafe way (including emotions that the therapist might not expect to be triggering, such as pride or joy), or any number of other fears about the therapist and the therapeutic process.

Beginning the treatment

It is vital for the therapist to be aware throughout the therapy of the breadth and intensity of the fears that these patients may have, and to begin addressing these fears directly at the beginning of treatment. If a patient has been in therapy before, part of the assessment can involve exploration of previous treatment experiences, including how the patient experienced the therapist and what relational challenges occurred in the dyad. In some cases, patients' fears may have roots not just in childhood but also in adulthood, as some patients will have been abused by previous therapists or health care providers, and this is important information to obtain. If the patient has not been in therapy before, exploration of other important attachment relationships in the past and present may provide similar information as to what relational templates may be activated in the therapy.

Once this information has been gathered, the therapist can explicitly normalize and validate fear of the therapist and link these fears to the TRD being treated. This issue may be discussed using different language in different therapeutic modalities (e.g., transference, core beliefs, schemas), but broadly, the patient should be told that it is common and understandable for people with TRD to fear the therapist and therapy. Therapists can highlight that while the patient may intellectually know that the therapist is not dangerous, for reasons we have discussed above, this information may not resonate on an emotional level. The therapist may use the material discussed in Chapter 3 to educate the patient that there is a neurobiological basis to this experience. This can reduce shame about fears that the patient might feel are "silly" and so would otherwise hide from the therapist. The initial phase of therapy also involves establishing as much relational safety as possible, but this task, and associated fears, will need to be revisited repeatedly throughout the treatment. Much of the establishment of safety is done through the therapist's behavior, as patients with TRD will need repeated concrete demonstrations of safety and predictability rather than words, as they may not trust the therapist to be truthful.

Establishing a dynamic of transparency

As much as possible, a dynamic should be established that counters the atmosphere of secrecy that characterizes many abusive relationships. One reason that we have recommended above that the therapist provide a clear treatment contract, explicitly discuss boundaries, and adhere as much as possible to the therapeutic frame is to reduce the sense of secrecy, as well as the degree to which patients may misinterpret aspects of the therapeutic frame (e.g., incidental touch, being asked to pay for missed sessions) as evidence of an impending violation or as a punishment or rejection. Patients with TRD may need more explicit explanations of what therapeutic techniques the therapist will use and what the rationale is for those techniques. Patients who have been sexually abused may need to be explicitly told that the therapeutic relationship will not be sexualized (though it is also important not to assume that stating this has actually dispelled the fear). Patients should be encouraged to tell the therapist if something is disturbing or confusing to them, and to ask any questions. Notably, however, patients may at times request or demand personal information about the therapist, asserting that this would make them feel safer. The therapist may choose not to answer questions that are unduly intrusive or personal, and may instead explore with the patient the meaning of having that information, how it would make them feel safer, and how else the therapist could address the patient's concern. In this situation, transparency may mean being explicit with the patient about why the therapist has chosen not to answer the question.

Establishing a dynamic of collaboration

Many patients with TRD have had experiences of authoritarian control in interpersonal relationships, and struggles around control can become central to the therapy. Patients can be told that they are not obligated to be in therapy, to disclose any specific information in therapy, or to work with that specific therapist (if this is in fact the case). Patients can also be allowed to have some choice about how the therapy is conducted, and in particular can be asked for consultation on what might make them feel the most safe and comfortable in the therapy office. For example, patients can be offered options as to where they would like to sit (e.g., to be closer to the door), how far away they would like the therapist to sit, or whether they use the therapist's first or last name (within the therapist's personal limits).

Continuing the treatment

Therapists can expect that establishing a sense of safety in the therapeutic relationship is a task that will continue throughout much of the therapy, and that the patient's sense of safety may fluctuate over time. Some patients may not be able to feel fully safe with the therapist for some time, though some degree of relative safety on the part of both therapist and patient is necessary for the therapy to continue. The therapist should continue to model curiosity about the patient's fears and willingness to respond with openness and flexibility to the patient's concerns about safety. The therapist should also monitor the patient's affect for evidence of fearfulness in response to the therapist's actions (e.g., standing up, reaching across the room, or speaking in a certain tone of voice) and can explicitly ask the patient about their reaction. For some patients, concrete reminders that the therapist will not harm or exploit them can be useful, but for others, only repeated behavioral demonstrations of safety are effective. The therapist can call the patient's attention to their track record together, including asking the patient to think of and name objective differences between the therapist and previous abusers, educate the patient on warning signs of abusive relationships, and discuss openly with the patient how either might know if the relationship was becoming unsafe, and how they could respond to restore safety. These kinds of open conversations can help reduce fearfulness and model appropriate self-protection in close relationships.

ATTACHMENT STYLES AND THEIR POSSIBLE IMPACTS ON TREATMENT

A patient's attachment style (see Chapter 1) can have a significant impact on treatment. Some traumatized clients may have an insecure but organized attachment style that remains generally consistent within the relationship. Insecure attachment can appear in the therapy in a number of ways, such as:

1. Avoidance of any dependency on the therapist (e.g., never making any requests, not acknowledging attachment needs, not calling when in serious crisis)
2. Flight from the relationship (e.g., missing sessions, lateness, long periods of silence, ending therapy)
3. Angrily attacking the therapist in response to perceived rejection (e.g., a cancellation or vacation)
4. Intense dependency needs (e.g., frequent phone calls, requests for more or extended sessions, difficulty with separations).

In clients who have a disorganized attachment style (see Chapter 1), all of these different behaviors may be present. The therapy may be characterized by rapid oscillations among the different modes described above. Given that the disorganized attachment style can be associated with childhood trauma and with dissociative symptoms (see Chapter 1), it makes sense that disorganized attachment is a frequent issue encountered in patients with TRD (Lyons-Ruth et al., 2006).

Liotti (2004) suggests that Karpman's triangle, which we reviewed above,, can be a useful model for understanding those with dissociative self-states, by recognizing that a child with a disorganized attachment style likely develops multiple representations of both the self and the caregiver as a way of making sense of the dilemma posed by a caregiver who is a source of both nurturance and danger. Clients who have dissociative self-states may show markedly different attachment styles in different self-states. This can be confusing for the therapist, who may have difficulty understanding why the patient's relational style changes so rapidly, and why any response from the therapist can seem unhelpful. The role of the therapist in this case is to begin to acknowledge the needs of different self-states and to find ways to "bridge" between them (Blizard, 2003).

Ultimately, the therapist's role is to move the patient toward an experience of greater attachment security. As discussed above, maintenance of the therapeutic frame and of appropriate boundaries is key in providing the patient with an experience of safety in an attachment relationship, and of an attachment figure who is reliable and benign rather than frightening and exploitative. (For further discussion on the management of dependency needs in the therapeutic relationship with patients with TRD, see also Steele et al., 2001.)

While the ultimate goal is for the patient to experience secure attachment with other people in the outside world and to be able to provide a felt sense of security and comfort to themselves, for highly traumatized patients, for whom human contact is often associated with abuse or neglect, this may not be possible until much later in the therapy. In these situations, it can be useful to help the patient to access the felt sense of secure attachment through imagery of nonhuman attachment figures, such as animals or even parts of nature (e.g., a sturdy tree with deep roots that has survived changes in weather and seasons for many years) (Steele et al., 2017). This "attachment resource" imagery might include the same components of secure attachment between humans, such as eye contact, physical proximity and physical contact, breathing together, and comforting messages, without directly involving imagery of other humans, which may transform into traumatic intrusions or trigger ungrounded states.

ROLEPLAYS ADDRESSING THE IMPACT OF RELATIONAL TRAUMA ON RELATIONAL FUNCTIONING

Difficulties with absences

PATIENT: I just can't stand it when you go away. I'm not going to see you for a whole week and it's just too long.

THERAPIST: It is very hard for you when I'm away, I know. Is there any part of you that knows I'm coming back?

PATIENT: No, when you're gone, it lasts forever. I barely remember you—I don't remember what you look like or sound like or what it is like to be with you. And I think you forget about me too.

THERAPIST: It's like when I'm away, you worry that our whole connection vanishes.

PATIENT: Well, doesn't it?

THERAPIST: Not for me—even though I'm away, I still remember you and feel connected to you. I wonder if there is anything we can do to help you stay more connected to me.

PATIENT: I don't know.

THERAPIST: What if you borrow something from my office? You can return it when I get back, and then you'll know I have to see you again to get it back from you. [Some therapists keep a collection of such objects, such as shells or rocks. Patients are allowed to select and keep one and can use it as a transitional object to hold to foster a greater sense of lasting connection with the therapist.]

Lateness

PATIENT: I didn't really want to come today and I almost didn't. That's why I was late.

THERAPIST: It seems like we have this conversation a lot lately—I wonder what makes it so hard for you to come here.

PATIENT: I just don't want to, I guess.

THERAPIST: It's interesting that you didn't want to come today, because I actually thought that we had a really good session last week.

PATIENT: I guess I thought so too, at the time. But then I got up this morning and I just thought, "I shouldn't go today. I don't want to see her."

THERAPIST: Last session you were saying that this is the longest you've ever stayed in therapy before. I wonder if there is some part of you that's reacting to feeling closer to me.

PATIENT: I guess. I just feel like I need to get away, that's all. Last week I remember thinking that you were really starting to understand me.

THERAPIST: Does any part of you feel shame or anxiety about that?

PATIENT: Yeah, I guess. I mean, if you really understood me, you definitely would kick me out of therapy, so I guess I just want to leave first, you know?

THERAPIST: Oh, so there's a fear that if I really get to know you, I'll reject you. That makes sense to me, given everything you've described about how your parents treated you. It's good that we are talking about this.

Difficulty ending the session

THERAPIST: I notice a pattern has developed over the last couple of sessions where it's difficult for us to end on time. It seems like there's always one more thing we need to discuss. Do you have any sense of what happens for you at those times?

PATIENT: I just feel really safe here; it feels like there's never enough time to say everything I need to say.

THERAPIST: Tell me about the feeling of not having enough time.

PATIENT: It just feels like people never really hear me, like they never really get it.

THERAPIST: This is important—maybe part of the reason it's hard for you to leave is that you aren't sure if I have really heard you during the session, if I have really understood what you've been trying to tell me. Do you think there is anything I can do to make you feel heard?

PATIENT: I don't know—it just feels like I need more time. Fifty minutes isn't very long when I have so much that I need to say.

THERAPIST: It's difficult to fit everything in, and, given that we are working within a 50-minute session, I wonder if there are ways that I could help you to feel more heard within those 50 minutes. Like, what if I checked in with you more often to see if you feel heard during our sessions?

PATIENT: Maybe that could help.

THERAPIST: Maybe we can try that right now. What's it like for you to have this conversation about having trouble ending the session? Do you feel like I'm hearing you right now?

PATIENT: I think it's good that we are talking about it—nobody has ever discussed it with me before. I'm glad that you're asking me about it—it does feel like you're starting to understand.

THERAPIST: It's really important for us to be able to talk about these things—and important for you to let me know if there are times when you don't feel heard. We can keep working together to make the end of the session less difficult.

PATIENT: I still think it will be hard—I mean, like I said, I feel so safe here, and as soon as I leave, I'm just all by myself again.

THERAPIST: That is hard—I know we've talked a lot about how really lonely you are. You know, one of the goals for our work together is to help you feel less lonely, so that you have more people you can rely on in your life.

PATIENT: I know, but right now I am just so lonely, and leaving is awful.

THERAPIST: Does it help to know that we will see each other again?

PATIENT: It doesn't feel like we will—it feels like I'll be alone forever and if I don't tell you everything right now before I go, I'll never get another chance.

THERAPIST: So when you leave and you feel so lonely, can you remind yourself that you and I are working together to help you get less lonely, and that in the meantime you will see me again in a week?

PATIENT: Yeah, I guess.

THERAPIST: Why don't you try that after our session today, and if it doesn't help, we can talk more next time and try to come up with another idea.

Patients who ask for a hug

PATIENT: This is really hard for me to talk about—it's so upsetting. I am so embarrassed. [Long pause] Can you hug me? I think that would make me feel better.

THERAPIST: I can totally understand why you would want a hug; let's talk about that more. What impact do you think my hugging you would have on you?

PATIENT: I would just know that you care about me, that I'm not alone with all this.

THERAPIST: It sounds like it would be really helpful for you to feel close to me—for you to feel comforted by me when you're feeling so upset. As we've talked about before, though, I worry that if I were to actually hug you, it might end up with you feeling more unsafe and worried about my boundaries. Is there a way that I could show my caring with my words, rather than a hug, that would give you that same feeling, of being cared about and not alone?

PATIENT: I don't know—it just seems like if you hugged me, I would know that you're really here with me—I feel so far away.

THERAPIST: It's hard for you to feel that I am really here with you. How about if you just listen to my voice as I tell you that I'm right here with you, listening to you, that you're not alone right now. How is that for you?

PATIENT: It's okay, I guess. I still feel upset.

THERAPIST: What if you try looking at me? Just notice that I am here with you, that I'm present, that right now you have my full attention in this moment.

PATIENT: I don't want to look at you. I can't stand looking you in the eyes and I don't want you to see me.

THERAPIST: OK. What if you try just looking at my feet, or at my knees, just so you can see that I'm really here with you?

PATIENT: I feel a little better. I guess it's just hard to know you're really listening, but if I pay attention, I guess it seems like you are.

THERAPIST: That's important—for a minute, you were able to start to feel closer to me while still staying within the boundaries of our relationship.

Too-frequent calls/not accepting advice

THERAPIST: At the beginning of our work together, we discussed that part of our agreement is that you can call me between sessions if you need to for crises. I notice that lately, we've been talking on the phone almost every day. What do you think is happening between us?

PATIENT: Yeah, it just seems like everything is so horrible right now, there's no way I can manage on my own.

THERAPIST: And how has it been to talk to me on the phone?

PATIENT: It doesn't make me feel better—it still doesn't feel like enough—but I just don't know what else to do other than call you. I'm at the end of my rope!

THERAPIST: I think I'm noticing the same thing you are—that it feels like nothing I say or offer seems to be helpful when we're on the phone—and actually it seems to me like when I try to help or try to suggest something, you don't even feel able to give it a try. It almost seems like the more suggestions I make, the more hopeless you get and the less able you feel to try anything. I bet that feels really frustrating for you, and to be honest it doesn't feel great for me either.

PATIENT: Yeah, I do feel frustrated. But like I said, I don't know what else to really do. I can't figure it out by myself. I wish you could just help me solve the problem.

THERAPIST: Well, I think sometimes phone calls can be a useful part of your treatment, and I think we might need to do some work together to make them more useful for you. It's just like a medication—if you take the right dose at the right time, it can really help, but if you take too much or too little, it can even make you worse. So we talk about the dosing of things like sessions and phone calls, and I think right now we need to talk about the dose of your phone calls.

PATIENT: When you say that, I feel like I'm in trouble and I've been bad. I really need to be able to call you or I won't be able to manage!

THERAPIST: It's not about being in trouble—it's about making sure that all of the parts of your treatment are working for you, and that you're getting the right doses of everything. Sometimes that takes a few tries, and some trial and error, to find what dose will work best for you. And I think the phone calls will work much better for you if we can find a way for you to take in what I am saying, so that I can be more helpful. So I think what would be really helpful would be that if you call me, you agree to try one of the things that I suggest—and if you're not ready to try anything, we will stop the phone call, and you can call me back when you feel ready to try something.

PATIENT: I don't know if I can do that.

THERAPIST: What do you think would get in the way? What happens for you in those moments when I make a suggestion?

PATIENT: It just feels like nothing could possibly work anyway—I'm too tired to even try—and I feel angry that you're expecting so much from me, expecting me to do all these things when I already feel so bad. I just want you to make me feel better.

THERAPIST: That makes sense—do you think it would help if I let you know that I know that? If I reminded you that I know how bad you feel inside and how hard it is to do these things?

PATIENT: I don't know—maybe.

THERAPIST: Maybe we can try that together. I will remind you that I know how bad you're feeling inside and that we agreed together that phone calls are only going to be helpful if you're willing to try some of my suggestions. And if you're still not willing to try, I will hang up the phone, and we can talk in the next session about what got in the way and try to figure it out together.

PATIENT: So you're going to punish me if I don't do what you say? How is that helpful?

THERAPIST: It's not a punishment—you haven't done anything wrong. If you were taking a high dose of a medication and getting all kinds of side effects, it wouldn't be a punishment to lower the dose or try a different medication, it would just be acknowledging that something wasn't working, and trying to make it work better. And it's not just you, either—maybe I'm doing something that isn't working too! The most important thing is that we work as a team to figure out what helps you the most, and keep adjusting things until we figure that out.

Managing fearfulness

THERAPIST: [Notices that patient is having a reaction, assesses if patient is grounded, and works to help patient get grounded if needed before continuing]

THERAPIST: What just happened? I noticed that when I reached across the room for a tissue just now, you jumped, and now you look really afraid.

PATIENT: Oh, it's nothing. Never mind [shakes head].

THERAPIST: Well, I think this might be important. It seemed like you were startled and now it looks like you're afraid of me. Given everything that you've told me about your past experiences, I wondered if you were afraid I might harm you, and if that's true, it would be really important for us to talk about together.

PATIENT: It's stupid. I know there's nothing to be afraid of.

THERAPIST: Part of you knows that. But I wonder if there is another part of you that is having some fears about me, and if talking about those fears might be really helpful in helping you feel safer in therapy.

PATIENT: I guess when you moved so quickly, it just seemed like you might be able to grab me or hit me or something. But I know that's dumb [hides face]. I've known you for years.

THERAPIST: I'm glad that you shared that with me. That's so important. Of course, I would never grab you or hit you, but I can completely see how you might be afraid of that, given everything you have been through.

PATIENT: Yeah, I guess so.

THERAPIST: It's really important for us to work together as a team to help you feel as safe as possible in this therapy. Is there anything you can think of that might help you feel safer right now?

PATIENT: I don't know. I still feel tense.

THERAPIST: Would it help if I moved my chair back a little bit to give you more space?

PATIENT: Maybe.

THERAPIST: Let's try that—we can try it together and see if it helps or not [moves backwards]. What do you think?

PATIENT: That feels a little bit better.

THERAPIST: That's great. If you think of anything else I can do to help you feel safer, please let me know so that we can talk about it.

CONCLUSION

Therapists should expect and develop skill in recognizing their patients' profound mistrust and avoidance borne from trauma- and attachment-related difficulties, compounded by underdeveloped emotion regulation skills and the patients' beliefs that they are worthless and others are unreliable or malevolent. When these relational patterns and difficulties emerge in treatment, repeatedly recognizing, naming, and discussing them with the patient, as well as working through possible ruptures in the therapeutic relationship, gradually bring about healing. The echoes of trauma in the therapeutic relationship serve as powerful opportunities to resolve the impact of victimization. Therapists show that they are, in fact, reliable, trustworthy, and caring, albeit human, as they repeatedly demonstrate their willingness to be open and flexible and to stay present while the patient learns about and repairs unhealthy relational patterns.

6

Addressing Challenges Related to Dissociation, Emotions, and Somatic Symptoms

Patients who are in a triggered state are typically not able to integrate new information or work productively in therapy. In these situations, they may be lost in reexperiencing past trauma, and have significant difficulty noticing what is actually happening in the here-and-now present moment. The goal is to conduct therapy in a grounded state, and to help the patient engage from within a grounded state, where they are alert enough to be curious and engaged but not so activated that they cannot focus on anything other than escaping the perceived threat.

Therapists will find that they cannot always anticipate or prevent a patient's triggers—nor should they, as learning to manage being triggered is an important part of a patient's therapeutic work. It can be expected that at some point in the therapy, perhaps quite early, the patient will become triggered during a session, either by the therapist or by some other cue, and the therapist will need to intervene to help the patient get grounded in the present moment.

Patients, especially early in the therapy, may enter ungrounded states quickly, without knowing the signs that they are becoming ungrounded, and be unable to either directly tell the therapist that they are dysregulated or to regulate the state for themselves. Therefore, it is important for therapists to be alert for signs of dysregulation and have a toolbox of strategies that they can use to coach patients how to notice they are becoming dysregulated and help themselves return into a state of relative regulation.

Here are steps to help patients ground themselves:

1. Identify the earliest signs that the patient is no longer grounded (i.e., hyperaroused and "feeling too much" or hypoaroused and "feeling too little").
2. Drop the content of the discussion and immediately attend to grounding the patient.

3. Flexibly use a variety of grounding strategies to identify what works best for the patient in that moment.

4. Continue using grounding strategies until the patient is clearly grounded.

5. If the patient consistently cannot get grounded, identify and work with barriers to getting grounded.

This chapter will address each of the above steps in detail, including practical techniques that the therapist can use with patients who are triggered.

STEP 1: IDENTIFY THE EARLIEST SIGNS THAT THE PATIENT IS NO LONGER GROUNDED

When patients become triggered in therapy, if the therapist does not intervene early, patients are likely to become more and more triggered and less and less in touch with the present. The more a patient becomes lost in past trauma or dysregulation, the more difficult it will be to help them reorient to the present. The goal is to intervene early to help the patient to self-regulate before the patient enters an overwhelmed state of emotion or a deep state of dissociation from which it is more difficult to reemerge. To this end, it is important to be aware of the variety of ways in which dysregulated arousal can manifest in session, and to monitor the patient closely for the beginning of these manifestations. In this section, we will focus on somatic changes that indicate loss of grounding. The material on the neurobiology of trauma-related disorders (TRD) presented in Chapter 3 can provide a useful complement to this section, as it provides explanatory material that can help the therapist understand the mechanisms behind these changes and present them to the patient in easy-to-understand language. This allows the patient and therapist to collaboratively attend to and address these changes more effectively.

Therapists may be more used to attending to patients' words than their bodies. Attention to the patient's body (including both subjective sensations and objective changes noted by the therapist) is essential in working with traumatized patients but is often overlooked in traditional talk therapy. The body gives a wealth of information about how the patient is experiencing and remembering their trauma, and the body is clearly a site of trauma-related symptoms (see also Ogden et al., 2006a; van der Kolk, 2014). Many patients have disconnected from their bodies as a way of escaping abuse, leading to experiences of numbness and dissociation in day-to-day life. By communicating that the patient's body is an important site of experience and memory, and teaching the patient about the ways in which trauma is held in the body (see Chapter 3), the therapist can help the patient to reconnect with and process their own somatic experiences, which gives them a powerful tool for recognizing their level of dysregulation. As they learn to attend to their body, they can gradually become more adept at recognizing earlier when they are becoming dysregulated, therefore providing themselves with more opportunity to regulate when it is easier to do so. This gradually leads to an increased ability to be present and to live a meaningful life (for further discussion of the importance of mindfulness, see Siegel, 2007, 2010).

One model for understanding the impact of trauma on the body, and the role of the body in dysregulated arousal, is the window of tolerance model (for a detailed discussion of this model, see Ogden et al., 2006a; Schore, 2003; Siegel, 1999). Briefly, all people have a range of activation or energy within which they feel comfortable (their window of tolerance; Figure 6.1). Dysregulated states can be thought of as being outside of that window in one of two ways: hyperarousal (too much activation in the system) or hypoarousal (too little activation in the system). These states are mediated by the autonomic nervous system, a part of the peripheral nervous system that controls multiple organ systems and basic bodily functions, including digestion, heart rate, and respiratory rate. The autonomic nervous system has two subdivisions, the sympathetic, which mediates hyperarousal, and the parasympathetic, which mediates hypoarousal. Of note, trauma survivors are typically very uncomfortable with somatic sensations and can be highly intolerant of and dysregulated by even small changes in arousal or minor physical sensations, leading to a very small window of tolerance and the capacity for wide, rapid fluctuations into ungrounded states.

Ungrounded states are typically characterized by the activation of one or more animal defense mechanisms, patterns of responding that are beyond conscious thought and are conserved across the animal kingdom due to their role in preserving life in the face of threat (Nijenhuis et al., 2004). When threatened, most people *without* extensive trauma histories will initially respond with hyperarousal as they attempt to assess, escape from, or stop the threatening situation. Most people are familiar with the concept of "flight" and "fight" as animal

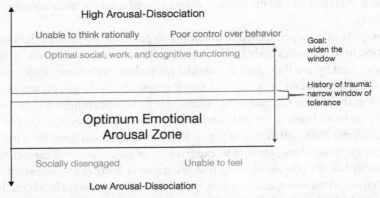

Figure 6.1. Window of tolerance. Individuals who have been traumatized often have a narrow range of emotions and physical sensations that they can tolerate. This increases the risk for unsafe, risky, and unhealthy behaviors and/or dissociation.
Based on Ogden, Pain, & Fisher, 2006b, Siegel, 1999.

defenses, which are mobilizing defenses that involve high levels of energy in the system and are associated with hyperarousal. When these options are not immediately possible, or when attempting to avoid attracting the attention of a potential threat, an animal or human may also respond with tonic immobility (feeling like they are unable to move their entire body or parts of their body), which may be followed by emotional shutdown/collapse. These are immobilizing defenses. While on the surface tonic immobility involves stilling, and so may be confused with hypoarousal, the internal experience remains one of hyperarousal and increased activation (e.g., racing heart, muscle tension). This corresponds to the colloquial idea of "playing dead" or "playing possum" in the face of danger. When these defenses fail, however, as in the case of a small child being abused, who is subjected to prolonged trauma without the capacity either to physically escape or interrupt the trauma, the only remaining survival strategy is a submissive, collapsed state characterized by profound hypoarousal and decreased muscle tension. In individuals who have been chronically traumatized, their experience is often that no other response to danger is ever possible, and so by the time they are adults and present for therapy, this may be their initial line of defense in response to any perceived threat. They may quickly slip into this collapsed, dissociative state when triggered, or may oscillate between states of hyperarousal, tonic immobility, and hypoarousal.

Hyperarousal

Hyperarousal is what is typically thought of as "flight or fight" mode. In this state, the body and mind are highly activated and energized and are primed to run away from or fight off a potential threat. While the internal experience is always of high energy, alertness, and activation, this high-energy state can sometimes lead to frozen/tonic immobility.

Signs of hyperarousal are as follows:

1. Change in color (face flushing or pallor)
2. Change in eye contact or visual focus—gaze darting around the room or fixed staring
3. Wide eyes
4. Shaking
5. Sweating
6. Rapid breathing
7. Fidgeting (knee shaking, foot tapping) or sitting rigidly still in preparation for movement
8. Speaking rapidly, getting louder or yelling
9. Standing up or pacing
10. Tense, rigid appearance (e.g., sitting very straight, clenched fists, clenched jaw, frozen gaze, frozen breath, inability to move)

Hypoarousal

When it is not possible to physically escape or fight off an attacker (e.g., in the case of an abused child), hyperarousal may not be a useful survival strategy, and high levels of activation and movement may attract attention and bring on more abuse. The most adaptive response in these situations may instead be to become numb and passive in order to minimize the abuse. This response, which may look like "spacing out," dissociation, or flatness, is referred to as hypoarousal.

Signs of hypoarousal are as follows:

1. Pallor
2. Shallow breathing or holding breath (cannot see chest rising)
3. Fixed, "unseeing" staring (e.g., the "thousand-yard stare"), or closing eyes
4. "Glassy," unfocused, or "unseeing" look in patient's eyes
5. Slumping or physically collapsing, or curling feet up underneath them and getting "small"
6. Limp appearance
7. Speaking slowly in a monotone, or long delay before responding
8. Lack of verbal response or movement

STEP 2: DROP THE CONTENT AND IMMEDIATELY ATTEND TO GROUNDING THE PATIENT

If the therapist realizes that the patient may not be grounded, it is important to stop the current conversation and attend to the patient's dysregulation. Not only will the patient be unable to integrate further information in an ungrounded state, but the patient will also become further dysregulated and triggered the longer the therapist continues talking without grounding the patient. No matter how important the content or material, there is no point in continuing to explore it if the patient is not grounded, because no meaningful processing will be done, and the patient will be unlikely to retain the information.

The therapist can begin by verbally reorienting the patient to the current situation. For instance, call their name and say, "You are here with me in [city]. Today is [date]. You are safe. No one is going to hurt you."

STEP 3: USE A VARIETY OF GROUNDING STRATEGIES TO IDENTIFY WHAT WORKS BEST FOR THE PATIENT

Grounding techniques help patients return to the present moment and are useful in assisting traumatized patients to regulate their level of emotion and dissociation. We teach a variety of these techniques in the Finding Solid Ground program. (See Appendix B, Grounding Script, for an introduction to orienting to and anchoring in the present; see the first module of the accompanying workbook for additional techniques and discussion of grounding skills.) Grounding techniques are fundamental skills for patients with TRD, including dissociative disorder. Teaching patients to use these skills inside and outside of therapy in response to feeling ungrounded is crucial toward helping them stabilize. Helping patients learn how and when to use grounding should be a focus from the beginning of therapy. The therapist must be able to coach the patient on when and how to use these skills until the patient can do it for themselves. Patients should be encouraged to repeatedly practice grounding skills, including at times they are not acutely needed so that they are more effectively able to use them when help with grounding is urgently needed.

While some grounding strategies are useful no matter which state the patient is in, it is also important to be aware of strategies that are particularly helpful for either hyperarousal or hypoarousal. When patients are hyperaroused, the goal is to bring down the energy in the body by activating the parasympathetic nervous system, or to target specific physiological features of hyperarousal (e.g., to target rapid, shallow breathing by encouraging slow, deep breathing). Similarly, when patients are hypoaroused, the goal is to increase the amount of energy in the body, by activating the sympathetic nervous system, or to target features of hypoarousal (e.g., collapsed body posture).

By definition, patients who are not grounded, or patients who are breathing very shallowly or holding their breath, are not fully aware of their bodies. The goal is to help the patient to return to the present, the here and now, by making use of their physical senses to notice and focus on what is happening in the moment, and by taking care of their body by ensuring that they are continuing to get the air they need to breathe rather than inadvertently creating a sense of panic due to a lack of oxygen. Although some patients may be phobic of the body, as will be described below, even these patients can usually begin to approach the body with modification of some of these techniques if they are taught the rationale for, and importance of, tuning in to their bodies. Use of the body, particularly the breath, is vital in working with these clients, as it helps them to reconnect with their body and learn to live in their body, which is a necessary precursor to being present and grounded, which is a precursor to therapy sessions being truly beneficial (Michael et al., 2019; Polak et al., 2015).

Attachment Resources

Attachment resources, such as a small rock or shell that the therapist provides, can be useful in bringing patients out of ungrounded states (Steele et al., 2017). Alternatively, some clients respond well to nonhuman attachment imagery such as animals (including pets) or objects in nature such as sturdy trees that have survived and thrived despite stormy weather. (We recommend avoiding imagery of humans, as this can cause some patients to become more ungrounded due to their history of repeated traumatization by human attachment figures.) Imagery tends to work best when the patient is only mildly ungrounded, as engaging in an imagery exercise may be too abstract if a client is already quite dissociated. In this case, engaging the client in movement and using the five senses for grounding are more likely to be successful.

Reorientation

The following techniques represent some ways that the therapist may help the patient to become more aware of the present moment, as opposed to being caught up in past trauma. These can be useful when the patient is experiencing either extreme of arousal:

1. Making eye contact with the therapist (although some patients may find this more threatening and may do better if instructed to look at the therapist's feet or a specific familiar feature of the room) or attend to the sound of the therapist's voice.
2. Look around the room and name objects that they see (or describe three objects, or look for items of a certain color, or count a certain kind of item).
3. Use strong sensations: holding an ice cube or ice pack, eating a mint or sour candy, or smelling a scented oil.
4. Coach the patient to normalize their breathing (as will be discussed below, breathing exercises should be used with caution and may require modification).

Hyperarousal

Techniques that can be helpful for *hyperarousal* include the following:

1. Taking slower, deeper breaths with a long outbreath[1]
2. Pressing feet into the floor or hands into the chair
3. Applying deep pressure with the use of weighted blankets or weighted vests
4. Other grounding or centering techniques, such as those taken from trauma-sensitive yoga practices (Emerson, 2015; Price et al., 2017).

If the patient is experiencing tonic immobility (internal experience of hyperarousal but unable to move their whole body or parts of their body), the therapist may consider increasing movement, including very small or even micro-movements (e.g., the imperceptible movement of a single finger).

Hypoarousal

Techniques that can be helpful for *hypoarousal* include the following:

1. Standing up, stretching, or walking around the room (although it is important to be cautious when asking patients to stand, as more profoundly hypoaroused patients may feel dizzy or be at risk of falls)

1. As will be discussed in a later section, some patients may be unable to tolerate working with the breath due to associations with past trauma.

2. Looking around the room instead of staring fixedly at a single point
3. Some yoga positions can be useful in helping patients to become more activated and mobilized (see Emerson, 2015, for a detailed discussion).

STEP 4: CONTINUE USING GROUNDING STRATEGIES UNTIL THE PATIENT IS CLEARLY GROUNDED

It may be necessary to use several grounding strategies for extended periods of time to get patients grounded, and the therapist should monitor the patient for evidence that they are getting more grounded rather than assuming that they are grounded because they have successfully completed one of the grounding strategies.

Signs that the patient is becoming more grounded include the following:

1. Breathing more easily and regularly
2. Making eye contact with the therapist (for patients who regularly do this). As noted above, eye contact is dysregulating for some patients, and encouraging it in these patients may lead them into an even more ungrounded state.[2]
3. Being able to engage in back-and-forth conversation
4. Being able to clearly tell the therapist that they are feeling more grounded.

STEP 5: IF THE PATIENT CONSISTENTLY CANNOT GET GROUNDED, IDENTIFY AND WORK WITH BARRIERS TO GETTING GROUNDED

It is crucial that therapists recognize that grounding "goes against the grain" of traumatized patients' longstanding coping through entering ungrounded states to prepare for danger and/or disconnect from overwhelming experiences. Individuals with childhood trauma, for example, understandably go into dissociative states to avoid overwhelming feelings and traumatic intrusions. When abuse was occurring, dissociation may have been their only escape. So learning grounding techniques, and actually remembering to use them outside of session, is a long process that requires psychoeducation and repeated discussion in session, including exploring the reasons why the patient may be subtly, or not so subtly, reluctant to get grounded (see Grounding Topics 1 through 3 in the Workbook for information on addressing potential obstacles and ways to help patients learn

2. Frewen and Lanius (2015) quote one patient as saying, "When I make eye contact, I feel like they're going to see a stain on my soul" (p. 204). This sense of vulnerability to making eye contact indicates why eye contact can be triggering for some patients. Other patients may perceive direct eye contact to be aggressive and threatening.

how to get and stay grounded). While these barriers may need to be addressed in moments of not being grounded, these conversations also need to be had at times when patients are grounded, so that they can engage in conversation and exploration around any difficulties with grounding.

It is useful for therapists to also be aware that some patients may find particular grounding exercises to be unhelpful or even triggering of further dysregulation. This is particularly common in working with the breath, or making eye contact with the therapist, but can occur with any grounding strategy. This does not necessarily indicate that the patient is resistant to getting grounded in general, and should not automatically be viewed as such. If the patient is reluctant to try a particular technique, or seems to get even more flooded or dissociated after using it, the therapist can try other strategies, or explore with the patient when the patient is grounded what makes some strategies more difficult than others.

It is important to note that clients may be profoundly phobic of the body, leading to general failure of grounding strategies that involve the body. Even the word "body," the naming of a specific body part, or directions to attend to sensations in the body (e.g., feet on the floor) may be triggering for these patients and may send them into further dysregulation. This will be discussed in more detail below with respect to working with the breath, but working with the body in general can also present difficulties. Working with the body, however, is also extremely important in the treatment of trauma, and should not be avoided entirely due to concern about dysregulating the patient. For patients who are phobic of the body, modification of body-focused techniques may help the client move toward working with the body. For example, instead of attending to the sensation of feet on the floor, patients may be asked if there is any part of their body where they do feel sensation, or the therapist may suggest attending to a very small part of the body, such as one little toe, or applying pressure to part of the body (e.g., with a finger).

Sometimes no technique seems to work in helping the patient to get more grounded. In these cases, it may be useful to explore perceived advantages to staying in an ungrounded state. Sometimes, there are specific reasons a patient is reluctant to get grounded, such as the following:

1. Getting grounded can make the present reality more real, which may be painful.
2. Getting grounded may make the impact of the traumatic past more real by bringing emotions or physical sensations into awareness.
3. Getting grounded may bring up grief over lost time or current chaos and/or loneliness.
4. Getting grounded may imply to the patient that they will "have to" start processing traumatic experiences if they are no longer overwhelmed by symptoms.
5. Getting grounded may mean being more vulnerable if someone hurts or traumatizes them, due to loss of coping through dissociation.
6. Getting grounded feels unfamiliar and therefore unsafe.

After identifying barriers, a frank conversation can be had with the patient about the advantages and disadvantages of getting grounded. It is important to acknowledge and validate the survival function of dissociation, and the advantages of remaining in a dissociated state. It is undeniably true that staying ungrounded has advantages and serves a protective function for patients, and this should be acknowledged. It is also important, however, to help patients to acknowledge the negative impacts of existing in a chronic state of high dissociation and move toward greater willingness to work on getting grounded. Therapists who are willing to explore and acknowledge advantages as well as disadvantages, and allow the patient to develop intrinsic motivation to get grounded through such conversations, are less likely to become polarized and caught in a power struggle around whether or not the patient should work on getting grounded.

ROLEPLAYS: ADDRESSING HYPER- AND HYPOAROUSAL THROUGH GROUNDING

Grounding hyperarousal

THERAPIST: I notice that when we start to talk about that experience, your hands start to shake, and it looks like you're breathing really quickly. Are you still feeling present in the room with me?

PATIENT: [Tapping foot] I don't know.

THERAPIST: Let's stop exploring that experience for right now and just help you get to a place where we're both sure that you're fully present, here in the room with me. Can you look around the room and name some things that you see?

PATIENT: I see . . . a lamp, a painting, the rug.

THERAPIST: Good. Can you describe them in detail? [Patient describes them.] Can you hear any sounds? [Therapist continues having patient use their senses to get grounded in the present moment.]

PATIENT: I think I hear a car, the sound of the fan, I hear your voice.

THERAPIST: How do you feel now?

PATIENT: A little better, but I still feel shaky.

THERAPIST: How about we do some breathing together? I notice that you are still breathing very shallowly, and if you breathe more deeply, it will help your nervous system know that you are safe here.

PATIENT: OK.

THERAPIST: Take a deep breath through your nose and breathe out slowly through your mouth. Make sure that when you breathe out, it's nice and long. Just do that a few times. [Therapist continues using different techniques until the patient no longer displays signs of dysregulation and confirms that they are present.]

Grounding tonic immobility

THERAPIST: I notice that all of a sudden you are very still and you look stiff—it looks like your breath has stopped or has frozen. [Therapist is noticing signs of tonic immobility.] Are you still present in the room with me?

PATIENT: [Long silence] I don't know.

THERAPIST: Let's stop discussing that event for a minute and just make sure that you are here in the room with me. Can you push your feet into the floor and move your hands a bit?

PATIENT: I can't feel my hand. I can't move my arms or legs.

THERAPIST: I wonder if you can even move just the tiniest bit—just move the very tip of your index finger and see what happens. It can even be such a small movement that nobody could even see it.

PATIENT: I can do that. I can move a little bit.

THERAPIST: OK, why don't you try making it just a little bit bigger? Moving the whole finger, for example?

PATIENT: OK.

THERAPIST: Now how about your hand? And your arm? [Keep working on grounding until patient reports they can feel and move their body.]

THERAPIST: You're moving more, but it looks like your breath is still very shallow or frozen [associated with tonic immobility]. Can you take a breath?

PATIENT: [Takes a breath]

THERAPIST: Good. Keep breathing and keep noticing what is happening with your breathing.

Grounding hypoarousal

THERAPIST: I notice that your head is falling forward and you're curling up. Are you getting ungrounded?

PATIENT: [Long pause] Umm . . .

THERAPIST: Let's get you grounded before we do anything else. Can you try sitting up a little bit straighter?

PATIENT: [Doesn't move]

THERAPIST: Can you hear me? It's 2022 and nobody here is going to harm you. Why don't you try looking around the room a little bit?

PATIENT: [Doesn't look up]

THERAPIST: It seems like it's really hard to get grounded right now. What's getting in the way?

PATIENT: It's not safe. I might feel too much.

THERAPIST: You're worried if you get grounded you will feel too much. That's important. In this therapy we both need to work together on helping you feel an amount that's safe for you. I will help you with that as much as

I can. But we need to get you grounded first. Can you look up just a little bit? Just at the rug?

PATIENT: [Looks up]

THERAPIST: Good job. [Therapist continues using strategies to regulate hypoarousal until the patient is grounded.]

GROUNDING PATIENTS WHO "CAN'T BREATHE"

While tools like deep breathing and diaphragmatic breathing are often recommended to patients with anxiety, there are particular issues to consider when working with the breath in the context of trauma. Working with the breath can be triggering for a variety of reasons, such as the following:

1. Patients who have experienced abuse that involved their body (sexual or physical) may be highly avoidant of, or triggered by, any mention of the body or by increasing awareness of physical sensations, including their breath.
2. Patients may experience a range of somatic symptoms, including chronic shortness of breath, that may interfere with breathing or worsen in the context of attention to the breath.
3. Patients may have had experiences of being choked, felt like they were suffocating, or otherwise had their breathing interfered with during trauma. With these patients, focusing on breathing, or noticing alterations in breathing, can lead to flashbacks and traumatic intrusions.
4. The sound of breathing may be a conditioned trigger that brings back recollections of an abuser breathing loudly.
5. Breathing may be associated with making noise, motion, or taking up space or oxygen, all of which may have been dangerous to the patient in the context of trauma. Alternatively, patients may feel like they do not deserve to take up space or oxygen.

Breath, however, is still a critical tool in helping these patients regulate their nervous system, if the exercises are modified for trauma survivors (Michael et al., 2019; Polak et al., 2015). Given the vital importance of the breath in grounding, and given that patients who are not breathing in a full, healthy way are by definition disembodied, the therapist should not give up on working with the breath even in patients who are triggered by the breath. The therapist should be creative in modifying strategies such that the patient can tolerate this work without becoming more triggered. For example, the therapist can work with the patient to find imagery that allows changes in the breathing pattern without directly referring to the breath. Some ideas might include the use of rhythmic imagery such as swinging on a swing, waves gently coming ashore, or balancing on a surfboard in the water (see the following roleplay). While the therapist should continue to work toward an ultimate goal of the patient's being able to consciously attend to the breath, alternatives can be useful in the initial states of treatment.

Roleplay: Offering an alternative to deep breathing

THERAPIST: I notice that when we talk about this, your breathing starts to get very slow and shallow. Why don't we try to do some deeper breathing together to help you get more grounded?

PATIENT: No, I don't like thinking about my breathing. I'm starting to feel really panicky now—it's like I'm being choked all over again.

THERAPIST: OK, let's just drop the focus on breathing for now. Instead, I want you to imagine that you are on a swing. Just see yourself sitting on a swing and starting to swing back and forth. Imagine that you are in a park, or some other place that feels safe and beautiful. As you swing, really focus on your body going back and forth.

CHALLENGES RELATED TO EMOTIONS

Alexithymia, or difficulty naming and processing emotions, is a common feature in patients with trauma-related disorders and is often related to dysregulation and nonsuicidal self-injury (NSSI) (Frewen et al., 2008; Zlotnick et al., 1996, 2001). These patients may describe their intense feelings with generic words like "out of control," "upset," or "unsettled" but may be unable to identify or differentiate specific emotions. Frewen and Lanius (2015) discuss two potential experiences of alexithymia that are common in patients with TRD: a neutral or "not feeling" state, and a state of high but undifferentiated arousal that cannot be described.

While we have emphasized the importance of the body and working with the body throughout, addressing disconnection from the body may be a particularly important aspect of improving alexithymia. Recent research has suggested that different emotions may be associated with statistically separable body sensation maps, which suggests that the ability to be in touch with and distinguish sensations in the body may be a key component of emotion processing. As we have discussed, emotion regulation is likely to be problematic in patients with TRD, who are frequently dissociated from, and phobic of, the body (Nummenmaa et al., 2014; Steele et al., 2017).

One way of clinically approaching alexithymia is to assist patients to begin to develop a vocabulary for emotions (through lists of emotions and education about different emotions) as well as for bodily sensations. Patients who cannot identify any sensations in their body can be encouraged to complete body scans, beginning at the feet, and systematically notice and describe sensations in their body. If they still cannot identify any sensations, they can be asked to apply pressure to a part of their body that feels relatively safe with their finger or hand and describe what they feel, as described in the following roleplay. Once clients have been helped to build a vocabulary of bodily sensations, they can then begin to match patterns of somatic activation with different emotions. This increases their ability to notice, describe, and tolerate emotions and link them with body sensations, while enriching their emotional vocabulary (Frewen & Lanius, 2015).

Roleplay: Working on identifying emotions

PATIENT: [Crying]

THERAPIST: What's coming up for you right now?

PATIENT: I don't know. My face is wet. I don't know why. I feel out of control.

THERAPIST: What kind of out of control?

PATIENT: I don't know—just out of control.

THERAPIST: Do you feel sad? Angry? Hurt?

PATIENT: I don't know.

THERAPIST: Sometimes when we don't know what we feel, the body can give us clues. What do you feel in your body right now?

PATIENT: Nothing. I feel nothing.

THERAPIST: What if you start at your feet and just scan up your body to see what sensations you notice?

PATIENT: [Pauses] I still don't feel anything.

THERAPIST: What if you take one finger and put some pressure on your other hand? Do you feel that?

PATIENT: Yes.

THERAPIST: What does it feel like?

PATIENT: I don't know.

THERAPIST: Does it feel heavy? Light? Cold? Warm?

PATIENT: Heavy and warm, I guess.

THERAPIST: Good. Now, do you notice anything else in your body?

PATIENT: I feel kind of heavy in my stomach. But not warm, more cold.

THERAPIST: Sometimes when people feel heavy in their stomach, it goes with feeling sad. I wonder if there's any chance you feel a bit sad when you talk about those things.

PATIENTS WHO AVOID/CANNOT TOLERATE POSITIVE EMOTIONS

While one goal of treatment in traumatized clients is to increase positive affect (joy, happiness, pride, pleasure, love), simply urging clients to increase positive life events is often not the solution. It is important to recognize that these individuals often experience barriers both to engaging in pleasurable activities and to experiencing pleasurable affect in the course of day-to-day life. In the histories of chronically traumatized clients, play and spontaneity may have been dangerous in their home environments, leading to overcontrol and difficulty engaging in hobbies or leisure activities that could be pleasurable. Due to lack of safe caregiving, they may never have been taught to value play, or even how to play. Many throw themselves into work (or surfing the internet, playing computer games excessively, etc.) to avoid traumatic memories through being perpetually distracted. In some clients, for example in some instances of familial sexual abuse, play may have been associated with abuse. That is, abuse may have been framed as a type of play, or abuse may have at times involved sexual arousal or pleasurable physical sensations. Therefore, play or pleasure in adulthood may be a trigger that is avoided. All of these associations represent barriers to engaging in potentially pleasurable activities and relaxation.

One study has found that people with posttraumatic stress disorder may have difficulty recognizing positive emotions in others, and that this may be more pronounced in those who have experienced more trauma (Passardi et al., 2018). Additionally, as we have discussed above, these patients are often quite alexithymic and therefore may struggle to even identify when they are feeling positive emotions, which makes it difficult to increase experiences that may result in positive emotions. Even if they are able to engage in theoretically pleasant activities, they may go through the motions of increasing pleasurable events without fully experiencing or being aware of any sense of enjoyment; therefore, the intervention does not produce any meaningful change.

Difficulties with positive affect are also linked to chronic shame, which is a common issue in TRD patients and which we discuss in further detail in the next section. While clients may experience acute shame in response to positive emotions, chronic shame may also lead patients to believe that they are not deserving of positive or pleasant things due to their sense of internalized badness and unworthiness. This can lead to avoidance of pleasurable activities as well as a reflexive response of increased shame and dysphoria when positive emotions begin to arise in any context. Experiences of positive feelings may also trigger increased trauma-related symptoms (including flashbacks), increased dissociation, and/or attempts at self-punishment (e.g., though NSSI).

This intolerance of positive affect can also manifest in the therapeutic relationship, such as when therapeutic gains are made. It can be perplexing to therapists that the patient may experience an exacerbation of symptoms following periods of apparent success in treatment or in their daily life. One of the most common reasons patients avoid and fear getting better is the sense that they do not deserve to feel good or get better. Therefore, patients may respond to therapeutic gains by increasing unsafe behaviors, missing sessions, coming late, or even dropping out of treatment entirely. Alternatively, patients may feel invalidated by the therapist's focus on positive affect and may worry that the therapist will abandon them or end therapy if they show improvement.

An important goal in treatment is increasing positive experiences. However, the therapist should be aware that such experiences may be immensely triggering. The therapist should be alert to the potential for the patient to become ungrounded when discussing or experimenting with these experiences and respond as discussed. If the patient does begin to worsen in some way or engage in treatment-interfering behaviors after making gains, the therapist can reflect this to the patient and explore any potential link. Similar to any difficult emotion, exposure should be titrated, and the patient can be encouraged to begin to experience small amounts of positive affect or minor pleasant events. The patient may need to be explicitly taught what kinds of activities might be pleasurable and how to integrate them into daily life.

ROLEPLAYS: WORKING WITH DIFFICULTIES RELATED TO EMOTIONS

The association between positive emotions and ungrounded states

THERAPIST: Imagine yourself in a peaceful place in nature. Is there a place you like?

PATIENT: There's a park by my house.

THERAPIST: Just imagine yourself there—what is it like?

PATIENT: I see the trees, I feel the breeze; it's relaxing.

THERAPIST: What else?

PATIENT: [Silent]

THERAPIST: All of a sudden, you stopped breathing—what happened?

PATIENT: [Silent]

THERAPIST: Open your eyes and look around the room; tell me three things you see.

PATIENT: Uh . . . a lamp, the painting, the box of tissues.

THERAPIST: Make sure you are breathing. Try to breathe a little bit more deeply.

PATIENT: [Breathes more deeply] All of a sudden I saw my abuser come out from behind the tree, and then I just . . . it was like it was happening all over again.

THERAPIST: That's interesting—it seems like just as you started to feel more relaxed, something changed and you started to slip back into the past.

PATIENT: Yes, I just don't like the feeling I had. I felt something nice in my body, and it just reminded me of what happened before.

THERAPIST: That makes sense to me. If feeling nice was coupled with abuse, you would of course start to feel ungrounded when something starts to feel nice. I wonder if we can work together on ways that you can feel nice feelings and know that you are in the present, where it's safe to do that. Maybe by taking it just a little bit at a time.

Inability to feel happiness

THERAPIST: How long has it been since you self-harmed? It's been a while, right?

PATIENT: [Smiling] Nearly a year.

THERAPIST: Wow, that's amazing. How does it feel?

PATIENT: I don't know. [Slumping and looking away] I guess I don't really feel anything.

THERAPIST: For a minute, it looked like you were smiling—I wondered if you felt happy, or proud of yourself—and then it just disappeared. What happened there?

PATIENT: I don't know. I guess I just felt scared.

THERAPIST: Does that fear remind you of anything?

PATIENT: I guess when I was a kid if I did something good and I talked about it, I'd usually get punished. My parents would say it wasn't really that good and I was just being stupid.

THERAPIST: So you learned that any time you feel good, you'll probably be punished. No wonder it's hard for you to feel good.

PATIENT: Yeah.

THERAPIST: At the same time, now that you're an adult, you're working on relearning how to feel good. Can we go back to that moment where you thought about not self-harming and you felt happy? What did the happiness feel like?

PATIENT: I was just thinking how hard I worked, and that I did it even though I didn't really think I could.

THERAPIST: I remember that, too, that you told me a lot of times that you really didn't think you could manage without self-harm. When you go back to the moment where you think about how hard you worked for this, what sorts of physical feelings do you notice?

PATIENT: Lightness, I guess. Sort of tingly. It makes me smile.

THERAPIST: So maybe just let yourself experience that positive feeling.

PATIENTS WHO FEEL CHRONICALLY ASHAMED

Shame is an inherently relational emotion with ties to attachment. Unlike guilt, which generally consists of self-disapproval with respect to a past action or behavior (e.g., forgetting to return a phone call), shame involves a sense of internal badness of the self, and a perception that others will disapprove of or be disgusted by the person (Frewen & Lanius, 2015; Herman, 2011). Given the relational nature of shame, it is expected that shame will emerge not just in these patients' daily lives and social interactions but also in the relationship with the therapist.

Patients with TRD frequently experience both acute high-arousal states of being flooded with shame and chronic dysphoric low-arousal shame, which is linked to their underlying negative sense of self that defines their identity (Frewen & Lanius, 2015). Typically, these patients experience themselves as inherently bad, damaged, defective, and/or inferior to other people. One result of this can be underachievement—patients may undersell their abilities or not work to their full potential in a variety of domains of life.

People who have experienced trauma typically have a sense of shame that is profound and related to aspects of themselves that are in fact normative and healthy, but were punished. Therefore, they may experience shame if they feel that the therapist has "discovered" aspects of themselves that feel disgusting. For example, trauma survivors may have been taught that it is "bad" to have needs, to have emotions (including or especially positive emotions), to display self-esteem, or to be successful. When they experience any of those aspects of themselves, they may experience crippling shame, even though each of these areas is necessary for a full adult life. Additionally, the shame and secrecy surrounding their abuse typically creates a sense of inner badness. Abused children typically blame themselves for their abuse, rather than blaming the perpetrator. Some abusers directly blame the child for causing the abuse. Thus, survivors may believe that their badness caused the abuser to harm them.

While most therapists are aware of the potential shame that is often triggered by discussing abuse, they should also be aware that many patients are triggered to feel severe shame, or to have other unexpected negative reactions, by seemingly innocuous events. Such events might seem to be positive experiences for the patient. Possible triggers for shame and/or other negative reactions include the following:

1. Making gains in therapy or accomplishing a goal
2. Receiving praise or positive regard from the therapist
3. Experiencing pride or happiness; feeling relaxed, sexual arousal, or other positive emotions or body sensations (see below)
4. Feeling "seen" by the therapist (this can take the form of feeling understood or validated by the therapist, or can simply be triggered literally by making eye contact)
5. Making a request or expressing a need
6. Needing the therapist's assistance to deal with a crisis
7. Simply being in therapy and needing help (as the patient may feel unworthy of help or support or may feel that it makes them vulnerable to being harmed)

Patients are unlikely to spontaneously volunteer that they are feeling ashamed and may not even have words for the experience. Because shame is held in the body, the therapist should be aware of, and alert for, somatic signs of shame. Intense shame can easily leave the patient in a state of profound hyperarousal and/or hypoarousal, dissociation, and/or relational disconnection, whereas intervening early can "keep the patient in the room" and engaged in the work.

Somatic indicators of shame include the following:

1. Avoidance of eye contact (particularly in patients who usually make eye contact)
2. Slumped body posture (slumped shoulders, physically collapsed torso)
3. Shallow breathing or seeming to not breathe
4. Covering the face, curling up, pulling clothes or blankets over the head, hiding behind hair, or otherwise hiding from the therapist

If the therapist believes that the patient is experiencing shame, the therapist can reflect what they have noticed in the patient—for example, "I notice that you have a hard time looking at me when we talk about this" (see the following roleplay about working with shame). The therapist can also label that they may be experiencing shame and provide psychoeducation about the association between trauma and toxic/chronic shame. While many therapists would provide a patient with reassurance (e.g., by telling them that they have nothing to be ashamed of), the shame experienced by these patients goes beyond the level of words. Talking about and providing education about shame is an important aspect of the therapy, but in addition, shame is yet another area in which it is vital to involve the patient's body in healing. Just as shame can be triggered by attachment, attachment resources, as discussed above, can be a valuable tool in addressing and healing shame through fostering a felt sense of connection and acceptance. For further discussion of addressing shame in TRD, see Dorahy et al. (2017a) and Herman (2011).

Roleplay: Working with shame

THERAPIST: I notice that all of a sudden, it seems like you're having trouble looking at me, and you're covering your face. I wonder if you're feeling ashamed right now.

PATIENT: Yeah, I feel really ashamed of what happened to me.

THERAPIST: What about it makes you feel ashamed?

PATIENT: I must have done something wrong—I must have done something to make him think that I wanted it.

THERAPIST: Really? How could that be true?

PATIENT: He said it was my fault and I wanted it. I can't talk about it. [Slumps over further]

THERAPIST: I wonder if part of what makes it hard to talk about is that you feel so ashamed that you're not really with me in the here and now anymore. I know it's hard for you to look at me—you don't have to—but what if you try sitting up just a little bit straighter and see if you can work on this shame, which is a really tough issue for all survivors.

PATIENT: [Sits up straighter]

THERAPIST: That's good. Do you notice any change when you sit up straighter like that?

PATIENT: I guess I feel a bit more grounded. It makes it less intense.

THERAPIST: That's really good. Working with the body is so important in helping this kind of shame, and helps us to be able to talk about it more effectively. And this kind of shame is so common. Do you know that many or even most people who were sexually abused blame themselves and feel tremendous shame about what was done to them as children? Do you think it is their fault? Should they be ashamed of themselves?

PATIENT: That's not right. It's the adult's fault. They were just kids. I know what you're trying to get me to say.

THERAPIST: So you can see how unfair that is for other sexual abuse survivors to blame themselves. But somehow it feels like you are the exception? That you alone are at fault for being abused?

PATIENT: Well, I can see it's a double standard.

THERAPIST: Yes. Why do you think your abuser may have said it was your fault and you wanted it? When in fact, what he was doing to you was against the law. It was so seriously wrong what he was doing that it was a felony.

PATIENT: Maybe he wanted to make it my fault rather than his?

THERAPIST: I think you might be right. What do you feel in your body when you say that?

PATIENT: I feel even straighter, like my body is uncurling a little bit. I feel more curious, like I can think clearly.

THERAPIST: You know, sometimes it's easier for children to blame themselves than to blame their parents, because if they blame themselves, it means that if they could find a way to be better, then maybe the abuse would stop. Otherwise, they have to believe that they are helpless and don't have anybody to protect them, and that can be even worse. And it can feel better to think your parent wouldn't really do anything awful to you unless you truly deserved it, because all of us need to feel we can count on our parents to take care of us and protect us.

PHYSICAL HEALTH PROBLEMS

Early exposure to trauma is linked to a variety of poor physical health outcomes. The Adverse Childhood Experiences (ACE) questions are one method used in the literature to quantify exposure to childhood trauma (Felitti et al., 1998). The ACE score assigns 1 point for exposure to each of 10 types of childhood adversity. (In other words, an ACE score of 4 indicates a person has experienced four types of adverse childhood experiences.) In the original study, an ACE score of 4 or more was associated with a significantly increased likelihood of a variety of chronic medical conditions, including diabetes, cancer, chronic lung disease, and ischemic heart disease. More broadly, a high ACE score has been associated with the presence of multiple medical conditions, high health care utilization, poor self-rated health, pain, and disability (Chartier et al., 2010; Felitti et al., 1998). High ACE scores have also been associated with a variety of health-harming behaviors, including smoking, unintended teenage pregnancy, morbid obesity, and heavy drinking (Bellis et al., 2014). However, it is also well documented that childhood trauma causes alterations in a number of physical systems that may also help to explain poor health outcomes. Childhood trauma has been associated with increased inflammation as measured by levels of multiple inflammatory markers, including heart disease, stroke, and diabetes (Baumeister et al., 2016). It is also associated with alterations in the cortisol stress response (Heim & Nemeroff, 2001; McGowan et al., 2009). Of note, the ACE score, while very useful in the context of population-level research, does not provide a nuanced or complete depiction of an individual's trauma history and cannot predict a particular individual's risk of specific adverse health outcomes (Anda et al., 2020). The most important implication of the research presented above is that therapists working with traumatized patients should be prepared to contend with high levels of medical illness and medical complexity.

It is important for therapists working with traumatized patients to be aware of the high likelihood of medical comorbidities in this population and to have some sense of the patient's physical health status (e.g., by routinely asking about medical conditions, somatic symptoms, medications, and other health care providers involved with the patient as part of the intake assessment, and by periodically updating this information). As a result of TRD patients' difficulties trusting others, discomfort interacting with authority figures or others who remind them of abusers, and avoidance of other situations that may remind them of past trauma, many patients have difficulty with medical examinations and routine health maintenance (e.g., cancer screening) and may avoid it. Some may not seek medical attention despite significant and potentially dangerous physical symptoms. Others may be high utilizers of the medical system and may have an overwhelming number of providers involved in their care. Even patients who are highly engaged in the medical system overall may have specific triggers related to specific types of medical exams (e.g., gynecological exams, dental cleanings) that are avoided, and it can be helpful for the therapist to inquire about such areas of focal avoidance specifically. The therapist may need to play a pragmatic role in patients' physical health care by helping them to overcome avoidance and cope adaptively with triggering medical situations and/or, with the patient's informed consent, by directly communicating with other providers to help them to understand the role of trauma in the patient's health behaviors.

Psychiatric medications are a frequent part of the treatment of TRD patients, and polypharmacy is common in this population, which can also be a source of physical health complications (Brand et al., 2009b; Loewenstein, 2005). For example, in the Treatment of Patients with Dissociative Disorders (TOP DD) naturalistic study, 80% of patients were receiving psychiatric medications, with the most common types of medications being antidepressants and antianxiety medications (Brand et al., 2009b). Some of the medications used in TRD patients can cause significant side effects and can also predispose patients to long-term metabolic consequences, including obesity and diabetes. Even when the therapist is not a physician and/or is not responsible for prescribing medications to the patient, a basic awareness of this possibility is important, as the therapist may be the first health care provider to whom the patient discloses that they are having side effects, or the only provider who sees the patient regularly enough to notice signs suggestive of a change in health status (e.g., significant weight gain).

MEDICALLY UNEXPLAINED SYMPTOMS

Aside from having multiple medical comorbidities, TRD patients frequently present with physical symptoms for which a demonstrable organic cause has not been found; these are referred to as somatic symptoms (previous term: somatoform symptoms). Common somatic symptoms include sexual dysfunction, pelvic pain, abdominal pain, nonepileptic seizures (sometimes called pseudoseizures or psychogenic seizures), headaches, and shortness of breath. Two studies of patients with dissociative disorders found that they report an average of 12.4 to 13.5 somatic symptoms, and measures of somatoform dissociation (which include pain, altered sensation, and other such physical symptoms) have been found to be sensitive and specific screening instruments for dissociative disorders (Nijenhuis et al., 1998a; Ross et al., 1989b; Saxe et al., 1994). In the TOP DD naturalistic study, 22% of patients had a comorbid somatoform disorder (Brand et al., 2009b).

Given the high prevalence of medical comorbidity in these patients, therapists should not overattribute medical symptoms to trauma. Rather, they should encourage the patient to appropriately seek care in response to changes in their physical health. When a physical cause cannot be identified, it is important to educate patients on the connection between trauma and somatic symptoms while emphasizing that they are not consciously produced. In the process of seeking care for medically unexplained symptoms, these patients may experience interactions with the medical system that leave them feeling invalidated, ashamed, or dismissed. Some medical providers may not be aware of the connection between trauma and the body or may not have language for discussing these symptoms with patients in a validating way. Therefore, therapists may need to provide extra psychoeducation to their patients and help them to come up with a nonpejorative understanding of their symptoms. Expressing compassion for these symptoms' very real impact on patients' lives is crucial to maintaining a therapeutic relationship. Some psychotherapeutic modalities may work directly with symptoms in the body (Ogden et al., 2006a; Steele et al., 2017). Even therapists who do not operate from a specifically somatic focus can explore the meaning of the symptoms to the patient and provide support in maximizing function, coping with uncertainty when a diagnosis cannot be found, and managing the impact of symptoms on day-to-day life (see the following roleplay).

Roleplay: Medically unexplained symptoms

PATIENT: I'm pretty sure my whole body is broken. I feel pain all the time.
I've been to a million doctors and they never find anything. I just want to
know what's wrong with me.

THERAPIST: That makes sense to me—it must be so difficult for you to feel
like you don't know what is happening with your body. Can you tell me
more about the pain?

PATIENT: I just have pain everywhere. I have headaches every day, I have
pain in my . . . you know . . . down *there* [looks ashamed]. I feel nauseated
all the time. It feels like every part of my body has something wrong with
it, but nobody can even tell me what's wrong.

THERAPIST: You know, oftentimes people who have experienced trauma
hold the trauma in their body in all kinds of ways. I wonder if there's
any chance that your pain could be connected to some of the traumatic
experiences we have been working on together.

PATIENT: What I'm feeling is *real*—everybody just wants to tell me it's all in
my head, but I have real pain and I know that something is wrong! I just
think if they did a few more tests, they would find something, and then
they'd be able to make it go away. I think they don't believe that my pain
is real, or they would be trying harder to fix it.

THERAPIST: Of course your pain is real. It's real whether or not there is
a diagnosis. And it's also true that the mind and the body are deeply
connected. Your body may express some of what you have experienced
through medical symptoms or physical sensations. It's going to be important for us to be curious about your body as well as your mind, and what
your body might be trying to tell us.

PATIENT: But that won't make it go away. We can talk about it forever and
I'll still be living with this same stupid pain.

THERAPIST: Neither of us knows what will happen with your pain, that's
true—it might change as we work through some of your traumatic
experiences, and it might always feel just like it does now. You don't have
to stop hoping for a diagnosis, but what we can work on together now is
helping you cope with your very real pain, and find ways to live your life
as fully as you can, and also on understanding how your trauma has impacted you and how you can find new ways to manage that as well.

CONCLUSION

Individuals who have been profoundly unsafe, unprotected, and repeatedly
victimized understandably struggle with a variety of challenges. As is clear from
this discussion, many of these challenges stem from difficulties with emotion regulation. When there is no escape from danger and interpersonal betrayal (Freyd,

1996), dissociation can enable the individual to survive, yet after the danger and victimization have ended, survivors need to develop a range of healthy ways of managing emotions, tolerating physical sensations, and living in their bodies so they can live more comfortably and live well in the present. Rather than avoiding these emotional and somatic difficulties, as well as the understandable fear about not dissociating, repeatedly addressing these patterns helps survivors heal from trauma.

7

Understanding and Working with Dissociative Self-States

Very few mental health service providers receive systematic training in the assessment and treatment of people with trauma-related dissociation (TRDs) and dissociative self-states (DSS) as part of their training programs. To further complicate matters, there are inaccurate descriptions of DSS in the media and professional literature. Unfortunately, inaccurate information about TRD and DSS is even found in psychology textbooks (see Chapter 1). As a result, few clinicians have a solid, research-based understanding of dissociation to guide them in recognizing and helping people who experience DSS. The paucity of training about TRD contributes to the frequent misdiagnosis of people with DSS and treatment that is not directed at their core difficulty—that is, TRD (see Chapter 1). Even after being diagnosed with TRD, many individuals have difficulty finding a clinician who has both training in treating dissociation and availability to accept a new patient because there are simply not enough trained clinicians available to treat individuals seeking treatment for DSS (Nester, Hawkins & Brand, 2022). Unfortunately, these factors often prolong the suffering of those with DSS. This is particularly lamentable given that treatment consistent with expert consensus guidelines and research (e.g., International Society for the Study of Dissociation, 2011) has been shown to result in positive treatment outcomes and reduced treatment needs (see Chapter 4).

This book and the Treatment of Patients with Dissociative Disorders (TOP DD) Network studies seek to ameliorate this situation. This chapter offers an introduction to understanding and working with people who have DSS. (For assessment recommendations, see Chapter 2. As a general guideline, however, please remember that to ensure accurate assessment and treatment, persons with trauma histories should be assessed for dissociative phenomena, including DSS.)

UNDERSTANDING DSS

To understand DSS, it can be helpful to think of them as a variation on a set of experiences that all of us can relate to. The experience of having different ways of being that are related to different relational situations is not unique to people with DSS, and is in fact a normal, adaptive, and healthy part of the human experience (Putnam, 2016). We each develop multiple identities/senses of self through the relationships we experience over the course of our lives (e.g., child, sibling, relative, friend, student, therapist, colleague, supervisor, parent), and different situations and relationships call for different aspects of ourselves/different sides of our overarching set of identities to be present. For example, relaxing with a friend we feel very comfortable with evokes different aspects of ourselves (including different behaviors, associations, and expectations) than a work-related activity.

Similarly, most people notice evidence of shifting between different aspects of themselves depending on their role and social context. For example, most therapists can readily identify at least some differences between how they engage with others when working—that is, when they are in their "professional self"—compared to when they are in their "home self." They might dress differently, speak in a different tone of voice, respond differently to others, and engage in different behavior when they are in their office compared to when they are at home. (One reason it can feel awkward to encounter a patient outside of the office is the sense that the patient is witnessing aspects of the therapist that are not typically part of the therapist's "professional self.")

Additionally, many people who do not experience dissociation nevertheless automatically think in "parts language" when faced with an internal conflict. For example, waking up on a weekend, a person might think "part of me wants to stay in bed for a couple more hours, and part of me wants to get up and go for a walk." (This is also an example of different states or aspects of the self coexisting, of the internal multiplicity present in nondissociative persons.) Many can also recognize experiences of nondissociative people suddenly "feeling" or acting younger when frightened, or engaging in old, less healthy behaviors when seriously overwhelmed for a prolonged time.

These normal experiences of shifts and divisions between different aspects of ourselves are generally functional, allowing us to successfully respond to and transition between different environments with different demands. In people who are not highly dissociative, these different aspects of themselves are experienced as part of the same single self ("me"). Such people can transition fairly fluidly between their different self-states while maintaining a relatively coherent overall sense of themselves and their actions over time, and the information contained within each state (memories, emotions, skills) is reasonably accessible to all aspects of the self. (For example, a therapist at home with their family can still call to mind the patients in their practice and remember the principles of the type of therapy they practice.) Transitions between self-states are smooth, appropriate, and to a large degree under conscious control—if a work-related phone call were suddenly to come in, most people would be able to shift relatively automatically. In addition, nondissociative self-states are generally oriented to the present day and to external events.

A crucial difference between DSS and nondissociative aspects of self is the presence of disconnection/dissociation between and within DSS. Due to dissociation *between* self-states, DSS are more separate from each other than nondissociative self-states; as a result of dissociation *within* self-states, DSS are also often disoriented to the present. As we will discuss below, there are reasons why this is the case: These qualities generally helped the person survive.

As with other forms of dissociation, the dissociation of self-states in TRD emerges as a means of escaping the emotional impact of overwhelming experiences that cannot be physically escaped or avoided. More specifically, DSS are most likely to develop in persons with disorganized attachment relationships ("Type D" attachment; see Chapter 1) when confronted with experiences the mind perceives as unmanageable or intolerable to be aware of, or to identify as "mine." The mind then disconnects (i.e., dissociates) memories and actions related to these experiences from other aspects of self, resulting in self-states that are perceived as more separate, foreign ("not me"), and autonomous.

Broadly speaking, DSS consist of memories, emotions, perceptions, relational patterns, and/or behaviors that are experienced as foreign or distinct from other memories, emotions, perceptions, relational patterns, and/or behaviors. DSS are a feature of more complex TRD—particularly, but not exclusively, the more severe TRD, such as OSDD-1 and dissociative identity disorder (DID). In complex posttraumatic stress disorder, borderline personality disorder, or OSDD, the individual may experience trance states with partial awareness, or frequent, prolonged alterations in the experience of the flow of time. At the most severe end of the TRD and dissociative spectrum, there can be periods of complete unresponsiveness, and in DID, periodic engagement in complex behavior associated with amnesia.

Depending on the degree of dissociation present, DSS vary in complexity (the range of experiences they contain) as well as the extent of separateness (i.e., "not me") and autonomy (ability to act independently). The degree of separateness and autonomy of DSS appears to vary based on what is tolerable to be known. For some, it is possible to tolerate partial awareness of the contents of one or more other states' awareness. In these cases, the individual may be aware of the emotions or memories contained in DSS but may continue to feel out of control of their actions when those DSS are more activated—or they might have the experience that those emotions "don't really belong to me." They may have some recall for the activities of various DSS, but these memories may be patchy, hazy, or fragmented. In others, especially those with the most extreme compartmentalization, such as in DID, there can be a complete absence of awareness of at least some other self-states. Notably, the diagnostic criteria for DID only require complete amnesia between some of the self-states some of the time; there may be partial awareness between some self-states and complete disownment of others.

Persons with DID perceive one or more DSS' thoughts, feelings, and actions as "not mine," although in some cases they perceive DSS as completely different "people" inhabiting the same body or taking over their body. Brain imaging research has shown that DSS experienced as distinctly "other" are associated with unique patterns of brain activation compared to other self-states within the same individual, lending scientific support to the subjective experiences described by those with DSS (see Chapter 3). Other terms used for DSS include parts, aspects, identities, and alters. (We discourage the use of the term "personalities," a hold-over from the earlier "multiple personality disorder" terminology, as this can seem to reify a sense of all DSS as more separate and complex than they necessarily are.) The collection of DSS within a given individual is often referred to as a "self-system" or simply a "system." The number and complexity of DSS in an individual appears dependent on the person's mind's need to keep experiences and actions separate from one another for the sake of safety and their ability to "carry on." Some clients report the experience of a central self with one or more DSS of varying degrees of lesser complexity. Others describe experiencing a complex system with multiple DSS with well-defined identities and significant influence within themselves and on their behaviors.

Functions of DSS in TRD

When we speak about DSS in the context of TRD, we are speaking about aspects of the self with varying degrees of (1) separateness (the extent to which DSS are experienced as "not me," including separation of memories, knowledge, and skills) and (2) autonomy (the extent to which the activity of the DSS is experienced as out of conscious control). Typically, the more severe the TRD, the more separate and autonomous at least some DSS have become.

For someone who has suffered protracted childhood trauma, DSS can afford a means of survival. The reality of a child being abused, for example, especially if by a trusted person such as a primary caregiver, can be intolerable. Keeping this reality out of conscious awareness is an essential survival strategy to make the intolerable tolerable. The development of DSS allows certain aspects of experience (and responses to them) to be kept out of awareness while continuing to function and maintain relationships, especially if these include an ongoing dependent and/or inescapable relationship with someone involved in their trauma. This can serve an emotional function (to allow a child to not know information that would be emotionally intolerable) as well as a practical one (to inhibit behaviors or emotional expressions that might increase the risk of further or greater harm). A child suffering abuse faces multiple interlocking, contradictory demands. For example:

1. Not wanting to know or believe that someone would do such a thing—especially someone in whom they, their family members, and/or the community have placed trust—and simultaneously needing to know what has happened in order to be able to protect themselves
2. Especially in the context of a caregiving relationship, being dependent on that person, having strong positive feelings for them, and needing and wanting positive experiences with them—and yet also being terrified of them
3. Distress about the abuse and intense terror of further abuse might result in the child wanting to tell others about what happened, yet abusers may directly or indirectly demand secrecy with threats of further or

greater harm to the person and/or loved ones should secrecy be broken. Similarly, the extraordinary distress that would naturally follow such trauma might impair functioning, resulting in other authority figures finding out about the abuse. This could put the abused child and/or their loved ones at great risk with the abuser.

4. Behaviors such as submissiveness that may be demanded and/or necessary for survival in a traumatic context could lead to significant problems in other contexts. Additionally, survival-necessary behaviors may be extraordinarily foreign to the youth's emerging sense of "who they are" and/or what is generally expected of them.

5. In addition to feeling shocked, confused, horrified, and sad, a child might naturally feel anger/rage at being abused, leading to a desire to fight back. However, attempts to fight back may provoke further abuse and greater injury. As a result, these feelings being kept out of awareness prevents overwhelm and reduces the risk of greater harm.

In such cases, each of these emotions and reactions may become compartmentalized into a DSS that functions to "manage" that particular perpetrator, trauma, or contradictory survival imperative. The dissociative child may manifest this compartmentalization externally (e.g., showing different sets of responses that appease a particular perpetrator or threatening situation in order to minimize harm) or internal (e.g., sometimes the only available means of regulating intense emotions is for the child to disown and compartmentalize them within their mind). It is impossible for a child to hold all of these intensely painful and often contradictory emotions, memories, and conflicting imperatives in mind at the same time. To survive, the child becomes unaware of some of them. As a result, the memories of those traumas may become compartmentalized within that DSS, and other DSS may not be aware that the trauma happened, or may have only a vague sense that something awful occurred. As these children grow into adulthood, conflicting information may be avoided, so that information is not shared among self-states. As a result, self-states holding trauma-related emotions and experiences often do not become aware that the trauma is over; instead, they continue to believe and react as if the past is happening in the present. Surviving in this way for years can create an array of DSS containing contradictory, unintegrated emotions, memories, and behaviors. This can lead to the adult reacting to present-day events as if the trauma were ongoing, and/or highly discrepant behaviors, emotional reactions, patterns of relating to others, and variable access to memory and skills that can cause significant impairment, as well as confusion in survivors, their loved ones, and their therapists.

Relational patterns of DSS

As noted above, DSS are often organized around responding to a particular kind of problem or situation. Although the characteristics of each DSS will be informed by the "problem" to be solved (discussed in greater detail in the following), the patterns they follow may occur automatically (i.e., not necessarily consciously) when responding to a highly stressful/potentially traumatic situation:

- **Flight/avoidance:** The most common response is to attempt to escape or avoid highly stressful/potentially traumatic situations.
- **Fight/interruption:** If it is not possible to avoid the situation, and it seems possible to interrupt it, this becomes an option. (This may include crying out for help.)
- **"Freeze" (i.e., tonic immobility) and/or dissociation:** Dissociation (disconnecting from the here and now) is the escape when physical escape/avoidance or stopping the situation is not possible.
- **Submit/submission:** To prevent worse things from happening, people may go along with what seems unavoidable/unstoppable. (This may include "please and appease" or shutdown types of reactions.)
- **Identify/identification:** To increase a sense of control in situations where they do not seem to have any, people may dissociate their own thoughts, feelings, and preferences and adopt the perspective of the person with the power/control of the situation, even if that means sounding or behaving like an abuser.

DSS tend to enact these trauma-related reactions in relation to others (and other DSS) as seemingly indicated by the situation. For example, after orienting to a threatening situation, a self-state may escape by "hiding inside the body." If it seems possible to defend "the body" (many people with DSS use language such as this, indicating active depersonalization symptoms), a DSS that has adopted a protective role may "come forward" to do just this (i.e., fight to prevent/reduce harm). Should this seem (or prove) unlikely to be successful, the person may go into tonic immobility (which is often associated with or "assigned to" a specific DSS). Should it appear more advantageous to "go along" with (i.e., submit to) what is going on to reduce greater or further harm, a self-state that has evolved to take on this kind of role may emerge. (Note that states that evolve to "take" trauma may dissociate their view of these situations as traumatic. This serves as a way for these states to continue to feel as if they are choosing to go along with an activity, even if in reality they have no real choice or control. This can be confusing to trauma survivors and can lead them to unfairly blame and shame themselves and/or that DSS.)

Finally, in order to reduce the prevalence and severity of trauma, some self-states may model themselves after an abuser (i.e., actually believe they are, or act/sound like, a particular abuser). Such "introject" or "inner critic" DSS enable the person to actively predict an abuser's likely actions and responses, and internally admonish (and/or punish) transgressions against "the rules" that the person has been implicitly or explicitly "taught" to follow to reduce risk and severity of harm. The harshly critical DSS provides a sense of control that is essential to surviving unpredictable, uncontrollable experiences of abuse. If the child grasped the reality that they truly had no control over the violence of the abuser, it would be unbearable and may have led to utter hopelessness, despair, and shutdown. Instead, highly critical DSS may develop who blame themselves (or another part of self) for the abuse; this self-blame gives them a sense of having control. Although this strategy means that later in life the person will likely continue to unfairly blame themselves for the abuse, during childhood it provides a modicum of control, a means for tolerating attachment to the abuser (in cases in which the abuser is also a caretaker or parent), and even a small glimmer of hope in the sense that "If I scrupulously berate and drive myself to be perfect, I may not get in trouble or be hurt as often."

In short, though not always readily obvious to other self-states (or other people), each state is reacting out of fear of further trauma or humiliation and is acting in the way it believes is most likely to result in the least amount of trauma. Because this is often not easily noticed by other parts, experiences of "inner war" in response to signals of possibly traumatic situations and/or reminders of trauma are common. Such inner wars about what to do are linked with having multiple trauma-related reactions (often in response to perceived double binds) at the same time.

When understood in this way, it becomes clear that, similar to many other dissociative symptoms, having trauma-related DSS is a survival strategy that stems from general human capacities taken to the extreme that were once necessary to survive extreme situations.

WORKING WITH PATIENTS WHO HAVE DSS

Dissociative disorder experts recommend working with DSS, particularly when the patient has amnesia for unsafe behavior that is not due to intoxication, medical conditions, or head trauma (Brand et al., 2012b; Fisher, 2017; International Society for the Study of Dissociation, 2011; Mosquera, 2019; Putnam, 1989; Steele et al., 2017; van der Hart et al., 2006). For example, if a patient does not recall repeatedly cutting themselves, and there is no indication that the patient's lack of memory is due to intoxication or medical illness (e.g., epileptic seizures), in order to stabilize their safety, it is important to assess whether these unsafe behaviors are occurring in dissociative states. If the therapist determines that the patient has DSS (see Chapter 2 on assessment) and that unsafe behavior occurred while in a dissociative state, it is likely that the safety problems will not be sufficiently stabilized unless the therapist addresses and includes the self-state(s) in which self-harm occurs.

Here we provide a brief discussion of working with DSS. We recommend that mental health professionals who are new to working with individuals with DSS seek specialized training, consultation with colleagues who have successfully treated patients with dissociative disorders, and seek out additional reading (see Appendix C for additional training and reading resources). The treatment perspective that we detail below is consistent with expert consensus guidelines and research about treatment recommendations with dissociative disorder experts (see also Chapter 4) (Brand et al., 2012b; International Society for the Study of Dissociation, 2011; Myrick et al., 2015).

Principles for working with DSS are as follows:

1. Patients may feel ashamed and terrified about having DSS and may be concerned that they will be seen and/or treated as if they are "crazy." It can be helpful for the therapist to normalize having DSS and related internal conflicts, as we strove to in the section above. The therapist may also use "parts" language to help the patient bring these internal conflicts into awareness—for example, "Even though part of you wants to be in therapy, it seems like there is a part of you that doesn't want to talk to me today." Several of the roleplays we will provide illustrate the use of parts language to explore a variety of therapeutic issues, which can be a powerful tool to help reduce shame and generate self-compassionate reflexivity in patients with and without DSS.

2. When working with someone with DSS, the overarching aim is to increase communication and collaboration between self-states toward shared goals (e.g., getting healthy needs met safely). The therapist should strive to foster mutual understanding and communication among parts, with the aim that the patient will become able to do this crucial work independently. This will take time and repeated practice, both in and outside of therapy.

3. When exploring internal conflicts (and when working with parts in general), it is important that the therapist maintain the stance of being the therapist for all parts, being interested in the concerns and experiences of all parts, and respecting all parts equally. (In other words, the aim is to help the person make decisions that address their parts' underlying concerns while working toward shared goals.) For example, if exploring the reasons for risky, unhealthy, or unsafe behaviors, and when making safety agreements/plans with the patient, the therapist should be actively inviting all parts' perspectives and concerns, and all parts should be involved in making and agreeing to follow these plans.

4. The therapist should maintain a generally consistent therapeutic frame regardless of which parts are present (e.g., continuing to end sessions on time, adhering to previous agreements about length and frequency of phone calls, speaking in their regular adult voice even if a DSS that identifies as being a child is present in the session).

5. While therapists should be interested in, and accepting of, all parts of the patient, therapists should not ascribe a greater degree of autonomy to self-states than is already present. For example, the therapist should not encourage the patient to name their parts if they do not already have names. Parts can instead be referred to using their needs, the emotions they embody, or their strengths—for instance, "the part of you that needs to feel cared for by others," "the part of you that can feel anger," or "the part of you that knows how to set boundaries."

6. With persons whose parts demonstrate greater separateness and autonomy, the therapist can help encourage improved communication/collaboration by using metaphors that speak to the person, such as the need for different members of the same music and/or dance group, sports team, and so forth to work together if they are to accomplish their goals. Toward these ends, over time, the therapist can help the person develop effective ground rules for and means of independently communicating across self-states. (Examples of communication formats that can be helpful: joint journaling or holding "meetings" in imagined meeting spaces that can be configured as needed to meet parts' safety and communication concerns.) Ground rules should ensure that communication is respectful and that parts' underlying concerns are meaningfully represented in decision-making processes.

7. Some patients' parts may fear or hope that treatment will result in some parts being lost, being "killed off," or "dying." It is important for patients to be explicitly educated that each part contains a critical strength that helped them to survive, and that the function of therapy is to help parts that are stuck in the past to come into the present and adapt their strengths to serve the patient in their present-day life—and that what this will specifically look like will be up to the person's self-system as a whole to develop over time in response to their goals and concerns. Some possibilities of eventual shifts that work for many: Childlike parts can bring a sense of joy and playfulness to time spent with friends, and protector parts can help the patient set appropriate boundaries with others and help more vulnerable parts keep themselves safe in healthy ways. (In persons with higher numbers of separate/autonomous DSS, after developing appropriate communication between self-states, many patients find it helpful to shift toward parts working together in groups, with "older" parts helping "younger" parts learn how to use healthy coping skills.)

8. After developing mutual understanding and mutual compassion, and engaging in constructive collaboration over an extended period of time, two or more self-states may choose to further increase their closeness by unifying (Kluft, 1993b; Steele et al., 2017) or "becoming one."

COMMON DSS

Although the characteristics of DSS in a person's self-system will vary based on trauma situation demands and individual experiences and characteristics, there are two kinds of self-states that are particularly common in persons with childhood trauma: young parts of the self (parts that are experienced by the individual as being children or adolescents) and angry parts that present as rageful, passive-aggressive, or disengaged. These parts are often particularly activated by the therapist's attempts to reduce dissociation and work on reducing unsafe behaviors. These parts may attempt to slow down or block the therapy because they perceive the encouraged changes as going against the "rules" they enforce (i.e., the "rules" the person learned to follow to reduce the likelihood or severity of trauma), and/or being unsafe. We have chosen to discuss these parts first, as the therapist must work with these parts early in treatment, particularly when they are disrupting treatment and/or causing unsafe behavior. These angry parts should typically be worked with before working with younger parts and before working with traumatic content. Until these parts can be enlisted to cooperate with or at least tolerate therapy, they will likely block the therapist's efforts to engage, sometimes in ways that are harmful to the patient or to the treatment (e.g., increasing self-harm, quitting therapy prematurely). Work with these parts often takes considerable time and may require repetition over the course of the therapy, as more material comes into the treatment, or as more parts become activated.

Working with angry/critical self-states

Often, angry and critical parts can be conceptualized as parts of the self "fighting" what feel like risky changes to how they are used to doing things, and/or internalizations of an abuser's perspective/reactions. (In persons with DSS systems demonstrating high degrees of separateness/autonomy, it is not uncommon for a self-state to identify not just with but *as* the abuser as a means of keeping the person as a whole/their body "safer" by proactively anticipating the actual abuser's reactions.) These parts have important protective functions for the patient and, like all parts, have valuable strengths that can be repurposed to assist the patient in living well in the present day. These parts may function to protect the patient from vulnerability in the therapeutic relationship and other relationships. They may attempt to keep the person at a distance from others (including the therapist) and maintain unsafe behaviors that serve a self-protective or regulatory function. These parts often perceive what others deem "unsafe behaviors" to be safer than other options because they believe that these behaviors reduce the likelihood and severity of future trauma. For example, these parts may cause a patient to self-harm after a therapy session if the patient discussed a particularly vulnerable or internally prohibited topic. Alternatively, they may verbally lash out at the therapist in response to a seemingly innocuous question.

While not all angry or self-destructive actions on the part of a patient are indicative of the presence of DSS, the therapist should listen carefully for the extent to which these actions are connected to a DSS, have the "not me" or disowned quality of dissociation, and/or are associated with poor or no recall. The therapist should also devote attention to noticing what types of situations or interactions trigger these parts to become active, so as to better anticipate and become aware of them in the moment and, eventually, before they become activated.

While these parts may appear unhelpful and can even be intimidating, recognizing their survival function is crucial to successful treatment. All parts of the patient contain important strengths and have served crucial functions toward reducing the impact and/or prevalence of trauma. These parts may be stuck in the traumatic past at the beginning of therapy, however, and believe that the old ways of functioning are still necessary. They may also slip into perceiving "now as then" throughout treatment. When helped to become aware of the nontraumatic present and the options that can now be available to the person, however, they can be extremely helpful in helping patients to assert themselves appropriately and set healthy boundaries.

Strategies for working with angry, critical, and/or "internalized abuser" self-states are as follows:

1. Model curiosity about and compassion for these parts by asking and speculating about their concerns, feelings, strengths, and reactions.
2. Provide the person with education about the adaptive functions of these parts and the role they typically play in a dissociative individual.
3. Help internalized parts orient to the present, recognize the roles they have been playing, and find ways to adaptively use their strengths in the present day. For example, in the case of "internalized abuser" parts, this would involve helping those self-states understand that the difficult and unpleasant job of acting and possibly "sounding and looking" like an abuser and enforcing "trauma rules" helped keep them and "the body" safer before moving toward exploring how they could more effectively keep the person safer in the here and now. Note that helping such self-states recognize these as the motivations driving their behaviors is often most effectively accomplished through (and may require a great deal of) compassionate questioning about their concerns. As part of this process, states that have been playing such roles may opt to change how they internally "appear" and/or "sound." (While not ignoring the need to adaptively address any safety concerns that emerge, it can be helpful to know that there is often a scared, lonely "young" self-state underneath the "mask" of an "internalized abuser" that would like to not have to keep playing this role in this way but doesn't feel it is safe not to.)
4. Help the patient's self-system reduce avoidance of these parts and increase compassion for them. This requires the therapist to be aware of and address any urges they might have to avoid engaging with these parts. These urges are understandable in light of reported/observed self-state behaviors and indicate a need for greater curiosity about and understanding of the concerns and dynamics involved.

Throughout this work, the therapist must remember the importance of continuing to maintain healthy boundaries and limits through compassionate confrontation, including transparently discussing the rationale for interventions. It can be helpful to be aware of the risk of falling into Karpman's (2011) triangle roles described in Chapter 5: Both therapist and patient can fall into passive, unprotective bystander or victim roles, and the therapist is at risk of playing an overinvolved rescuer role rather than facilitating improved relationships between the patient's DSS. The goal is to work with parts to develop effective internal communication and collaboration, and to stop any behaviors that threaten the emotional or physical safety of the patient, the therapist, or the therapy.

This crucial work can take time and often needs to be revisited as therapy progresses. It is also important for therapists to monitor their reaction to these parts, as they can be frustrating or frightening to work with for therapists. If the therapist has strong negative reactions toward these parts and/or feels unable to work with them, this is an important indication to seek consultation. For further discussion of working with angry parts and voices, see Chefetz (2015); Loewenstein (1993, 2006); Mosquera & Ross (2016); Putnam (1989); and Steele et al. (2017).

Working with young self-states

Some patients may have parts that are experienced as infants, children, or adolescents. Child parts can be compelling and endearing, and the presence of young parts may tempt the therapist to treat them as actual children, sometimes in ways that are not healthy for the patient as an adult person. The role of the therapist is not to provide parenting for young parts but to support *the patient* to care for these young parts. This is yet another place where the dynamics described by Karpman and others can be enacted: The patient may have little understanding how to soothe and regulate disowned childlike self-states (and as a result will act like an "unprotective bystander") and/or may be aggressive (i.e., act like a "perpetrator") in relation to these states due to the vulnerability and trauma-based memories they often encapsulate. Each of these scenarios leaves the childlike states in a "victim" role. It is crucial for the patient's healing to recognize when they are enacting these roles and to learn how to attend to all self-states' needs in safe, healthy ways.

Attachment resources (as discussed in Chapter 6), can be very useful for helping patients care for these parts, as young parts often incapsulate intense unmet attachment needs and attachment insecurity. The ultimate goal is for the patient's adult self to become the secure attachment figure for these young parts. (This can be accomplished through imagery, as demonstrated in a roleplay below.) However, in many cases, the adult and child parts are phobic of each other—especially if previous attachment figures were frightening or involved in trauma. The therapist should be aware that it may take considerable work and time for the patient to be able to tolerate even very small doses of connection between child and adult parts due to the degree of disowned emotions, needs, and trauma-based recollections these disowned parts hold. Imagery related to attachment, such as animals or elements from nature, can be used as soothing surrogates in cases where either the adult or the child part is unwilling or unable to provide or receive attachment (Boon et al., 2011; Steele et al., 2017). Another useful regulation intervention is safe/peaceful place imagery (International Society for the Study of Dissociation, 2011). Used in this way, imagery can provide a sense of security, self-control, and self-regulation.

ROLEPLAYS: WORKING WITH DSS

Working with self-states in relation to safety

In this roleplay, the therapist encounters silence when confirming what seemed to have been a collaboratively developed plan, suggesting that there is a part of the patient that disagrees with this course of action. Thankfully, the therapist gets curious about and verbalizes this possibility.

THERAPIST: So we have set up and agreed that the plan is that next time you want to self-harm, you're going to get out of your apartment away from the things you use to hurt yourself, and instead go to a coffee shop or call a friend. Do you know which friends you can call?

PATIENT: [Silent]

THERAPIST: Do you think that's something you can do?

PATIENT: [Silent]

THERAPIST: Hmm, it seems like there's a part of you that doesn't want to talk about this anymore, that just shuts everything down as soon as we start to make a plan together. Is that what's happening?

PATIENT: [Silent]

THERAPIST: It's really important that all parts of you have a voice in the plan to manage your self-harm, so let's be curious together about the part of you that shuts everything down. What do you think that part might be thinking or feeling?

PATIENT: I don't know, it's just stupid. When we start to talk about it, I can't think straight anymore.

THERAPIST: Most times, when parts shut things down, there's a reason that makes sense. What about if we put the judgment to the side for now and try to really understand that part of you?

PATIENT: Well, I guess self-harm is how we have managed all these years; it's been really helpful in some ways.

THERAPIST: Oh, that makes sense. Is it possible that that part of you is worried about how you will manage without it? That that part might not realize that you're an adult now and that you have other ways of managing difficult feelings?

PATIENT: I guess.

THERAPIST: Can you ask inside and see if that is their concern?

PATIENT: Yes, that's right. And I don't want to be a burden.

THERAPIST: I think it's really important to appreciate and thank that part of you for looking out for you and making sure you can cope—and it's also really important to remind that part of you that you have more tools now, and you can manage in a different way.

PATIENT: Why? That part of me is just getting me into trouble.

THERAPIST: I think that part of you is pretty strong for helping you manage all this time. The goal is for you and that part to work together on keeping you safe. I actually think that that part of you could be really helpful in working on that goal. The problem is, I think that part doesn't realize that the abuse isn't happening anymore. If we can help that part to truly realize that you are safer now, that part might actually have some really valuable skills.

PATIENT: Maybe. I also worry about being a burden to my friends.

THERAPIST: You have friends now that care about you. You don't have to tell them details about your safety struggles so that it is a burden. You can just say you'd find it helpful if you can get together for some distraction and fun.

Investigating the underlying concerns of a change-fighting self-state

In the midst of problem-solving, the patient starts to get distant and show signs of getting ungrounded.

THERAPIST: It seems like as we're talking about this, you're drifting away. You've gone quiet and you aren't looking at me anymore.

PATIENT: [Silence]

THERAPIST: It seems like you're getting ungrounded. Let's do a grounding exercise together. Can you sit up straighter and put your feet on the floor?

PATIENT: [Doesn't move]

THERAPIST: Can you hear me? It's 2022 and you're here in my office. It's safe here. Remind all your parts that it's safe to be here, and invite them to look around the room to see this for themselves.

PATIENT: [Slumps in the chair]

THERAPIST: It seems like you're getting very dissociated. Can you move any part of your body? Maybe just start by moving one of your fingers the tiniest bit.

PATIENT: [Quietly] No.

THERAPIST: Oh, it seems like some part of you really doesn't want to get grounded right now. Can the part of you that just said "no" let us know why they doesn't want to get grounded?

PATIENT: [Silence]

THERAPIST: I think this is very important. I would really like to know what that part of you is concerned about so that I can help. I'm sure there's a very good reason why that part is worried.

PATIENT: You can't help.

THERAPIST: I would certainly like to try. Why does that part think I can't help?

PATIENT: It isn't safe.

THERAPIST: Something isn't safe about me helping? Or about getting grounded?

PATIENT: Both.

THERAPIST: Can the part of you that thinks it's unsafe to get grounded let us know what makes it unsafe? It's really important that all parts feel safe in therapy, so if something feels unsafe, I really want to know about it.

PATIENT: It's not safe for you.

THERAPIST: What do you mean?

PATIENT: If you help us, you'll get hurt. So I can't let you.

THERAPIST: Why would I get hurt?

PATIENT: We can't rely on you. It makes us weak. If we're here with you, part of me will hurt you so that you stay away.

THERAPIST: It sounds like part of you is really worried about being in a relationship with me. It's really important that we find ways for us both to be safe in this relationship—and I think there might be ways to do that without you being ungrounded.

Working with patients who cannot remember their behavior and/or experiences

Particularly with patients with DSS and a high degree of separateness between parts, there may be amnesia or periods of memory loss, including memory loss for work done in therapy sessions. In these cases, it can be useful to explore the function of the memory loss—patients can be asked, for example, if there is any part of them that is afraid to remember the contents of the session. Patients with DSS can be asked to check inside to see if any other parts may hold the missing information or if any other parts were present during the time they indicate not remembering. It is important not to give up too quickly, as the patient may simply need more time to retrieve the information. Sometimes patients may also be avoiding trying to recall what they do not easily have recollections of due to it being uncomfortable to remember. The therapist may want to simply sit with the patient, sometimes even for 10 or 15 minutes, encouraging the patient to take their time, as in the following roleplay.

PATIENT: Can you tell me what happened in our last session?

THERAPIST: What do you remember about it?

PATIENT: Well, I remember walking in the door. We agreed to talk about the anniversary of my father's death, and then, nothing, it's just a black hole. I don't remember anything at all after that.

THERAPIST: I wonder if it's that you don't remember, or if you, or some part of you, is afraid to remember.

PATIENT: I don't know.

THERAPIST: I think the information might be there. We just need to help you retrieve it. What if we just sit together while you try to remember it? You can take all the time you need; there's to rush. [Waits]

PATIENT: [Silence] Well, I felt really tired after the session and my eyes were all red when I looked in the mirror. I kind of remember crying. I guess I would just rather not have let you see all that emotion. I kind of wish it hadn't happened. I don't want to think about that.

THERAPIST: Why not?

PATIENT: I don't know. It gives you a lot of power over me. Before, if someone knew I was emotional about something, they would always use it against me.

THERAPIST: You know, in this relationship, it's a chance for you to have a different experience. You've brought feelings here before. Have I used it against you?

PATIENT: I guess not. You're generally OK. It just feels vulnerable.

Working with a patient with childlike self-states

Here, the patient asks for something from the therapist in a way that acknowledges vulnerability, which can pull for the therapist to act in a manner that (1) is counter to helping the patient's self-system learn how to be there with and for each other, (2) can scare other aspects of the patient, and/or (3) can cross therapeutic boundaries.

PATIENT: This is just really hard for me to talk about—it's so upsetting. I am so embarrassed. Can you hug me? I feel so little right now. I think my young parts need a hug.

THERAPIST: It sounds like the young parts of you really need comfort right now. One of the things we agreed to work on together is helping you learn to give that to them. I think this a really important chance for you to try comforting them. I wonder if we can try something together, to see if it helps those young parts feel a little bit more held.

PATIENT: I don't like thinking about those parts of me. It's embarrassing and I feel grossed out.

THERAPIST: What if we try just a little bit, just to see what it's like? I think it could be really important for you to start relating to those parts more. Remember how we've talked about how easy it is to slip into the role of being the unprotective bystander? You don't want to ignore their needs like your needs were once ignored.

PATIENT: Fine, but I'm not going to like it.

THERAPIST: If you look inside, can you see that young part of you?

PATIENT: Yuck. I don't want to see her. She's gross; she's so needy.

THERAPIST: What if you even just try looking from across the room, just so we can get a sense of that part of you.

PATIENT: It would have to be a really big room.

THERAPIST: That's OK. It can be as big as you both need it to be. Right now, the goal is just to learn more about that part of you, what she might be struggling with, and what might help her feel less upset.

PATIENT: I guess if I'm really far away, then I can try to look at her.

THERAPIST: If you look at her, what do you see?

PATIENT: She is maybe 5 years old. She looks like me—she has longer hair, like I did when I was that age. She is sitting in the corner and crying. She is so sad.

THERAPIST: How do you think that part of you would react if you moved a little closer to her?

PATIENT: I don't think I can.

THERAPIST: OK, why don't you just stay there for now, and just practice being aware of her. Is there anything you can think of that might help her?

PATIENT: I don't know. Maybe if she wasn't alone.

THERAPIST: Why don't you ask her what she needs to feel less alone? It doesn't have to be a person. It could be an animal, or something in nature.

PATIENT: She wants to have a dog.

THERAPIST: OK, that's good. What kind of dog is it?

PATIENT: A big black one.

THERAPIST: Why don't you let her spend some time with the dog? Feel the dog's fur, notice the dog breathing, look into its eyes. See what that feels like in the body to have the younger part of you have a dog for comfort.

PATIENT: She can't look yet. It's too overwhelming for her.

THERAPIST: That's OK—she doesn't have to look until she is ready. Just focus on breathing together, really noticing the breath rising and falling [pauses]. What does that feel like in the body?

PATIENT: It feels warmer, less upset.

THERAPIST: That's wonderful. It's so important to build experiences of safe connection for that part of you. Just keep breathing together and taking in what it feels like to be connected.

CONCLUSION

Therapists should anticipate and expect that individuals with TRD and DSS will struggle with a variety of challenges in treatment. As is clear from this discussion, these challenges typically stem from trauma- and attachment-related difficulties with emotion regulation, a sense that the patient is undeserving and bad, and a sense that others are going to harm and/or leave the patient if the patient comes to rely on them, lets down their guard, or is otherwise vulnerable. Rather than avoiding these difficulties, repeatedly discussing them (and the possible disruptions they can sometimes cause in the therapeutic relationship) is a powerful method for helping the patient heal from interpersonal trauma. These emotional and interpersonal difficulties can serve as crucial moments for repeatedly working through the damage wrought by chronic traumatization and caregivers who may not have been able to provide healthy attachment experiences.

8

Stabilizing Unhealthy and Unsafe Behaviors

In traumatized patients, the therapist is frequently working not just with past experiences of trauma and abuse but also with present-day retraumatization and unsafe behaviors. As mentioned throughout this book, these patients may engage in a variety of behaviors that can broadly be considered unsafe, including using too many drugs, drinking too much alcohol, nonsuicidal self-injury (NSSI), suicide attempts, disordered eating, aggression toward others, placing themselves in physically hazardous situations, and entering and remaining in unsafe interpersonal relationships (Ford & Gómez, 2015; Myrick et al., 2013; Najavits & Walsh, 2012; Webermann et al., 2014, 2017). People who engage in unhealthy, risky, or unsafe behaviors need to gradually develop an understanding of the reasons why they engage in these behaviors, and learn and begin to use healthier ways of managing the feelings, needs, and urges that drive these behaviors. Many people with trauma-related disorders (TRDs) have engaged in NSSI and other risky behaviors (see Chapter 1). As one of their primary ways of coping with stress, emotions, and trauma-related symptoms, it is often highly threatening for them to consider "getting safe." They often have no idea of what the word "safety" even means. Clinicians need to be aware of what a challenge it is for many of these individuals to, from their perspective, "give up" one of the few methods of being in control and managing their chaotic inner world. Clinicians need to strive to be empathic about how profoundly frightening and difficult it may be for TRD patients to decrease using potentially unsafe behavior, given what may be decades of reliance on this form of self-regulation.

An addictions model approach is often useful (Loewenstein, 2006). Early in treatment, it is often easier to commit to being safe for "one day at a time" rather than the overwhelming prospect of a long-term, seemingly permanent commitment to safety. This approach acknowledges that these behaviors have served crucial functions, such as calming a highly traumatized child, thereby decreasing the feelings of being utterly alone, helpless, ashamed, and betrayed. These behaviors often developed in childhood or adolescence to manage experiences and emotions that were intolerable. Due to repeatedly, chronically using unsafe methods to manage such overwhelm, the prospect of relinquishing the use of unsafe behaviors can be utterly terrifying.

It is imperative that clinicians recognize and openly discuss how difficult it is to make the decision to begin to develop healthy methods for dealing with dangerous urges and emotions that have felt catastrophic and unending in the past. To draw an analogy of what clinicians are requesting when we ask people to give up risky or otherwise potentially damaging behaviors, it is useful to think of giving up these behaviors as similar to agreeing to give up anesthesia for a major surgery. Dissociation and self-injurious behaviors may have served as a patient's "anesthesia" throughout life when they could not rely on caretakers to protect and soothe them. It requires tremendous courage and daily, even hourly, conscious effort to not "give in" to using the "quick fix" of cutting, drinking alcohol, or whatever other form(s) of unsafe behavior the individual has relied upon for respite from emotional pain. It is essential to help these patients learn recovery-focused ways to regulate their emotions, bodies, symptoms, stress, and relationships.

As with addictions, however, patients with TRDs will sometimes relapse into unsafe behaviors, potentially even after long periods of being safe. For this reason, it is important for healthy management of dysregulation to be a focus in all stages of treatment. To reduce the negative impact of potential relapses, encourage patients to not hide them, but instead to talk openly about what happened and how to immediately engage sufficient support and healthy alternatives to meet the underlying vulnerability that drove the relapse. This approach detoxifies the shame most patients feel when they engage in unhealthy behaviors. For example, after learning that a patient has relapsed into cutting, the clinician can thank him or her for having the honesty and trust to reveal the relapse. Together they can work to determine what feelings, stressors, symptoms, or other factor(s) created the urges to be unsafe, and identify supportive others and alternative, healthy methods for managing the feeling or stressor both currently and in the future in similar situations. Such patients need to develop an understanding of what gets in the way of actually using healthy coping skills in addition to what causes them to engage in unsafe or potentially risky behaviors.

It is quite common for patients who have learned these self-regulation strategies to not use them or "forget" to use them. One of the most common reasons is that mistreatment and attachment difficulties have contributed to believing they do not deserve to feel or live well. Additionally, they may experience anxiety about what they imagine the treatment process or healthy living will involve. For example, they may believe that if they get safer, the chaos in their lives will settle down, and then there will be enough stillness in their minds that memories of traumatic and painful attachment experiences may emerge. Such fears are not necessarily "cognitive distortions"—it *is* common for traumatized people who get sober from addictive substances or behavior to begin to think about the painful traumas and, more critically, feel the painful emotions that they were striving to numb via staying high or drunk. However, the "costs" of living amidst such chaos and self-destructiveness often become so high that, if encouraged to nonjudgmentally explore their unsafe behaviors and trauma-based beliefs, these individuals typically realize their unsafe behaviors and critical self-judgments are no longer as helpful as they likely were in the past at times they truly had little or no control.

Therapists may have their own judgments about these behaviors and may instinctively lean toward telling patients to end abusive relationships and stop unsafe behaviors. Therapists may feel helpless when dealing with seriously self-injuring or suicidal patients. They may have a wish to protect or rescue the patient. They may also be frightened that the patient will die or be seriously injured or worry about potential medicolegal consequences. All of these reactions are understandable. It is worth keeping in mind how powerfully the issue of safety pulls for the roles described in Karpman's triangle, which we have discussed in other chapters.

It is important, however, to recognize that these behaviors are strategies that have helped the person to survive their traumatic experiences and excruciating present-day feelings. Although it may seem counterintuitive, these behaviors serve a function in the patient's life (Brand, 2001). Typically, they represent attempts to meet natural and healthy human needs, to survive overwhelming experiences, or to manage intense suffering. There are many possible functions of such behaviors:

1. To soothe or escape overwhelming emotions (particularly related to trauma-related triggers; Nester, Boi et al., 2022) in the absence of more adaptive self-soothing strategies (or to increase feelings of numbness in traumatized patients who prefer to feel numb)
2. To reawaken feelings (physical or emotional) and decrease numbness
3. To meet attachment needs for connection and closeness through caretaking that they may receive after an unsafe behavior (e.g., medical care, concern from friends or family, or even caring for their own injuries)
4. To replace or prevent more immediately life-threatening behaviors (e.g., binge eating in place of overdosing, drinking alcohol instead of injecting opiates, cutting rather than committing suicide)
5. To punish themselves in response to deep feelings of shame and worthlessness
6. To show others (including the therapist) how much they hurt, especially if they have difficulties describing feelings in words, or to validate their own pain for themselves.

It is important to nonjudgmentally explore with patients what they perceive to be the functions or benefits of an unsafe behavior or relationship. Questions might include the following:

1. What do you like or find helpful about this relationship?
2. How does drinking alcohol help you?
3. How do you feel before and after you self-harm?
4. What were you hoping self-harm would do for you?
5. When did the binge eating start?

It is important to spend time assessing the perceived advantages and benefits of unsafe behavior. By spending some time understanding the behavior or relationships, the therapist strengthens the alliance with the patient and may build the patient's motivation to change the behavior. This information about the functions the behavior serves lays the groundwork for a more tailored and detailed plan for how the patient can change. Once the therapist understands the function of the behavior, the therapist can provide psychoeducation about and validation of the fact that the patient's underlying needs are likely normal and healthy, and that the patient does not (currently) know any other ways to meet those needs (or is not currently willing to meet them in ways that may not work as well or as quickly, or that are perceived as "healthy"). The therapist can then work to explore disadvantages of remaining unsafe, and to reach an agreement with the patient to work on finding other ways to meet their needs, as patients may equate giving up unsafe behaviors with giving up the possibility of getting their needs met.

In traumatized patients, who have often experienced authority figures as controlling, authoritarian, and frightening, a collaborative approach that emphasizes autonomy is especially important. Any attempts by the therapist to control the patient's behavior are fertile ground for reenactments and therapeutic stalemates and may, in fact, increase the behavior in question or lead to the patient continuing the behavior but hiding it from the therapist. It may be particularly helpful to emphasize and explore disadvantages that hinder the patient's own goals for themselves rather than framing a particular behavior as inherently "bad" or focusing on those consequences that seem the most problematic from the therapist's perspective. For example, the therapist may remind the patient that they have noted that they fight more with their partner when they are drunk, if the patient has a goal of improving their relationships and has in fact noted that alcohol use interferes with that goal. This may be more effective and more patient-centered than, for example, focusing on the impact of drinking on the patient's liver and future physical health if the patient does not seem concerned about this. In fact, some clients who drink heavily may actively do so in part because they want to harm their body so they can "die sooner."

This type of collaborative, harm-reduction approach does not preclude the need to carefully assess risk and intervene in a more directive way when necessary to prevent serious harm to the patient or to others or to maintain the therapeutic frame. For example, patients who use substances should be provided with resources for education about harm-reduction strategies (e.g., needle exchanges, infectious disease testing, naloxone). Patients who remain in abusive relationships should have a safety plan in case violence escalates, and child protection services should be involved if children's safety is possibly imperiled. Patients who are chronically suicidal or who engage in physically hazardous behaviors should be monitored and hospitalized (involuntarily if necessary) at times when their risk rises above baseline (e.g., failure to maintain a medically safe weight, increasingly medically serious suicide attempts or NSSI). The therapist may also set reasonable limits on the patient's behavior as it plays out in the therapy (e.g., self-harming during a session).

Many struggles with safety relate to conflicts within a person that are enacted among dissociative self-states. We addressed these conflicts and methods for addressing them in Chapter 7.

ROLEPLAYS

Exploring ongoing interpersonal violence

PATIENT: My boyfriend and I have been arguing a lot lately—it's been really triggering for me. We've been talking about breaking up, but I don't want to.

THERAPIST: What does the arguing bring up for you?

PATIENT: Well, we usually argue more when he has been drinking. You know, when I was a kid, my father used to get really violent when he would drink. I didn't tell you this before because I felt so embarrassed, but my boyfriend can get pretty rough too when he drinks.

THERAPIST: What do you mean by "rough"?

PATIENT: Well, he yells and calls me names a lot when he's drunk.

THERAPIST: Does it ever get physical?

PATIENT: Sometimes he pushes me. He pushed me against the wall yesterday and I hurt my arm.

THERAPIST: I am glad you told me that this is happening—it is so important for me to know. Can you say more about not wanting to tell me?

PATIENT: I guess I just don't want you to tell me to break up with him. And I don't want you to think that I'm bad like he thinks I am. I know it's not good that he does this, but I just don't want to leave.

THERAPIST: It sounds like there's a part of you that worries that this relationship isn't safe—and what you're saying does make me worry about your safety—but it also sounds like there's a big part of you that finds this relationship really important. Can you tell me what makes this relationship so important? It isn't my job to tell you what to do, but it *is* my job to understand what is happening for you so that we can figure out together what will work best to help you heal.

PATIENT: Well, I just really love him. When he's not drinking, he's really sweet to me and he apologizes for everything. And what if I can't find anybody else? It's not like people are lining up to be with me. At least he loves me. And he gets me—he's been through a lot, too.

THERAPIST: It makes sense that you want a partner who loves you. All people want to feel connected to others—we are social creatures. Is there anything else that keeps you in the relationship?

PATIENT: Well, I just don't feel like a very good person inside anyway. I probably do things to make him angry. I don't really deserve any better.

THERAPIST: We can agree to disagree on that part. I don't think anybody deserves to be called names and pushed into walls. Are there any children at home with you?

PATIENT: No—well, my daughter is living at home, but she's an adult.

THERAPIST: You've told me before that you really want your daughter to have better relationships with men than you have.

PATIENT: Yeah, I do think about that. I don't like that she sees me and my boyfriend fight. Her last boyfriend was a total jerk, and I want her to know that she deserves better.

THERAPIST: That's important—it sounds like on one hand, the relationship makes you feel connected to another person and loved, and at the same time, you worry about the impact on your daughter. Maybe at some point, when you're ready, we can talk about if there are ways that you can increase your sense of connection with other people that don't result in you being unsafe or mistreated.

PATIENT: I guess, maybe. But for now I want to stay with him.

THERAPIST: If you are staying with him, are you willing for us to spend some time working on a plan for how to stay safe at home if things get worse?

CLIENT: OK, I guess we can do that.

Clothing that is sexually provocative and interpersonal safety

THERAPIST: You know, we've spent a lot of time in therapy talking about your safety, some of the things that make it hard for you to be safe, and things you have decided to work on to help yourself get and stay safer, like setting and keeping healthy boundaries. Lately, I've been wondering about whether your clothing choices might be related to your difficulty setting and holding healthy boundaries.

PATIENT: What do you mean? I like dressing like this! Are you saying there's something wrong with my clothes? Are you saying I deserve to be hurt because of what I wear?

THERAPIST: Not at all. There's nothing right or wrong about dressing a particular way, and no clothing choice gives anyone the right to hurt someone. I just wonder how the way you dress is connected to how you relate to yourself and other people, and think it might be worth exploring that together.

CONCLUSION

The emotional pain caused by trauma is often expressed through a range of unsafe and unhealthy behaviors. Although safety struggles can become chronic in patients with TRD, their safety and self-care *can* improve, as shown in the

Treatment of Patients with Dissociative Disorders (TOP DD) studies as well as other studies. The approach to improving safety and self-care that underlies the Finding Solid Ground program is described more fully in the next chapter and in the accompanying workbook (*The Finding Solid Ground Program Workbook: Overcoming Obstacles in Trauma Recovery*). With treatment and education, dissociative individuals can deepen their self-compassion and self-care skills so that they can finally feel safe. By working with these patients, we can help them achieve *solid, safe ground.*

9

The Finding Solid Ground Program and How to Use It in Individual and Group Settings

The challenges that trauma survivors often face can feel overwhelming to patients and clinicians. Trauma-driven neurobiological changes can lead people with trauma histories to have a variety of struggles, including:

- Feeling that further trauma is imminent
- Frequently experiencing intense emotions that can lead to dissociation (feeling "too much" or "too little")
- Having difficulty noticing when they are safer
- Feeling like the present is "just like" the past, even when they are safer and have different capacities, options, and resources
- Having emotions, memories, and physical sensations related to past traumas intrude into the present without warning or understanding
- Struggling to develop and maintain healthy self-care and relationships
- Suffering from a variety of medical problems and illnesses.

In addition, each of these difficult experiences interferes with attention, concentration, and retention, making it difficult for trauma-related disorder (TRD) patients to take in, remember, and use new information, including information about healthy, healing-focused coping skills that can help them progress toward getting and feeling safer.

Despite wanting to get and feel safer, trauma survivors may not believe that it is possible to feel better and get safer—or that they deserve anything better than their current level of symptoms and difficulties. In the absence of healthy coping skills that work—and when doubting that they deserve to be safe—they may rely on unhealthy, risky behaviors that seem to help in the short term. They are often not aware that these unhealthy behaviors contribute to keeping them feeling unsafe and interfere with making progress toward recovery. They may not recognize that engaging in unhealthy behaviors implicitly reinforces the idea that they do not deserve to be safe and healthy.

Learning new ways of doing things is hard for all of us—particularly if someone feels conflicted about being safer and doing things differently, as TRD patients often do. It may not feel acceptable to make changes that go against trauma-born "lessons" or "rules" that are based on lived experience in a past that still feels present. Further, being reminded of trauma by talking about trauma-related reactions (including engaging in risky or unhealthy behaviors) can lead to yet more trauma-related reactions. This in turn may increase the urges to engage in unhealthy, risky, and unsafe behaviors.

These are the interrelated challenges faced by complex trauma survivors. This seemingly unending cycle of symptoms, unhealthy and risky behaviors, and "roadblocks" to progress can be confusing, frustrating, and daunting to patients and therapists alike. It is understandable that treatment providers who have not received training in the diagnosis, management, and treatment of TRD can feel perplexed about how to treat these individuals.

As the research discussed in Chapter 4 shows, however, patients with complex TRD *can* make meaningful and important progress in treatment. Research and expert consensus suggest that progress is most likely to occur within treatment that emphasizes symptom management and safety stabilization from the beginning of, and throughout, treatment.

The Finding Solid Ground program's psychoeducational materials are aimed at facilitating this approach. This program, which is focused on symptom management and safety stabilization, targets each of the challenges just discussed. Initially the program was developed for use in the Treatment of Patients with Dissociative Disorders (TOP DD) Network study. The program addresses the symptom management and stabilization commonly needed by TRD patients. The Network study version of the Finding Solid Ground program was informed by years of discussions among TOP DD research team members, who are experts in treating and researching TRDs, and feedback from TRD patients.

The Finding Solid Ground psychoeducational program was the core of the TOP DD Network study. As reviewed in Chapter 4, TOP DD Network Study patient participants demonstrated meaningful improvements while using the program as an adjunct to individual psychotherapy. We then used Network study patient and therapist feedback to refine the program materials, which TOP DD Network study co-investigator Dr. Hugo Schielke has been using in trauma symptom management treatment groups. The Finding Solid Ground program was further refined based on these patients' feedback. Thus, the TOP DD team's philosophy of "working together, learning together, healing together" guided the exchange of ideas that led to the initial development and repeated refinements of the Finding Solid Ground program.

This book provides the theoretical and clinical rationale and research basis for the program. This chapter provides an overview for therapists of the content presented in *The Finding Solid Ground Program Workbook: Overcoming Obstacles in Trauma Recovery* (Schielke et al., 2022). This workbook provides the

information sheets and written and practice exercises that serve as the foundation
for the Finding Solid Ground program. Below, we provide an overview of the
materials and recommendations for using the Finding Solid Ground program in
individual and group contexts, followed by discussion of practical considerations
for using the materials.

THE FINDING SOLID GROUND PROGRAM MATERIALS: AN OVERVIEW

The overarching goal of the program is to help people who have experienced
trauma get and feel safer by learning healing-focused ways to manage and reduce
trauma-related difficulties. We aim to increase self-compassion, in part by helping
patients understand that these difficulties make sense given a history of trauma,
and strive to teach them how to help themselves heal from trauma, starting with
healthy ways to manage trauma-related reactions and symptoms.

The materials are presented in an order that aims to provide the information
most helpful toward managing dysregulation first. We then provide information in
a sequence that builds on previous work and seems most likely to offer manageable
next steps toward making progress in getting and feeling safer. Throughout this
process, we emphasize the importance of managing and reducing dysregulation
with healthy coping skills when first noticing signs of feeling "too much" or "too
little" (i.e., at the earliest possible signs of being at risk of getting outside of their
window of tolerance).

The Finding Solid Ground program materials discuss 30 topics and include
psychoeducational information sheets as well as written and practice exercises
for each topic. Information sheets offer succinct summaries of what we have
found most important and helpful. To help patients follow discussions, focus attention, and be less likely to get overwhelmed, information sheets are kept brief,
and each subtopic is presented within its own "focus box." Information sheets
are also meant to serve as a resource that patients can keep handy and use as
needed. The program also provides a set of written and practice exercises for each
topic. These are designed to help patients reflect on, apply, and practice the information discussed in the topic's information sheet. Throughout the materials,
we encourage participants to work at a manageable pace, pausing to manage any
dysregulation that may emerge with healthy coping skills, and to talk to treatment
providers about any difficulties or questions that may come up as they work on
the program.

When using the materials in group or individual contexts, we recommend beginning with sharing the program's overarching frameworks (see "Setting the
Stage" in Table 9.1), including the principles of trauma-informed care (reviewed
in the "Using Finding Solid Ground Program Materials" section below) and
the stages of trauma treatment (discussed in Chapter 4). We also describe the
program's goals and offer recommendations on how to engage with the program.
(The workbook's introduction to the program, "Welcome to the Finding Solid

Table 9.1 FINDING SOLID GROUND OVERVIEW

Category (Goals)	Topics (Notes)
Setting the Stage *(Preparing to work through the program modules. Goals: Understanding the program's frameworks, aims)*	Recovering and Healing from Trauma *(the stages of trauma treatment)* and Principles of Trauma-Informed Care *(Information sheet in the "Resources" section of the workbook)* Welcome to the Finding Solid Ground Program *(introduction in the workbook; offers context to increase self-compassion and recommendations to get the most out of the program)*
Grounding *(Goal: Reducing risk of overwhelm by learning how to connect to the present and regulate emotion when feeling too much or too little)*	Grounding: When, How, Why *(when, how, and why to use grounding skills to orient to and anchor in the present)* Signs That You Are Starting to Get Ungrounded and Healthy Ways to Get Grounded *(mental and physical signs of getting ungrounded or starting to dissociate, healthy mental and physical ways to get grounded)* 101 Healthy Ways to Get Grounded *(ways to get grounded that patients have found to work well for them, organized into categories of sensory/physical, mental, and creative grounding activities)*
Separating Past from Present *(Goals: Noticing when the present is safer, better than the past, being aware of current resources/options, learning how to manage and contain trauma-related intrusions)*	Separating Past from Present: When, How, Why *(actively working to notice how the present is different when a situation feels "like" or "just like" the past; Loewenstein, 2006)* Using Imagery to Help Separate Past from Present *(including split screen, containment imagery)* Separating Past from Present: Managing 90/10 Reactions *(i.e., managing strong/intense feelings in the present triggered by similarities to the past; Lewis et al., 2004)*
Additional Foundations *(Goal: Learning additional ways to help make progress toward getting and feeling safer)*	More Healthy Ways to Help Yourself When You're Feeling Too Much *(including deep breathing; slow swing imagery; peaceful place imagery; gauge, regulator, pause button imagery)* How to Help Yourself Heal the Impact of Trauma on the Brain *(how trauma changes the brain, how trauma symptom management skills help heal the brain, anticipating the process)* Managing Crisis-Level Feelings *(combining skills to help manage intense feelings)* The Importance of Self-Compassion in the Healing Process *(developing self-compassion, including curiosity about what is happening and what can help; how self-neglect and harsh self-criticism get in the way of healing)*

Table 9.1 CONTINUED

Category *(Goals)* | **Topics *(Notes)***

Managing Trauma-Based Thoughts
(why they can happen, signs of trauma-based thoughts, steps to manage them)

Getting and Feeling Safer, Part 1
(Goal: Learning how to recognize and interrupt patterns that can contribute to risky, unhealthy, or unsafe behavior, or get in the way of getting and feeling safer)

Recognizing and Planning How to Manage Challenging Situations *(identifying and managing triggers)*

Getting Healthy Needs Met Safely *(how this helps heal trauma, why this can be difficult for people with trauma histories, and how to work toward this with self-compassion)*

Why People Who Have Experienced Trauma Sometimes Do Risky, Unhealthy, or Unsafe Things, and How to Get Healthier and Safer *(why people with trauma histories sometimes do unhealthy or unsafe things, how these behaviors get in the way of healing from trauma/keep people stuck in a cycle of feeling unsafe, how to get healthier and safer)*

The Cycle of Unhealthy Behavior, and How to Break Out of It *(how to understand and interrupt this cycle that keeps people feeling unsafe)*

Understanding and Reducing Trauma-Related Reactions

Addressing Trauma-Based Thinking
(Goal: Identifying and reducing trauma-driven cognitive distortions)

Shifting from Trauma-Based Thoughts to Healing-Focused Thinking *(what to know about trauma-based thoughts, how to recognize them, how to shift them with/toward healing thinking)*

Making the Decision to Get Healthier and Safer *(why it can be so hard, how to help prepare to make the decision)*

Getting and Feeling Safer, Part 2
(Goal: Learning more ways to recognize, interrupt, and reduce patterns that can contribute to risky, unhealthy, or unsafe behavior)

Working to Calm Your Alarm System *(how to do this)*

Feeling Too Much or Too Little and Your Window of Tolerance *(i.e., range of manageable sensation [Siegel, 1999]; what it is, why it is important to be aware of, how to notice risk of getting outside of it, how to reduce likelihood of this and work toward healing/widening the window)*

Helping Yourself Recognize Signs That Your Risk of Doing Unhealthy or Unsafe Things Is Increasing *(how to recognize and reduce risk)*

Improving Your Relationship with Emotions, Body Sensations, and Aspects of Self

How to Help Your Feelings Help You *(why emotions/body sensations might feel scary/bad/wrong, why to work toward having a better relationship with them, how to do this)*

Why Naming Feelings Can Be Difficult *(why this can be the case, why to not just suppress emotions, recommendations)*

(continued)

Table 9.1 CONTINUED

Category *(Goals)*	Topics *(Notes)*
	Naming Feelings *(basic feelings, related feelings, related sensations, what each feeling discussed tries to help you notice)*
	Self-Understanding Through Compassion: Accepting All Your Feelings *(what it does and does not mean to accept feelings and dissociated parts; important information for people with parts; how to develop healthy relationships with emotions, parts)*
	Safely Practicing Noticing and Naming Feelings *(preparation, and steps to manageably practice)*
	Guilt, Shame, and Self-Compassion *(what are guilt and shame; how to determine if you are being unfair with yourself; differences between healthy guilt [an emotion that raises awareness of discrepancy between values and action] and toxic shame [symptom of depression]; how to help get yourself out of toxic shame)*
Sticking With the Process and Building on Progress	Feeling Safe Takes LOTS of Practice *(reminders of how practice helps, how important it is, how to approach this work)*
	Let the Good Times Roll—Learning How to Allow Good Feelings and Positive Experiences *(why this might be difficult, how to help yourself feel better, managing trauma-based thoughts about feeling good)*
	You Have Learned a Lot—How You Can Keep Healing *(review of what was covered in the program, how to keep building on progress made)*

Ground Program: An Introduction to the Program and How to Get the Most Out of It," presents information and language that you may find helpful with this.) It is important to emphasize that patients work on the program materials at a manageable pace, with patience, persistence, and a self-compassionate recognition that learning new ways of doing things takes repeated practice over time.

With respect to program content, we begin with modules teaching foundational trauma symptom management skills, including grounding (orienting to and anchoring in the present) and separating past from present (noticing how the present is different than the past) as well as imagery skills that help with separating the past from the present (e.g., containment). These skills facilitate participants' ability to connect to, and remain in, the here and now (versus the "there and then" of past trauma), regulate emotion when feeling too much or too little, and reduce risk of overwhelm. As patients make improvements in these areas, they reduce dysregulation and therefore the risk of engaging in risky or unhealthy behaviors. Progress in using these skills may also improve their ability to focus and attend to and retain information. The Finding Solid Ground program next presents education on self-soothing techniques, trauma's impact on neurobiology and how to help heal the impact of trauma, managing crisis-level feelings, the importance of self-compassion and suggestions for how to remember to give themselves the care they need, and suggestions for managing trauma-based thoughts.

In the first series of information sheets and exercises explicitly focused on recognizing and interrupting patterns related to risky, unhealthy, and unsafe behaviors, we provide information on identifying and managing triggers; getting healthy needs met safely; and understanding the reasons traumatized people may engage in risky, unhealthy, or unsafe behaviors. Patients are much more likely to feel motivated to engage in the hard work that is required to get safer if they can self-compassionately understand how unhealthy coping that seems like a "quick fix" in the short term ultimately impedes getting and feeling safer and healing from trauma by keeping them stuck in a cycle of unhealthy behavior. This information hopefully increases patients' self-awareness and self-compassion. We encourage them to work on learning to recognize and respond to early warning signs, as well as methods for breaking out of any cycles of unhealthy behavior they may be engaging in.

The next materials offer information about trauma-related reactions and how to reduce susceptibility to them in safer situations, and recognizing and shifting trauma-based beliefs that get in the way of people's ability to feel they deserve to get and feel safer. This is followed by material on recognizing, reducing, and interrupting patterns related to engaging in risky or unhealthy behaviors. We provide instruction about increasing awareness of their windows of tolerance (i.e., noticing the earliest signs of beginning to feel too much or too little) and when they may be at risk for unhealthy behaviors. We then teach them how to develop a plan to address such risks by using recovery-focused emotion regulation and self-soothing skills.

The program then focuses on improving self-awareness and tolerance of emotions, body sensations, and aspects of self (including dissociative self-states [DSS], if applicable). Because shame is particularly challenging, we address it directly and indirectly repeatedly throughout the program. However, because shame is so often triggering, we address it only briefly until this point in the Finding Solid Ground program; thus, patients will have hopefully developed sufficient emotion regulation skills that they can begin to work on addressing even this highly challenging trauma-related emotion.

The final series of materials emphasizes recognizing and building on the progress they have made by continuing to practice what they have been learning. We emphasize that getting and feeling safer requires lots of practice, and that this practice is essential to helping their brains develop new healthy patterns and pathways. We also emphasize the importance of working to allow themselves to tolerate "feeling good" and having positive experiences. The program ends with a review of all they have learned and encouragement to keep building on this work to continue their healing process.

Consistent with the program's emphasis on managing dysregulation, participants are repeatedly encouraged to work through the materials at a pace that feels manageable. We also encourage going through no more than one topic (i.e., reading one information sheet and completing its accompanying written and practice exercises) per week. Going too quickly precludes participants from engaging in the practice required to incorporate what they are learning into healthy habits that will improve their lives, contradicting the point of the program. Going too quickly also increases the risk of participants getting overwhelmed—an experience that we are trying to help participants reduce. It is for these reason that, in the words of trauma expert Dr. Richard Kluft, "The slower you go, the faster you'll get there."

USING THE FINDING SOLID GROUND PROGRAM IN INDIVIDUAL SETTINGS

While we believe there is a sound rationale for the presented sequence, which appears well suited for general application in individual and group settings, it is helpful to adapt the length of time focused on each topic area to the patient's needs. With this in mind, clinicians working with patients in individual therapy may find that patients further along in treatment have sufficient strengths in some areas, and so may not need extended focus on those skills. Therapists may find that some patients would benefit from reviewing certain materials earlier in the process than the standard sequence. We encourage therapists who are familiar with the materials and the principles underlying the presented organization to use their discretion to individualize the sequence and pacing of the materials for each patient. We encourage careful assessment and thoughtful consideration in making such decisions, however, as patients may not be aware of what they do not yet know (or might get overwhelmed by). Alternatively, patients may be able to readily identify and describe various skills, but have difficulty implementing these skills when needed, and so would benefit from active focused attention on putting intellectually understood information into practice before proceeding to later-sequenced topics.

USING THE FINDING SOLID GROUND PROGRAM IN GROUP SETTINGS

When using the materials in group settings, we recommend that groups be facilitated by two providers to enable increased attention to patient comprehension and regulation (i.e., to see if someone needs help with understanding content or self-regulating). We recommend meeting with potential participants individually to screen for fit, increase likelihood of sustained commitment, and gain informed consent about the group and its goals. In screening meetings, we recommend giving potential participants an overview of the group's goals, the importance of confidentiality, and the frameworks structuring the group, including the three-stage trauma treatment model and the principles of trauma-informed care (discussed below) (the "Resources" section of the workbook offers a handout describing both of these frameworks). We believe that in most settings, it is best to conduct closed group sessions—that is, to only add new group members mid-cycle when this is assessed to be appropriate/manageable for both the group and the potential new member. This, too, should be shared/discussed as indicated in pre-enrollment meetings.

Sharing the principles of trauma-informed care (e.g., Huang et al., 2014) during the screening process can help increase potential participants' sense of safety and increase their willingness to join and meaningfully engage with the group. These principles are aimed at facilitating healing from trauma and reducing the likelihood of triggering trauma-related reactions. Briefly stated, trauma-informed care involves striving to consistently demonstrate the following:

- Safety (physical and emotional)
- Trustworthiness (including transparency about what you are doing and why)
- Collaboration (through curiosity and mutuality)
- Empowerment (sharing power, including through offering meaningful choices; encouraging participants to give voice to their perspectives and preferences)
- Attentiveness to cultural, historical, and gender-related issues, trauma (including racism, sexism, LGBTQIA discrimination)
- Peer support and mutual self-help (working and learning together, recognizing that mistakes are part of the process and striving to learn from these).

Sharing these principles with group members can help clarify otherwise potentially unspoken rationale for specific recommendations that providers might make in the facilitation of the group. (It can be helpful to articulate and embody these principles as a framework for individual therapy for the same reasons.)

A sense of group safety tends to increase when these principles are put into action. For example:

- Trustworthiness increases with clear descriptions of rationales for recommendations and demonstrated interest in collaboration.
- Meaningful collaboration is possible if each person's preferences and concerns are encouraged to be given voice, recognizing that these preferences and concerns can be difficult to give effective voice to as a result of the impact of trauma.
- It is easier to learn and work together in an atmosphere that recognizes that we all make mistakes along the way.

When describing the three-stage treatment model to potential group members, it is important to note that the group will focus on symptom management and stabilization. In keeping with this, it is important to emphasize that the group will not involve discussing details of trauma or unsafe behavior, as this can be dysregulating to themselves and others. (Discussing trauma details can quickly lead to reexperiencing and flashbacks, and so is contraindicated for this stabilization-focused group.) Stated differently, discussing trauma details is part of *processing*, the second stage of trauma treatment, which is made possible by learning healthy, healing-focused ways to manage trauma-related reactions and symptoms—the focus of this program.

A useful group guideline is that members agree not to share details about trauma or unsafe behaviors in group or outside the group with other group members because of the possibility of dysregulating each other and blurring boundaries. (If patients need to be assessed due to safety concerns, this should done individually with the group member.) Group members are instead encouraged (both prior to joining and as necessary) to keep references to traumatic material in a nonspecific "headline" level of detail (Loewenstein, 2006) in the group setting (e.g., "I was triggered by a reminder of trauma"; "I was having a flashback"; "I was having urges to do something risky and/or unhealthy"). (Note: If therapists are concerned about participants discussing unhealthy/risky behaviors at even a headline level in a group setting, it is possible to conduct the group with guidelines disallowing such discussion and reserving the materials that make headline mention of these behaviors for individual work.)

Most patients will find this approach reassuring. Others may need reassurance that these guidelines are meant to protect them and others and are offered out of concern for all group members' well-being (as opposed to the group being yet another place where people do not want to hear about what happened to them).

The initial group meeting should include a review of the group's frameworks and rationales and should make space for the suggestion and discussion of additional potential guidelines that participants and therapists collaboratively feel are consistent with these frameworks.

We recommend that group meetings begin with grounding (orienting to and anchoring in the present; see, e.g., the Grounding Script in Appendix B), initially led by a provider, but inviting a participant to take the lead when they feel ready. (Later in the program, it can also be helpful to have participants lead the group through other healthy forms of grounding that they use, such as those listed in the 101 Healthy Ways to Ground handout.)

We also recommend having participants take turns reading the information sheet content, with providers rephrasing and adding information as well as making space for participants' questions and comments, redirecting if needed to ensure emotional safety and reduce risk of overwhelm. To be of greatest help, therapists should be responsive to signs of possible dysregulation, checking in and initiating the use of grounding and other coping skills as indicated (see Chapter 6). Patients who get triggered are at risk of getting overwhelmed; the longer therapists wait, the harder time patients will have trying to reorient and reconnect to the present.

In general, we recommend that detailed work with written exercise topics take place outside of group. In group, the therapists should encourage participants to share their experiences related to this work (without including trauma details). Having said that, some settings include patients who are not as well suited for this approach; in these instances, topics suggested for written exercises can be useful to inspire group discussions while reminding and enforcing the guideline against discussing details about trauma.

Adapting group schedules to needs of setting/population served

Although the standard sequence appears well suited for settings that afford long cycles, each setting—and population—may have different needs and demands. To facilitate responsiveness to group participants' needs and differing rates of progress, it can be helpful to run different groups focusing on different aspects of the program, with participants progressing to subsequent groups as indicated. (Of note, a number of group participants have reported finding it helpful to repeat subsets of the program, noting that they are better able to make use of the information—and apply it to different difficulties—with the additional practice that repetition provides.) In groups focused on later-module materials, it is not uncommon for group discussions to tend to be more extensive and deeper—developments made possible by group members' ability to apply the skills learned in earlier groups. Group assignments and modifications in the materials' sequence should be informed by careful consideration of potential participants' abilities and the principles underlying the presented organization, including ensuring participants have sufficient ability to make use of the foundational skills presented in early modules before progressing on to the work presented in later modules.

PRACTICAL CLINICAL CONSIDERATIONS

The program was intended to assist TRD patients in learning new skills and building upon strengths they already have, and to assist their therapists in helping patients attain greater stabilization in treatment. It is important to convey a sense of compassion and respect, acknowledging that each individual has tremendous strengths because otherwise they would not have been able to survive trauma.

As discussed above, we encourage participants to pace themselves as they work through this program, to pause to use healthy coping to manage any dysregulation that may emerge, and to reach out to treatment providers as necessary. Therapists may wish to emphasize a phrase used often in the Finding Solid Ground program: "Step by step, you are getting there," meaning that each time they make the effort to practice the techniques and self-awareness fostered by the program, they are helping themselves "get there"—to finding more stability and feeling safer, with a healthier, higher quality of life.

It was challenging to develop a program that presents interrelated skills and ways of thinking about trauma's impact in "bite-sized chunks" that would slowly introduce challenging topics in manageable pieces. The following language from the TOP DD Network study's introductory video may be of help:

> The more you practice these skills, the better you will become at managing your symptoms and dealing with your emotions. It is crucial that you practice the skills several times each day because it takes many, many practices to remember and learn a skill. No one can get good at a new skill right away. The only way to get comfortable and remember to use these skills is if you practice them so that they become new healthy habits. . . . We will teach you a variety of skills throughout the program. Please keep using the earlier skills as you move through the later weeks. The skills complement each other and work well together. We also encourage you to discuss your reactions to the writing and practice exercises.

A great deal of consistent, daily practice and work is required to heal from chronic trauma. The educational materials often repeat this message. In clinical practice, many TRD patients (as well as most other people!) fail to make the daily effort at practicing new, healthy behavior and shifting from trauma-based to recovery-focused thinking. In the Network study, we conveyed the importance of concerted, daily work in multiple ways, including the following:

> Sticking with it is the most important part [of healing]. Because change is often difficult for lots of understandable reasons, it can be difficult to get and stay motivated to do things that will help you feel better, but working at developing skills is the only way to heal. It takes real effort—every week. If you want to build muscle, you have to use your muscles often—it's the same with developing skills that will give you better control in your life. If you want to understand and get better at managing your symptoms, you have to practice the skills every day.

AREAS TO ATTEND TO THROUGHOUT THE FINDING SOLID GROUND PROGRAM TO INCREASE EFFECTIVENESS OF ITS USE

Improving self-understanding and self-compassion

Assisting patients in developing self-compassion is a fundamental component of treating TRD individuals, particularly those who have experienced chronic childhood abuse and neglect. Without the development of some degree of self-compassion, it is exceptionally difficult for these individuals to fully embrace working on developing self-care and recovery-based skills. Encouraging curiosity is a core part of fostering self-compassion, and is an antidote to learned self-neglect. This is why, throughout the workbook, we model and emphasize the importance of being interested in and curious about what is being experienced internally, what is happening in the external situation, and what might help. This is also why we explicitly highlight how central curiosity is to treating oneself with self-compassion in the handout "The Importance of Self-Compassion in the Healing Process."

Being mistreated and unprotected during the years when identity, social cognition, and interpersonal patterns develop creates a profound sense of being unworthy of love and protection. The belief that one is unworthy of feeling better and deserving help is a major hurdle to recovery from trauma. Without some degree of self-compassion, these individuals may be so overcome with shame and self-hatred that they cannot fully, actively put in the effort to overcome the damage that trauma and neglect have wrought. The treatment of complex trauma is intensive and requires a good deal of effort. Self-hatred and shame undermine the energy and motivation required to fully engage in this work. Self-compassion is an antidote to shame. As such, it is of critical importance to the successful treatment for TRD.

RESOLVING FEAR-DRIVEN AMBIVALENCE WITH RESEARCH-INFORMED HOPE AND CARE

Recognizing and addressing trauma-driven ambivalence about feeling better, making progress in treatment, and becoming safer is crucial in treating chronically traumatized individuals. For example, it is common for these individuals to have developed the belief that they are so flawed and unworthy that they do not have the right to feel good, much less heal. (This is why helping develop a sense of self-compassion is so important.) in addition, they often are terrified of change because they have grown so accustomed to feeling miserable and living a chronically impaired, disabled lifestyle. Change also brings up fears of losing control—after all, in childhood they may have been terribly out of control with adults behaving unpredictably and dangerously. Unpredictability is frightening to most people, but it is usually profoundly threatening to people who grew up in chaotic, abusive, and/or dysfunctional families. Severely neglected and abused children learn through repeated experience that when events are unpredictable, adults may become harmful, or events can feel life-threatening to a small, terrified child who is at the mercy of his or her caretakers. Over the years, change and unpredictability may have become fused with the feeling that extreme danger, or death, was possible, even if the actual risk of death was low. In the aftermath of such experiences, lingering dread and fear of change can be paralyzing, sometimes accompanied by patients demonstrating their fears by sabotaging their progress in treatment.

It may have been utterly crushing to hear statements in childhood such as "I hate you" or "I wish you were never born" for the TRD patients who were psychologically abused. Feeling crushed and endangered tremendously impairs a child's initiative, self-confidence, and ability to tolerate change. Being terrified of making a mistake and being verbally or physically attacked can impair a child's ability to identify and follow through on behaviors that could be seen as independent or as challenging the authority figure. Being assertive or even simply making eye contact can increase an abused child's risk of being "seen" or noticed, which to a maltreated child may be equated with "being hurt." Abused children may have coped with this precarious environment by trying to make themselves small or invisible, by not trying to excel or do well, by hiding or avoiding people, and/or by staying frozen. In adulthood, taking active steps to change, and thereby taking on the perceived risks involved in behaving differently, can stir up deep-seated fears of failure and or being singled out for mistreatment or abandonment. Behavioral and attitudinal changes may make TRD patients feel "visible," which can bring up profound fears that they will be noticed and vulnerable to attack or being abandoned. Making changes in adulthood runs counter to these childlike but nonetheless deeply engrained ways of dealing with stress and emotion.

Clinicians need to understand how profoundly deep such conditioned beliefs and behaviors are, and why change can sometimes occur only at what seems like a snail's pace. Yet clinicians should not condone or grow "numb" and seemingly uncaring when a patient engages in poor self-care or high-risk behaviors. If clinicians show no concern or seem to be indifferent to unsafe behaviors, they may be enacting the role of the unprotective bystander who did little or nothing to protect the child from maltreatment (see Chapter 5).

Repeated exposure to betrayal, lack of protection, and ongoing trauma may contribute to patients consciously or unconsciously sabotaging their progress in treatment. They may fear facing talking and thinking about the trauma that was originally so overwhelming as a child. They may fear losing the therapist if they get better. They may also fear "having" to socialize or return to work if they get better. Unless these and many other sources of ambivalence are routinely discussed repeatedly throughout treatment, treatment can stall.

Therapists should provide encouragement to patients to keep working on these issues despite fear, and to make ambivalence about change a universal experience rather than something shameful to hide. They should attempt to build a sense that these difficulties are understandable given a trauma history to further reduce shame, and empathize with the difficulty of making changes in long-term patterns while providing a vision of the road ahead and stabilization as an achievable reality using tools such as those provided in the program. One way we put this in the study:

> Human beings are often afraid of change—this is part of being human. Many people . . . will therefore sometimes feel a fear of getting better, or a fear of change. This is normal. Whenever this occurs, please bring it up with your therapist. You don't need to be ashamed of those feelings. We will help you work through those feelings, as can your therapist. Take good care of yourself this week. We'll get there, working together!

IMPROVING MANAGEMENT OF TRAUMATIC INTRUSIONS

Chronic developmental trauma has serious long-term effects on the stress response and brain. This program explains some of the basic ways in which trauma impacts the brain, emotions, and coping. This information can increase participants' self-understanding, enhance self-compassion, and motivate them to frequently practice healthy skills to recover from the lingering impact of trauma.

We explain fear conditioning and traumatic intrusions in simple terms:

As a result of trauma, your brain is sensitized to pick up on danger. Having a brain that is telling you that you're in danger when you are actually safe can be very draining. So we'll begin working on helping you determine when you're really in danger versus when you're not currently in danger. Keep in mind that the old conditioned brain pathways can be changed. You can help your brain heal and develop new, calmer pathways with practice—lots and lots of practice. Gradually, some of those old fear pathways can get pruned away.

The materials explain that it is common to react very strongly to current situations with heightened emotionality due to trauma conditioning. Specifically, the traumatized person may react much more strongly than would most people in a given situation due to the person sensing threat or betrayal, even when the current situation is not actually as threatening as it is being perceived. These trauma-based emotional intrusions can make the person believe that emotions are dangerous and unmanageable. Some individuals even feel as if they are "crazy" and out of control due to how intensely and unpredictably their emotions can surge without them understanding why they are having the emotion or how to manage it. (Note: These baffling emotions can also be related to other phenomena, such as shifting to DSS.)

During these "emotional flashbacks" or "90/10 reactions" (Lewis et al., 2004), a significant amount of the emotion they are feeling (i.e., possibly 90%, as a rough estimate) does not relate to the current situation; instead, most of the emotion represents trauma-related feelings triggered by a reminder of past trauma. Only a small portion of the person's current emotional reaction (i.e., possibly 10%, as a rough estimate) relates to what the individual is currently experiencing.

To help participants feel less controlled by traumatic intrusions and related emotions, we teach methods for distinguishing past from present, the use of containment imagery, and ways to recognize and manage 90/10 reactions. As individuals begin to recognize that they are sometimes highly emotional due to triggers of past mistreatment, they typically feel less out of control and more self-compassion. Understanding their reactions, they are better prepared to soothe themselves and use recovery-focused techniques when triggered rather than engaging in potentially unsafe behavior or dissociation.

DISSOCIATION VERSUS GROUNDING

Children who are repeatedly exposed to maltreatment and who do not have secure attachment with caregivers who can provide protection and soothing may develop dissociative coping (see Chapter 1). In the absence of caregivers to help them regulate the intense states of emotional and physiological arousal that

maltreatment creates, disconnecting from their bodies and emotions via dissociation can be an essential method of survival. Individuals with TRDs may develop
discrete behavioral states as a result of childhood maltreatment; these self-states
are structured around emotion and traumatic experiences (see Putnam, 1997,
2016; Frewen & Lanius, 2015). Unprotected and maltreated by powerful adults
who are often attachment figures, abused children must manage overwhelmingly
painful experiences and resultant intrusive flooding and hyperarousal without
soothing from caregivers.

People who are repeatedly traumatized may learn to tune out their bodies,
emotions, and the world around them as a means of not feeling or fully
acknowledging the betrayal, helplessness, terror, and physical pain that they experienced. "Tuning out," or dissociating, during trauma, may have been one of the
only ways they could cope with childhood trauma. As Frank Putnam has noted,
"Dissociation is the escape when there is no escape."

Continuing to repeatedly dissociate in adulthood, when the person has more
power and is much safer, actually puts them at risk, however: By being out of
touch with their body and the world in adulthood, they are increasing the risk
of being victimized in the present. They may tune out emotions that could give
them warning that someone or some place is unsafe, and be so out of touch with
current danger that they may not see what is happening around them. A crucial
part of healing is shifting from habitually dissociating, so that they are frequently
out of touch with the here and now, to learning and using grounding skills to get
oriented to and anchored in the present (Boon et al., 2009).

Because getting grounded can be frightening to some trauma survivors with
significant dissociation, it is helpful to raise awareness of the benefits of being
grounded. These include that being grounded can enable a person to learn to feel
solid and connected to their body so that they literally may walk more steadily
and have better balance, and gradually experience more confidence and power.
Being grounded could help them have fewer falls or accidents while driving (if
they dissociate while driving). Being more aware of themselves and the world
around them can help individuals "hold their ground" in relationships and at
work. When grounded, they might notice things around them in nature or pick
up on subtleties in social situations such as humor, kindness, or even indications
that someone is potentially dangerous. One of the authors had a client who, after
attending therapy for several years during which the office furniture remained the
same, suddenly remarked one day, "I thought these chairs were blue, but they are
actually green!" This awareness of her environment coincided with her coming
more alive in her daily life as she reduced her overreliance on dissociation. Note,
however, that for some people, "tuning in" to their bodies may initially make
them dissociate more. This means that dissociation has become a habitual way of
"leaving" their body. Therapists should encourage such participants to proactively
practice grounding techniques many times throughout each day and to use the
program's grounding check-sheet to help notice when they have dissociated.

IMPROVING AWARENESS AND ACCEPTANCE OF DSS

Rather than gradually developing a relatively stable sense of self, individuals with complex DD may develop discrete behavioral states as a result of childhood mal-treatment and attachment disruptions (see Chapter 1). These discrete behavioral states, which we refer to as DSS, may encapsulate conflicting aspects of affect, identity, autobiographical memory, behavior, and cognition, among other impor-tant domains (Putnam, 1997, 2016). In patients with partial or full amnesia be-tween DSS, the individual may suffer from dissociative identity disorder (DID). Because DSS are often structured around emotion, one way of conceptualizing them is as a form of emotion regulation (complex neurobiological, genetic, and socioemotional influences play pivotal roles in the development and mainte-nance of DSS, but these are beyond the scope of this book; see Putnam, 2016, and Frewen & Lanius, 2015).

Unprotected and maltreated by powerful adults who are often attachment fig-ures, abused children must manage overwhelmingly painful experiences and re-sultant intrusive flooding and hyperarousal, without soothing from caregivers. DSS develop as state-dependent compartmentalized aspects of self that enable the child to avoid continually remembering, thinking about, and feeling the full blow of betrayal. They can provide some level of avoidance of trauma-related emotions and hyperarousal, thereby allowing the child to have periods of relative discon-nection from trauma-based emotions and conflicted attachment to caregivers. Viewed through this lens, DID can be conceptualized as a complex trauma-based disorder of emotion and attachment regulation, although there are additional crit-ical aspects that are influential, including neurobiology, genetics, social supports, and sociocultural variables (Brand & Lanius, 2014).

Over time, these DSS can increasingly be experienced as "not me," leading the individual to have less awareness of these disowned aspects of themselves and, gradually, less knowledge about the emotions and autobiographical memories that these states embody. Among many complex dissociative patients, this can contribute to a sense of being confused about who one is and a sense of inner conflict or, in some cases, even an "inner war" among markedly different feelings, values, behaviors, goals, and sense of self and others. This lack of ac-ceptance and sense of being fragmented often contributes to phenomena such as hearing voices and urges to engage in nonsuicidal self-injury (NSSI) or even attempt suicide.

Experts in DD emphasize the importance of working directly with DSS to as-sist complex dissociative patients to develop awareness, acceptance (even if be-grudgingly), and cooperation among DSS (International Society for the Study of Dissociation, 2011; Myrick et al., 2015). Research demonstrates that as individuals with DD participate in DD treatment, their sense of being fragmented and hearing voices decreases, which suggests that treatment may be associated with a gradual healing of compartmentalization and disowning of DSS (see Chapter 4).

STABILIZING SAFETY

The Finding Solid Ground program attempts to assist TRD patients in thoughtfully considering what beliefs, needs, and emotions put them at risk for unsafe and risky behavior, including NSSI and suicide attempts. The program's materials urge patients to discuss these crucial issues with their therapists. We strive to guide patients to consider whether they would be willing to make changes in how they view and treat themselves. Therapists can guide an exploration of what the individual believes "healing" would mean for them. Therapists' involvement is crucial in helping nudge TRD patients to test out any potentially unfounded assumptions about themselves and the process of healing.

It is important to be aware that TRD patients often begin to show healthy changes in establishing self-care, only to repeatedly relapse into NSSI or other risky behaviors. These repeated regressions to firmly entrenched, unhealthy ways of coping can be tremendously frustrating to patients and therapists alike, making both question if treatment is helpful. Therapists need to repeatedly strive to feel and show empathy about how panic-stricken the patient may be as they make what can seem like infinitesimally small steps toward change, as well as continually encourage them to keep making small steps, without shaming the person for inevitable missteps.

We convey an attitude of patience and self-compassion about the slow pace of change in the Finding Solid Ground materials. We advise participants to persevere in the face of setbacks in safety and symptoms, and to be undaunted by them because they are common. Here is one example of the Network study's information about slow change and relapses:

Safety is the foundation of healing. It is hard work to learn skills that will help you heal, so be patient with yourself as you learn and practice. Unlearning old habits and putting new skills into place takes time. Improvement over time happens by making steady progress each day. Most people will notice that sometimes they have more symptoms or more struggles with safety, even after days of things being easier. This may feel like a setback. However, our clients have taught us that that is just what happens to most people: ups and downs over time. You want to look for improvement gradually over months, not day to day. So don't get mad at yourself and don't give up. Just keep practicing no matter what happens and be patient.

The Finding Solid Ground program strives to reduce shame and self-attack about the difficulties many TRD patients have with establishing and maintaining safety. It is crucial for clinicians to manage their own frustration and assist their patients to manage their frustration and shame about setbacks. Clinicians are encouraged to seek peer consultation as needed, and to talk—repeatedly—with clients about these patterns, or related ones such as "forgetting" to practice healthy techniques such as the ones taught in the program.

IMPROVING EMOTIONAL TOLERANCE AND EFFECTIVE USE OF EMOTIONS

The program provides education about why people have feelings, how to identify them, and a variety of healthy ways to tolerate and deal with feelings. TRD patients are often terrified of emotions and strive to avoid them. This avoidance and difficulty managing feelings is one of the core difficulties underlying most trauma-related disorders (see Chapter 1). In our clinical practices, TRD patients often react with panic when we suggest that they need to learn how to tolerate emotions. Yet emotional overwhelm is often what triggers unsafe behaviors, including addictive behavior, cutting, and suicide attempts. This suggests that emotion regulation difficulties are likely to fuel much of these individuals' NSSI and other unsafe behavior. If these individuals can develop healthier ways of tolerating emotions, they would likely be able to decrease their reliance on unsafe behaviors and dissociation to manage emotions.

Yet learning to "sit with" emotions and tolerate them safely is very challenging. We tailored the program to gradually and repeatedly address healthy emotion regulation, including repeatedly stating the reasons why it is important to learn to healthfully deal with feelings. We introduce the concept of the "window of tolerance" to explain the link with being overwhelmed by emotions (Ogden et al., 2006b; Siegel, 1999).

Many traumatized people have trouble with too much or too little feeling. We illustrate the window of tolerance in a diagram in Chapter 6 (see p. 120). The narrow band of feelings in the middle of the diagram signifies the amount of feeling or body sensation that a person can comfortably experience. For trauma survivors, this range of tolerance for emotion tends to be very narrow. If a feeling gets too strong, many TRD patients begin to have difficulty. A little bit of feeling may be somewhat manageable, but if it becomes strong, these individuals may want to harm themselves, or eat too much or sleep too much, or do other unhealthy, risky, or unsafe behaviors. For example, if a feeling of frustration becomes too strong, they may begin to feel anger or even rage, and that may make them feel so bad about themselves, and so anxious, that they may have urges to be self-destructive or take their anger out on someone or something.

Similarly, many trauma survivors are uncomfortable with feeling OK or safe, or having happy feelings. Feeling nothing might seem acceptable and safer. If they begin to feel some happiness, they may feel guilty and ashamed. They may think they do not have a right to feel happy, or any of the positive feelings. If they begin to have those "good" feelings, some people have urges to harm themselves. People with DSS may hear voices telling them that they should harm themselves to "pay for" having felt better or for other perceived failures. In addition to feeling too much, for some people, feeling too little is challenging. For some TRD patients, it is frightening to feel numb because they feel dead. They may engage in cutting to the point where they feel pain and/or see blood because it proves to them that they are alive.

Because having feelings can be so challenging, we recommend that participants engage in grounding before doing program-related work, and the therapist should teach that developing affect regulation skills can increase the person's control over behavior, particularly potentially unsafe behavior. Addressing this in the Network study videos, we noted that:

Feeling too much or too little can lead people to make decisions with unsafe consequences. Feeling flooded with emotion can lead people to turn to drinking too much alcohol or using drugs to help numb out overwhelming emotions. Some people turn to overeating or undereating to get the same effect. Others cut or pick or burn their skin or use other forms of self-destructive behavior to try to manage the strength and chaos of their feelings. Being overwhelmed with feelings can lead people to choose to make suicide attempts or hurt other people or other unsafe behaviors. It is therefore absolutely essential to learn skills to help you feel "in the middle" range of emotion, and therefore be more in control of your behavior.

We provide a nonshaming, biological explanation about why a traumatized individual's emotions may be so intense and overwhelming. Our intent is to detoxify shame and fear about feelings and increase motivation to practice emotion regulation strategies. Specifically, we state:

When children are very frightened and upset, fear networks are created in the brain. These fear networks make you more likely to be easily triggered and afraid now. So, being exposed to danger back then created a stress-reactive brain now. You likely react strongly to potential danger or upsetting situations now. And if you stay in fearful, painful, upsetting situations or relationships now, fear networks can stay strong. If you want those old fear-based networks to gradually lose their power, you need to work to get them pruned away, so that healthier new patterns and networks form in your brain. To help your brain heal, you have to stop being around danger, harm, and violence. Being seriously frightened or stressed in childhood or adulthood is not good for your brain or body. In order for your brain to heal from the past, you must get safe and learn to cope using healthy coping skills. It is crucial that you develop a greater ability to deal with feelings safely, without dissociating and without feeling overwhelmed. As you gradually learn how to take care of yourself better, it will help your brain and body heal.

Traumatized individuals are often phobically avoidant of emotions for a variety of reasons, including shame about having feelings and their difficulty tolerating emotions. Another approach we provide to detoxify the shame and avoidance of feelings is this:

People who have been traumatized often have feelings *about* having feelings. Specifically, they tend to be embarrassed or ashamed or afraid of their emotions. We've talked about that already in this program. We hope that you've been able to soften your judgments about having feelings, and that you are beginning to recognize how important feelings are to being healthy and living a good life.

We also offer compassion about how daunting it is to deal with emotions, in addition to providing education about emotions. It is important to emphasize that by dealing with emotions, patients can gradually learn to accept all of who they are, which helps to decrease the tendency to compartmentalize emotions and, for some, to disown them via fragmented self-states. We link learning to deal with emotions as a method of helping heal their traumatized brain:

> You can unlearn the fear of feelings. You can create new pathways in your brain that are healthy and that will help you feel whole and connected to yourself and, gradually, to others. If you work hard to face your fear of feelings, and gradually the feelings themselves—and then gradually also to face the compartmentalized parts of yourself—you can heal your brain. You can reclaim all of who you are, including your feelings. You can do this step by step, at a pace that you can manage. You can heal your brain and learn to accept all of who you are.

IN SUMMARY, THERE IS HOPE

Research results from TOP DD and other studies, our work with patients, and feedback from patients and therapists around the world illustrate that people have a tremendous capacity for resilience and healing, even after devastating trauma and attachment disruptions. Although tremendous suffering and symptoms can endure for decades after trauma, a carefully staged trauma treatment approach can enable patients to gradually develop self-understanding and self-compassion, awareness and ability to accept their emotions, skill in managing their symptoms, and healthier coping and relationships. With treatment and education, traumatized individuals can reclaim all of who they are, increase their capacity to feel peaceful and safe, and create a life they feel good about. By working, learning, and healing together, patients, therapists, and researchers can assist patients in *finding solid, safe ground.*

Assessment Measures: PITQ-t and PITQ-p

PROGRESS IN TREATMENT QUESTIONNAIRE — THERAPIST (PITQ-T)

Circle the number to show what percentage of the time your client has demonstrated the following behaviors, cognitions or experiences in the **last 6 months**.

1. Engages in self-injurious behavior (e.g., cutting, burning) or suicide attempts.
   0%   10   20   30   40   50   60   70   80   90   100%
   (never)   (always)

2. Engages in potentially self-damaging acts such as abusing substances, purging, shoplifting, driving unsafely.
   0%   10   20   30   40   50   60   70   80   90   100%
   (never)   (always)

3. Identity is strongly tied to being a victim of abuse.
   0%   10   20   30   40   50   60   70   80   90   100%
   (never)   (always)

4. Understands that they have a dissociative disorder (DD) and generally acknowledges that this diagnosis is accurate.
   0%   10   20   30   40   50   60   70   80   90   100%
   (never)   (always)

5. Able to maintain a fairly strong treatment alliance, and when there are disruptions to the alliance, able to work productively to repair it.
   0%   10   20   30   40   50   60   70   80   90   100%
   (never)   (always)

6. Knows and uses self-soothing strategies (e.g., any type of calming strategy that is not used explicitly to contain PTSD symptoms or prevent dissociation) when they are needed.

0%   10   20   30   40   50   60   70   80   90   100%
(never)   (always)

7. Knows and uses containment strategies (e.g., hypnotic or imagery techniques used to contain intrusive PTSD symptoms) when they are needed.

0%   10   20   30   40   50   60   70   80   90   100%
(never)   (always)

8. Knows and uses grounding techniques to prevent self from going numb, zoning out, having amnestic lapses when they are needed (e.g., techniques such as muscle contractions, movement, or touching an object to avoid dissociating).

0%   10   20   30   40   50   60   70   80   90   100%
(never)   (always)

9. Keeps oriented in the present (i.e., does NOT get confused about past and present).

0%   10   20   30   40   50   60   70   80   90   100%
(never)   (always)

10. Shows good awareness of his/her emotions and feels his/her body sensations.

0%   10   20   30   40   50   60   70   80   90   100%
(never)   (always)

11. Shows good affect tolerance (can feel emotions without getting overwhelmed).

0%   10   20   30   40   50   60   70   80   90   100%
(never)   (always)

12. Shows good impulse control (e.g., can feel angry or depressed without acting it out).

0%   10   20   30   40   50   60   70   80   90   100%
(never)   (always)

13. Is aware that the trauma was not his/her fault.

0%   10   20   30   40   50   60   70   80   90   100%
(never)   (always)

14. Manages daily functioning well (e.g., managing hygiene, maintaining a home, paying bills).

0%   10   20   30   40   50   60   70   80   90   100%
(never)   (always)

15. Has continuous awareness of behaviors; that is, the patient does not report time loss or other signs of amnesia (e.g., no behaviors done out of their awareness, no possessions for which they can't recall how they obtained them).

0%   10   20   30   40   50   60   70   80   90   100%
(never)   (always)

16. Able to deal with stressful situations without dissociating.

0%   10   20   30   40   50   60   70   80   90   100%
(never)   (always)

17. Able to maintain healthy personal and professional relationships with other people.

0%   10   20   30   40   50   60   70   80   90   100%
(never)   (always)

18. Able to experience grief stemming from trauma-related losses.

0%   10   20   30   40   50   60   70   80   90   100%
(never)   (always)

19. Has found ways to make life feel meaningful and rewarding.

0%   10   20   30   40   50   60   70   80   90   100%
(never)   (always)

20. Has a generally positive view of him/herself.

0%   10   20   30   40   50   60   70   80   90   100%
(never)   (always)

21. Has a generally positive view of other people.

0%   10   20   30   40   50   60   70   80   90   100%
(never)   (always)

22. Able to experience sexual intimacy without difficulties such as intense shame, flashbacks, or dissociation and with some pleasure.

0%   10   20   30   40   50   60   70   80   90   100%
(never)   (always)

23. Able to tolerate doing trauma-focused abreactive work (i.e., able to express intense affect about past trauma, talk in detail about traumatic events, as well as explore the meaning, impact, and conflicts related to trauma).

0%   10   20   30   40   50   60   70   80   90   100%
(never)   (always)

Parts-related questions: The following questions are for persons who have dissociative self-states/"parts." If these items do not apply to your patient, please circle "not applicable." Otherwise, please circle the percentage of time each statement applies to your patient.

24. Has awareness that all dissociative self-states are part of himself/herself and share one body (i.e., does not believe one alter can "kill" another and survive the suicide).
0%   10   20   30   40   50   60   70   80   90   100%
(never or not applicable)   (always)

25. Knows parts and understands their functions (i.e., what purposes they serve, such as helping manage feelings related to trauma).
0%   10   20   30   40   50   60   70   80   90   100%
(never or not applicable)   (always)

26. Shows good internal communication and cooperation among parts.
0%   10   20   30   40   50   60   70   80   90   100%
(never or not applicable)   (always)

27. Has reliable co-consciousness with all parts.
0%   10   20   30   40   50   60   70   80   90   100%
(never or not applicable)   (always)

28. Has integrated at least two parts.
0%   10   20   30   40   50   60   70   80   90   100%
(never or not applicable)   (always)

29. Has integrated all parts and no longer experiences amnesia, voices, passive influence, or other signs of identity fragmentation.
0%   10   20   30   40   50   60   70   80   90   100%
(never or not applicable)   (always)

PITQ-t scoring: To score the PITQ-t, treat the percentages endorsed as points (e.g., 0% = 0 points, 100% = 100 points). *NOTE*: Items 1, 2, and 3 are reverse-scored (i.e., 0 = 100 points, 10 = 90, 20 = 80, 30 = 70, 40 = 60, 50 = 50, 60 = 40, 70 = 30, 80 = 20, 90 = 10, 100 = 0 points).

The procedure for calculating a PITQ-t score is different for patients with and without dissociative self-states. For patients without dissociative self-states, add the points corresponding to the percentages endorsed for items 1 through 23 and divide by 23 (i.e., maximum score = 100, minimum score = 0). For patients with dissociative self-states, add the points corresponding to the percentages endorsed for items 1 through 29 and then divide the total by 29 (i.e., maximum score = 100, minimum score = 0).

The use of this measure is free of charge. Please note, however, that norms for the PITQ-t have not yet been established. If you use the PITQ-t in research, please share your feedback and findings with BBrand@towson.edu and Hugo.Schielke@gmail.com.

PROGRESS IN TREATMENT QUESTIONNAIRE—PATIENT VERSION (PITQ-P)

Hugo Schielke, PhD, and Bethany Brand, PhD

Please circle the number that reflects what percentage of time each of the following statements has been true of you in the **last week**.

1. I have been diagnosed with a dissociative disorder and agree that this diagnosis is correct.

   0%   10   20   30   40   50   60   70   80   90   100%
   (never true)   (always true)

2. I collaborate well with my therapist, and when there are problems between us, I talk to my therapist about them so that we can resolve them together.

   0%   10   20   30   40   50   60   70   80   90   100%
   (never true)   (always true)

3. I am compassionate and fair with myself; that is, I respond to myself with as much empathy as I would show someone else in the same situation.

   0%   10   20   30   40   50   60   70   80   90   100%
   (never true)   (always true)

4. I'm aware of the thoughts, feelings, and body sensations that indicate I'm getting anxious or overwhelmed.

   0%   10   20   30   40   50   60   70   80   90   100%
   (never true)   (always true)

5. I use relaxation techniques (such as relaxation exercises, safe place imagery, music) to safely help myself relax and feel better when I begin to get anxious or overwhelmed.

   0%   10   20   30   40   50   60   70   80   90   100%
   (never true)   (always true)

6. I manage intrusive memories and flashbacks using containment strategies (imagery techniques used to contain and manage PTSD symptoms).

   0%   10   20   30   40   50   60   70   80   90   100%
   (never true)   (always true)

7. I use grounding techniques when I need to prevent myself from going numb, zoning out, or losing time. (Examples: focus on my surroundings; pay attention to my five senses; tense and relax my muscles.)

   0%   10   20   30   40   50   60   70   80   90   100%
   (never true)   (always true)

8. If I begin to confuse the past with the present, I notice this and work to see differences between how things are now versus how they were when I was being traumatized.
0%   10   20   30   40   50   60   70   80   90   100%
(never true)   (always true)

9. I am aware of my emotions and body sensations.
0%   10   20   30   40   50   60   70   80   90   100%
(never true)   (always true)

10. I am able to feel my emotions without getting overwhelmed.
0%   10   20   30   40   50   60   70   80   90   100%
(never true)   (always true)

11. I am aware of, able to think about, and can control my impulses. (Example: I can feel angry or depressed without doing something unhealthy.)
0%   10   20   30   40   50   60   70   80   90   100%
(never true)   (always true)

12. I reach out to treatment providers if I have difficulty controlling severe unhealthy impulses despite using recovery-focused coping skills (e.g., grounding, past vs. present, containment).
0%   10   20   30   40   50   60   70   80   90   100%
(never true)   (always true)

13. I know that the traumas that I experienced were not my fault.
0%   10   20   30   40   50   60   70   80   90   100%
(never true)   (always true)

14. I manage everyday life well (examples: I regularly eat, bathe, pay bills on time).
0%   10   20   30   40   50   60   70   80   90   100%
(never true)   (always true)

15. I am able to account for all that I do; that is, I don't "lose time" or find evidence of having done something I do not remember.
0%   10   20   30   40   50   60   70   80   90   100%
(never true)   (always true)

16. I am able to deal with stressful situations without dissociating.
0%   10   20   30   40   50   60   70   80   90   100%
(never true)   (always true)

17. I am able to maintain healthy personal and professional relationships.

0%   10   20   30   40   50   60   70   80   90   100%

(never true)   (always true)

18. I value my physical well-being, and do not do things that hurt my body (examples: I don't cut or burn my body or attempt suicide).

0%   10   20   30   40   50   60   70   80   90   100%

(never true)   (always true)

19. I value my health and do not do things that put me at risk (examples: I do not abuse drugs, throw up after eating, drive unsafely, have unsafe sex).

0%   10   20   30   40   50   60   70   80   90   100%

(never true)   (always true)

20. I am able to experience sadness and grieve the losses related to trauma.

0%   10   20   30   40   50   60   70   80   90   100%

(never true)   (always true)

21. Life feels meaningful and rewarding.

0%   10   20   30   40   50   60   70   80   90   100%

(never true)   (always true)

22. I have a generally positive view of myself.

0%   10   20   30   40   50   60   70   80   90   100%

(never true)   (always true)

23. I have a generally positive view of other people.

0%   10   20   30   40   50   60   70   80   90   100%

(never true)   (always true)

24. My sense of myself includes many important things beyond having been traumatized.

0%   10   20   30   40   50   60   70   80   90   100%

(never true)   (always true)

25. I am able to experience sexual intimacy without intense shame, flashbacks, or dissociation, and with some pleasure.

0%   10   20   30   40   50   60   70   80   90   100%

(never true)   (always true)

26. I can explore the meaning and impact related to the traumas
I experienced; I can feel and express the emotions related to these
traumas.

0%   10   20   30   40   50   60   70   80   90   100%
(never true)   (always true)

The following questions are for persons who have dissociated parts/self-states. If these items do not apply to you, please circle "not applicable." Otherwise, please circle the percentage of time the statements apply to you.

27. All parts of myself know that we are part of the same person and that
we share one body.

0%   10   20   30   40   50   60   70   80   90   100%
(not applicable/never true)   (always true)

28. All parts of myself are oriented to the present (know what day, month,
and year it is).

0%   10   20   30   40   50   60   70   80   90   100%
(not applicable/never true)   (always true)

29. I pay attention to and am curious about what different parts of myself
are feeling.

0%   10   20   30   40   50   60   70   80   90   100%
(not applicable/never true)   (always true)

30. I'm aware of which parts of myself are contributing to my actions.

0%   10   20   30   40   50   60   70   80   90   100%
(not applicable/never true)   (always true)

31. All parts of myself know and can independently use recovery-focused
coping skills (e.g., grounding, past vs. present, containment).

0%   10   20   30   40   50   60   70   80   90   100%
(not applicable/never true)   (always true)

32. All parts of myself communicate and cooperate well.

0%   10   20   30   40   50   60   70   80   90   100%
(not applicable/never true)   (always true)

PITQ-p scoring: To score the PITQ-p, treat the percentages endorsed as points (e.g., 0% = 0 points, 100% = 100 points). The procedure for calculating a PITQ-p score is different for patients with and without dissociative self-states. For patients without dissociative self-states: Add the points corresponding to the percentages endorsed for items 1 through 26 and divide by 26 (i.e., maximum score = 100, minimum score = 0). For patients with dissociative self-states: Add the points corresponding to the percentages endorsed for items 1 through 32 and then divide the total by 32 (i.e., maximum score = 100, minimum score = 0).

The use of this measure is free of charge. Please note, however, that norms for the PITQ-p have not yet been established. If you use the PITQ-p in research, please share your feedback and findings with Hugo.Schielke@gmail.com and BBrand@towson.edu.

For group settings: Since grounding is the foundational coping skill for people who struggle with trauma-related reactions, we recommend practicing grounding at the beginning of each group. We also recommend leading the group through grounding before going through the grounding handout. One potential script for this follows.

Grounding is a recovery-focused skill that offers powerful help toward managing and reducing the symptoms related to trauma, including feeling "too much" or "too little."

There are two core grounding skills: *orienting yourself to the present* and *anchoring yourself in the present.* Let's try them now.

GROUNDING, STEP 1: ORIENTING YOURSELF TO THE PRESENT

Orienting yourself to the present involves using your mind to help yourself connect to the here and now. Think to yourself: "What year, month, day, and time is it?" "How old am I?" "Where am I?" and "What's the situation?" Orienting yourself is especially good at helping you connect with the "now" part of the here and now.

GROUNDING, STEP 2: ANCHORING YOURSELF IN THE PRESENT

Once you've oriented yourself to the present, use your five senses to help yourself actively notice and connect to your surroundings in the here and now. This is referred to as *anchoring yourself in the present,* which is especially good at helping you further connect to the "here" part of the here and now.

Try doing this now: Look around, describing to yourself what you see. For example: What are the colors of the objects you see? What materials are the objects you see made of? How close or far away are objects from one another? Try describing what you see to yourself in enough detail that if you wrote them down, someone else could imagine them.

What are you hearing? Describe the mixture of different sounds in the environment in detail. Are they high-pitched? Low-pitched? Quiet? Loud? Try describing the sounds to yourself in a way that if you wrote them down, someone else could imagine them.

What smells can you notice? Describe these in detail. (Are they subtle? Strong? Sweet? Spicy?)

What tastes can you notice? If you are drinking or eating something as you do this, notice and describe the colors, flavors, textures, and temperatures of your food or drink to yourself. If your food or drink makes a sound, like crunching (when chewing food) or fizzing (when drinking a soda), describe that to yourself, too.

How about the surfaces around you—what do they feel like? Describe their textures to yourself: Are they rough or smooth? Are they cool or warm to the touch? Try intentionally choosing different kinds of surfaces to touch and comparing how they feel while describing them to yourself.

Now take a moment to notice how you feel now compared to how you felt before you started grounding yourself. You may notice feeling at least a little more connected to (grounded in) the present. You may also notice feeling a little calmer, more "solid," less confused or scared, and more able to notice and think about what's happening.

Different senses work differently well for anchoring at different times. For example, many people find that the sense of touch and noticing and describing different textures and temperatures helps them get grounded fastest when they most need it. Others like to always start with a deep breath in through their nose (smelling the air) to make sure they're breathing while grounding. (Forgetting to breathe is common among people with trauma histories, and can lead your brain to think that something bad is happening even if it isn't.) To find out what works best for you, try experimenting with the order you describe your senses to yourself in different situations.

Like doing anything new, grounding can be difficult at first, so be sure to give yourself credit for each time you practice and to notice the improvements as they happen. And keep practicing—the more often you take the time to practice orienting to and anchoring in the present, the easier it will get and the more it will help. Also, practicing when you are not overwhelmed will make it much easier to help yourself ground faster when you really need it!

Resources, Training, and Suggested Readings

TRAINING RESOURCES FOR GENERAL TRAUMA-RELATED DISORDERS

- Teachtrauma.com: website with facts about trauma including types of trauma, dissociation, traumatic memory, debates in the trauma field; slideshows for educators; evaluations of textbooks' coverage of trauma; classroom activities to teach about trauma; and additional resources
- International Society for Traumatic Stress Studies: istss.org
- International Society for the Study of Dissociation and Trauma: www. ISST-D.org
- American Psychological Association Trauma Division (Division 56): apatraumadivision.org/
- National Child Traumatic Stress Network: www.NCTSN.org
- European Society for Trauma & Dissociation: www.estd.org
- Blue Knot Foundation in Australia: www.blueknot.org.au

TRAINING RESOURCES FOR DISSOCIATIVE DISORDERS

- International Society for the Study of Dissociation and Trauma: www.ISST-D.org
- European Society for Trauma & Dissociation: www.estd.org
- Blue Knot Foundation in Australia: www.blueknot.org.au
- Teachtrauma.com: website with facts about trauma including dissociation, dissociative disorders, and traumatic memories; reviews about psychology textbooks, including their coverage of dissociation and dissociative disorders

RESOURCES FOR SURVIVORS OF TRAUMA

- Sidran Institute: traumatic stress education and advocacy: www.sidran.org
- Blue Knot Foundation in Australia: www.blueknot.org.au
- Male Survivors: overcoming sexual victimization of boys and men: www.malesurvivor.org
- 1in6: site for men who have been sexually abused or assaulted: https://1in6.org
- Adult Survivors of Child Abuse: www.ascasupport.org
- David Baldwin's Trauma Information Pages: www.trauma-pages.com/support.php
- Survivors Network of Those Abused by Priests: www.snapnetwork.org
- National Sexual Assault Hotline: https://hotline.rainn.org/online
- PTSD Coach Online: https://www.ptsd.va.gov/apps/ptsdcoachonline/default.htm

BOOKS AND GUIDELINES ABOUT COMPLEX TRAUMA-RELATED DISORDERS WITH AN EMPHASIS ON DISSOCIATION

Allen, J. G. (2005). *Coping with trauma: Hope through understanding* (2nd ed.). American Psychiatric Publishing, Inc.

Allen, J. G. (2013). *Restoring mentalizing in attachment relationships: Treating trauma with plain old therapy* (1st ed.). American Psychiatric Publishing, Inc.

Boon, S., & Draijer, N. (1993). *Multiple personality disorder in the Netherlands: A study on reliability and validity of the diagnosis.* Swets & Zeitlinger Publishers.

Boon, S., Steele, K., & van der Hart, O. (2011). *Coping with trauma-related dissociation: Skills training for patients and therapists.* W. W. Norton & Company.

Brenner, I. (2001). *Dissociation of trauma: Theory, phenomenology, and technique.* International Universities Press, Inc.

Briere, J. (2004). *Psychological assessment of adult posttraumatic states: Phenomenology, diagnosis, and measurement* (2nd ed.). American Psychological Association.

Briere, J. N., & Scott, C. (2015). *Principles of trauma therapy: A guide to symptoms, evaluation, and treatment* (2nd ed., DSM-5 update). Sage Publications, Inc.

Brown, D. P., & Elliott, D. S. (2016). *Attachment disturbances in adults: Treatment for comprehensive repair.* W. W. Norton & Co.

Brown, L. S. (2008). *Cultural competence in trauma therapy: Beyond the flashback.* American Psychological Association.

Chefetz, R. A. (2015). *Intensive psychotherapy for persistent dissociative processes: The fear of feeling real.* W. W. Norton & Co.

Chu, J. A. (2011). *Rebuilding shattered lives: Treating complex PTSD and dissociative disorders* (2nd ed.). John Wiley & Sons Inc.

Cloitre, M., Courtois, C. A., Charuvastra, A., Carapezza, R., Stolbach, B. C., & Green, B. L. (2011). Treatment of complex PTSD: Results of the ISTSS expert clinician survey on best practices. *Journal of Traumatic Stress, 24*(6), 615–627.

Cloitre, M., Courtois, C. A., Ford, J. D., Green, B. L., Alexander, P., Briere, J., Herman, J. L., Lanius, R., Stolbach, B. C., Spinazzola, J., Van der Kolk, B. A., & Van der Hart, O. (2012a). The ISTSS Expert Consensus Treatment Guidelines for Complex PTSD in Adults. https://istss.org/ISTSS_Main/media/Documents/ComplexPTSD.pdf

Cook, J. M., & Newman, E. (2017). Training in trauma: New Haven Consensus Conference conclusions on core competencies. In S. N. Gold (Ed.), *APA handbook of trauma psychology: Foundations in knowledge* (Vol. 1, pp. 145–157). American Psychological Association.

Courtois, C. A. (2010). *Healing the incest wound: Adult survivors in therapy* (rev. ed.). W. W. Norton.

Courtois, C. A., & Ford, J. D. (Eds.). (2009). *Treating complex traumatic stress disorders: An evidence-based guide.* Guilford Press.

Courtois, C. A., & Ford, J. D. (2013). *Treatment of complex trauma: A sequenced, relationship-based approach.* Guilford Press.

Courtois, C. A., Ford, J. D., & Cloitre, M. (2009). Best practices in psychotherapy for adults. In C. A. Courtois & J. D. Ford (Eds.), *Treating complex traumatic stress disorders: An evidence-based guide* (pp. 82–103). Guilford Press.

Daitch, C. (2007). *Affect regulation toolbox: Practical and effective hypnotic interventions for the over-reactive client.* W. W. Norton & Co.

Dalenberg, C. J. (2000). *Countertransference and the treatment of trauma.* American Psychological Association.

Davies, J. M., & Frawley, M. G. (1994). *Treating the adult survivor of childhood sexual abuse: A psychoanalytic perspective.* Basic Books.

Dell, P. F., & O'Neil, J. A. (Eds.). (2009). *Dissociation and the dissociative disorders: DSM-5 and beyond.* Routledge.

Dorahy, M. J., Gold, S., & O'Neil, J. (Eds.). (2022). *Dissociation and the Dissociative Disorders: Past, Present, Future (2nd Ed).* New York: Routledge Press

Fisher, J. (2017). *Healing the fragmented selves of trauma survivors: Overcoming internal self-alienation.* Taylor & Francis.

Forner, C. C. (2017). *Dissociation, mindfulness, and creative meditations: Trauma-informed practices to facilitate growth.* Routledge/Taylor & Francis Group.

Frewen, P. A., & Lanius, R. (2015). *Healing the traumatized self: Consciousness, neuroscience, treatment.* W. W. Norton & Co.

Freyd, J. J. (1996). *Betrayal trauma: The logic of forgetting childhood abuse.* Harvard.

Freyd, J. J., & Birrell, P. J. (2013). *Blind to betrayal: Why we fool ourselves we aren't being fooled.* John Wiley & Sons Inc.

Gartner, R. B. (1999). *Betrayed as boys: Psychodynamic treatment of sexually abused men.* Guilford Press.

Gartner, R. B. (Ed.). (2018). *Healing sexually betrayed men and boys: Treatment for sexual abuse, assault, and trauma.* Routledge/Taylor & Francis Group.

Gold, S. N. (2000). *Not trauma alone: Therapy for child abuse survivors in family and social context.* Brunner-Routledge.

Gold, S. N. (2017a). *APA handbook of trauma psychology: Foundations in knowledge* (Vol. 1). American Psychological Association.

Gold, S. N. (2017b). *APA handbook of trauma psychology: Trauma practice* (Vol. 2). American Psychological Association.

Gold, S. N. (2020). *Contextual trauma therapy : overcoming traumatization and reaching full potential:* American Psychological Association.

Herman, J. L. (1997). *Trauma and recovery: The aftermath of violence—from domestic abuse to political terror.* Basic Books.

Howell, E. F. (2005). *The dissociative mind.* Analytic Press/Taylor & Francis Group.

Howell, E. F. (2011). *Understanding and treating dissociative identity disorder: A relational approach.* Routledge/Taylor & Francis Group.

Hunter, M. E. (2004). *Understanding dissociative disorders: A guide for family physicians and healthcare workers.* Crown House Publishing Limited.

International Society for the Study of Dissociation. (2011). Guidelines for treating dissociative identity disorder in adults, third revision. *Journal of Trauma and Dissociation, 12*(2), 115–187. doi:10.1080/15299732.2011.537247

Johnson, S. (2005). *Emotionally focused couple therapy with trauma survivors: Strengthening attachment bonds.* Guilford.

Kezelman, C., & Stavropoulos, P. (2019). *Practice guidelines for treatment of complex trauma and trauma-informed care and service delivery.* Blue Knot Foundation (ASCA). www.blueknot.org.au

Kinsler, P. J. (2018). *Complex psychological trauma: The centrality of the relationship.* Routledge.

Kluft, R. P. (Ed.). (1985). *Childhood antecedents of multiple personality.* American Psychiatric Press.

Kluft, R. P. (2013). *Shelter from the storm: Processing the traumatic memories of DID/ DDNOS patients with the fractionated abreaction technique (a vademecum for the treatment of DID/DDNOS).* CreateSpace Independent Publishing Platform.

Kluft, R. P., & Fine, C. G. (Eds.). (1993). *Clinical perspectives on multiple personality disorder.* American Psychiatric Press.

Lanius, U. F., Paulsen, S. L., & Corrigan, F. M. (2014). *Neurobiology and treatment of traumatic dissociation: Toward an embodied self.* Springer Publishing Company.

Levine, P. A. (1997). *Waking the tiger: Healing trauma: The innate capacity to transform overwhelming experiences.* North Atlantic Books.

Lewis, L., Kelly, K., & Allen, J. G. (2004). *Restoring hope and trust: An illustrated guide to mastering trauma.* Sidran Press.

Ogden, P., & Fisher, J. (2015). *Sensorimotor psychotherapy: Interventions for trauma and attachment.* W. W. Norton & Co.

Putnam, F. W. (1989). *Diagnosis and treatment of multiple personality disorder.* Guilford.

Putnam, F. W. (1997). *Dissociation in children and adolescents: A developmental perspective.* Guilford Press.

Putnam, F. W. (2016). *The way we are: How states of mind influence our identities, personality, and potential for change.* International Psychoanalytic Books.

Ross, C. A. (1997). *Dissociative identity disorder: Diagnosis, clinical features, and treatment of multiple personality.* Wiley.

Rothschild, B. (2000). *The body remembers: The psychophysiology of trauma and trauma treatment.* W. W. Norton & Company.

Rothschild, B. (2017). *The body remembers: Revolutionizing trauma treatment* (Vol. 2). W. W. Norton & Co.

Schore, A. N. (2003). *Affect dysregulation and disorders of the self.* W. W. Norton & Company.

Siegel, D. J. (1999). *The Developing Mind:* Guilford Press.

Siegel, D. J. (2007). *The mindful brain: Reflection and attunement in the cultivation of well-being.* W. W. Norton & Company.

Siegel, D. J. (2010). *Mindsight: The new science of personal transformation.* Bantam.

Siegel, D. J. (2015). *The developing mind: How relationships and the brain interact to shape who we are.* Guilford Press.

Silberg, J. L. (2013). *The child survivor: Healing developmental trauma and dissociation.* Routledge/Taylor & Francis Group.

Steele, K., Boon, S., & van der Hart, O. (2017). *Treating trauma-related dissociation: A practical, integrative approach*. W. W. Norton & Co.

Steinberg, M. (1994). *Interviewer's guide to the Structured Clinical Interview for DSM-IV Dissociative Disorders (SCID-D)* (rev. ed.). American Psychiatric Association.

Steinberg, M. (1995). *Handbook for the assessment of dissociation: A clinical guide*. American Psychiatric Press.

Steinberg, M. (2000). *The stranger in the mirror: Dissociation—the hidden epidemic* (Vol. 2). Cliff Street/Harper-Collins.

van der Hart, O., Nijenhuis, E. R. S., & Steele, K. (2006). *The haunted self* (Vol. 2). W. W. Norton & Co.

van der Kolk, B. A. (2014). *The body keeps the score: Brain, mind, and body in the healing of trauma*. Viking.

Walker, D., Courtois, C. A., & Aten, J. (Eds.). (2015). *Spirituality oriented psychotherapy for trauma*. American Psychological Association Press.

Watkins, J. G., & Watkins, H. H. (1997). *Ego states: Theory and therapy* (1st ed.). W. W. Norton.

REFERENCES

Addy, P. H., Garcia-Romeu, A., Metzger, M., & Wade, J. (2015). The subjective experience of acute, experimentally-induced *Salvia divinorum* inebriation. *Journal of Psychopharmacology, 29*(4), 426–435.

Ainsworth, M. D. S., Blehar, M. C., Waters, E., & Wall, S. (1978). *Patterns of attachment: A psychological study of the strange situation.* Lawrence Erlbaum.

Akiki, T. J., Averill, C. L., & Abdallah, C. G. (2017). A network-based neurobiological model of PTSD: Evidence from structural and functional neuroimaging studies. *Current Psychiatry Reports, 19*(11), 81.

Allen, J. G. (2005). *Coping with trauma: Hope through understanding* (2nd ed.). American Psychiatric Publishing, Inc.

American Psychiatric Association. (2000). *Diagnostic and statistical manual of mental disorders* (4th ed., text revision). American Psychiatric Press.

American Psychiatric Association. (2013). *Diagnostic and statistical manual of mental disorders* (5th ed.). American Psychiatric Press.

Anda, R. F., Porter, L. E., & Brown, D. W. (2020). Inside the adverse childhood experience score: Strengths, limitations, and misapplications. *American Journal of Preventive Medicine, 59*(2), 293–295. doi:10.1016/j.amepre.2020.01.009

Armour, C., Elklit, A., Lauterbach, D., & Elhai, J. D. (2014a). The DSM-5 dissociative-PTSD subtype: Can levels of depression, anxiety, hostility, and sleeping difficulties differentiate between dissociative-PTSD and PTSD in rape and sexual assault victims? *Journal of Anxiety Disorders, 28*(4), 418–426. doi:http://dx.doi.org/10.1016/j.janxdis.2013.12.008

Armour, C., Karstoft, K.-I., & Richardson, J. D. (2014b). The co-occurrence of PTSD and dissociation: Differentiating severe PTSD from dissociative-PTSD. *Social Psychiatry and Psychiatric Epidemiology, 49*(8), 1297–1306. doi:10.1007/s00127-014-0819-y

Bakermans-Kranenburg, M. J., & van Ijzendoorn, M. H. (2009). The first 10,000 adult attachment interviews: Distributions of adult attachment representations in clinical and non-clinical groups. *Attachment & Human Development, 11*(3), 223–263. doi:10.1080/14616730902814762

Barach, P. M. (1991). Multiple personality disorder as an attachment disorder. *Dissociation: Progress in the Dissociative Disorders, 4*(3), 117–123.

Battle, C. L., Shea, M. T., Johnson, D. M., Yen, S., Zlotnick, C., Zanarini, M. C., Sanislow, C. A., Skodol, A. E., Gunderson, J. G., Grilo, C. M., McGlashan, T. H., & Morey, L. C. (2004). Childhood maltreatment associated with adult personality disorders: Findings from the collaborative longitudinal personality disorders study. *Journal of Personality Disorders, 18*(2), 193–211. doi:10.1521/pedi.18.2.193.32777

Baumeister, D., Akhtar, R., Ciufolini, S., Pariante, C. M., & Mondelli, V. (2016). Childhood trauma and adulthood inflammation: A meta-analysis of peripheral C-reactive protein, interleukin-6 and tumour necrosis factor-α. *Molecular Psychiatry, 21*(5), 642–649. doi:10.1038/mp.2015.67

Bellis, M. A., Hughes, K., Leckenby, N., Perkins, C., & Lowey, H. (2014). National household survey of adverse childhood experiences and their relationship with resilience to health-harming behaviors in England. *BMC Medicine, 12,* 72. doi:10.1186/1741-7015-12-72

Bernstein, E. M., & Putnam, F. W. (1986). Development, reliability, and validity of a dissociation scale. *Journal of Nervous and Mental Disease, 174,* 727–735.

Blevins, C. A., Weathers, F. W., Davis, M. T., Witte, T. K., & Domino, J. L. (2015). The Posttraumatic Stress Disorder Checklist for DSM-5 (PCL-5): Development and initial psychometric evaluation. *Journal of Traumatic Stress, 28*(6), 489–498. doi:https://doi.org/10.1002/jts.22059

Blevins, C. A., Weathers, F. W., & Witte, T. K. (2014). Dissociation and posttraumatic stress disorder: A latent profile analysis. *Journal of Traumatic Stress, 27*(4), 388–396. doi:10.1002/jts.21933

Blizard, R. A. (2003). Disorganized attachment, development of dissociated self states, and a relational approach to treatment. *Journal of Trauma & Dissociation, 4*(3), 27–50. doi:10.1300/J229v04n03_03

Bluhm, R. L., Williamson, P. C., Osuch, E. A., Frewen, P. A., Stevens, T. K., Boksman, K., Neufeld, R. W. J., Thebérge, J., & Lanius, R. A. (2009). Alterations in default network connectivity in posttraumatic stress disorder related to early-life trauma. *Journal of Psychiatry & Neuroscience, 34*(3), 187.

Boon, S., & Draijer, N. (1991). Diagnosing dissociative disorders in the Netherlands: A pilot study with the Structured Clinical Interview for DSM-III-R Dissociative Disorders. *American Journal of Psychiatry, 148,* 458–462.

Boon, S., & Draijer, N. (1993a). Multiple personality disorder in the Netherlands: A clinical investigation of 71 patients. *American Journal of Psychiatry, 150,* 489–494.

Boon, S., & Draijer, N. (1993b). The differentiation of patients with MPD or DDNOS from patients with a cluster B personality disorder. *Dissociation: Progress in the Dissociative Disorders, 6*(2–3), 126–135.

Boon, S., Steele, K., & van der Hart, O. (2011). *Coping with trauma-related dissociation: Skills training for patients and therapists.* W. W. Norton & Company.

Bowlby, J. (1969). *Attachment.* Basic Books.

Bowlby, J. (1980). *Attachment and loss.* Basic Books.

Brand, B. L. (2001). Establishing safety with patients with dissociative identity disorder. *Journal of Trauma & Dissociation, 2*(4), 133–155. doi:10.1300/J229v02n04_07

Brand, B. L. (2016). The necessity of clinical training in trauma and dissociation. *Journal of Anxiety and Depression, 5*(4), 251. doi:10.4172/2167-1044.1000251

Brand, B. L., Armstrong, J. A., Loewenstein, R. J., & McNary, S. W. (2009a). Personality differences on the Rorschach of dissociative identity disorder, borderline personality disorder, and psychotic inpatients. *Psychological Trauma: Theory, Research, Practice, and Policy, 1*(3), 188–205.

Brand, B., Classen, C., Lanius, R., Loewenstein, R., McNary, S., Pain, C., & Putnam, F. (2009b). A naturalistic study of dissociative identity disorder and dissociative disorder not otherwise specified patients treated by community clinicians. *Psychological Trauma: Theory, Research, Practice, and Policy*, *1*(2), 153–171.

Brand, B. L., Classen, C. C., McNary, S. W., & Zaveri, P. (2009c). A review of dissociative disorders treatment studies. *Journal of Nervous and Mental Disease*, *197*(9), 646–654. doi:10.1097/NMD.0b013e3181b3afaa

Brand, B. L., Dalenberg, C. J., Frewen, P. A., Loewenstein, R. J., Schielke, H. J., Brams, J. S., & Spiegel, D. (2018). Trauma-related dissociation is no fantasy: Addressing the errors of omission and commission in Merckelbach and Patihis (2018). *Psychological Injury and Law*, *11*, 377–393. doi:10.1007/s12207-018-9336-8

Brand, B. L., & Frewen, P. (2017). Dissociation as a trauma-related phenomenon. In S. N. Gold & S. N. Gold (Eds.), *APA handbook of trauma psychology: Foundations in knowledge* (pp. 215–241). American Psychological Association.

Brand, B. L., Kumar, S. A., & McEwen, L. E. (2019a). Coverage of child maltreatment and adult trauma in graduate psychopathology textbooks. *Psychological Trauma: Theory, Research, Practice, and Policy*, *11*(8), 919–926. https://doi.org/10.1037/tra0000454

Brand, B. L., & Lanius, R. A. (2014). Chronic complex dissociative disorders and borderline personality disorder: Disorders of emotion dysregulation? *Borderline Personality Disorder and Emotion Dysregulation*, *1*, 13. doi:10.1186/2051-6673-1-13

Brand, B. L., Lanius, R., Vermetten, E., Loewenstein, R. J., & Spiegel, D. (2012a). Where are we going? An update on assessment, treatment, and neurobiological research in dissociative disorders as we move toward the DSM-5. *Journal of Trauma & Dissociation*, *13*(1), 9–31.

Brand, B. L., Loewenstein, R. J., & Lanius, R. A. (2014a). Dissociative identity disorder. In G. O. Gabbard (Ed.), *Gabbard's treatments of psychiatric disorders* (5th ed., pp. 439–458). American Psychiatric Publishing, Inc.

Brand, B. L., Loewenstein, R. J., & Speigel, D. (2014b). Dispelling myths about dissociative identity disorder treatment: An empirically based approach. *Psychiatry*, *77*, 169–189.

Brand, B. L., McNary, S. W., Myrick, A. C., Classen, C. C., Lanius, R., Loewenstein, R. J., Pain, C., & Putnam, F. W. (2013). A longitudinal naturalistic study of patients with dissociative disorders treated by community clinicians. *Psychological Trauma: Theory, Research, Practice, and Policy*, *5*(4), 301–308. doi:10.1037/a0027654

Brand, B. L., Myrick, A. C., Loewenstein, R. J., Classen, C. C., Lanius, R., McNary, S. W., Pain, C., & Putnam, F. W. (2012b). A survey of practices and recommended treatment interventions among expert therapists treating patients with dissociative identity disorder and dissociative disorder not otherwise specified. *Psychological Trauma: Theory, Research, Practice, and Policy*, *4*(5), 490–500.

Brand, B. L., Sar, V., Stavropoulos, P., Krüger, C., Korzekwa, M., Martínez-Taboas, A., & Middleton, W. (2016a). Separating fact from fiction: An empirical examination of six myths about dissociative identity disorder. *Harvard Review of Psychiatry*, *24*(4), 257–270. doi:10.1097/HRP.0000000000000100

Brand, B. L., Schielke, H. J., & Brams, J. S. (2017a). Assisting the courts in understanding and connecting with experiences of disconnection: Addressing trauma-related dissociation as a forensic psychologist, Part I. *Psychological Injury and Law*, *10*(4), 283–297. doi:10.1007/s12207-017-9304-8

Brand, B. L., Schielke, H. J., Brams, J. S., & DiComo, R. A. (2017b). Assessing trauma-related dissociation in forensic contexts: Addressing trauma-related dissociation as a forensic psychologist, Part II. *Psychological Injury and Law, 10*(4), 298–312. doi:10.1007/s12207-017-9305-7

Brand, B. L., Schielke, H. J., Putnam, K. T., Putnam, F. W., Loewenstein, R. J., Myrick, A., Jepsen, E. K. K., Langeland, W., Steele, K., Classen, C. C., & Lanius, R. A. (2019b). An online educational program for individuals with dissociative disorders and their clinicians: 1-year and 2-year follow-up. *Journal of Traumatic Stress, 32*(1), 156–166. doi:10.1002/jts.22370

Brand, B. L., Webermann, A. R., & Frankel, A. S. (2016b). Assessment of complex dissociative disorder patients and simulated dissociation in forensic contexts. *International Journal of Law and Psychiatry, 49*(Part B), 197–204. doi:10.1016/j.ijlp.2016.10.006

Brandão, M. L., & Lovick, T. A. (2019). Role of the dorsal periaqueductal gray in posttraumatic stress disorder: Mediation by dopamine and neurokinin. *Translational Psychiatry, 9*(1), 1–9.

Briere, J., & Scott, C. (2006). *Principles of trauma therapy: A guide to symptoms, evaluation, and treatment.* Sage.

Briere, J. N., & Scott, C. (2015). *Principles of trauma therapy: A guide to symptoms, evaluation, and treatment* (2nd ed., DSM-5 update). Sage Publications, Inc.

Briere, J., Weathers, F. W., & Runtz, M. (2005). Is dissociation a multidimensional construct? Data from the Multiscale Dissociation Inventory. *Journal of Traumatic Stress, 18*(3), 221–231.

Brown, D. P., & Elliott, D. S. (2016). *Attachment disturbances in adults: Treatment for comprehensive repair.* W. W. Norton & Co.

Butler, L. D. (2006). Normative dissociation. *Psychiatric Clinics of North America, 29*(1), 45–62.

Butler, L. D., Duran, E. F. D., Jasiukatis, P., Koopman, C., & Spiegel, D. (1996). Hypnotizability and traumatic experience: A diathesis-stress model of dissociative symptomatology. *American Journal of Psychiatry, 153*(7), 42–63.

Byun, S., Brumariu, L. E., & Lyons-Ruth, K. (2016). Disorganized attachment in young adulthood as a partial mediator of relations between severity of childhood abuse and dissociation. *Journal of Trauma & Dissociation, 17*(4), 460–479. doi:10.1080/15299732.2016.1141149

Calati, R., & Courtet, P. (2016). Is psychotherapy effective for reducing suicide attempt and non-suicidal self-injury rates? Meta-analysis and meta-regression of literature data. *Journal of Psychiatric Research, 79*, 8–20. doi:10.1016/j.jpsychires.2016.04.003

Carlson, E. A. (1998). A prospective longitudinal study of attachment disorganization/disorientation. *Child Development, 69*, 1107–1128.

Carlson, E. B., Putnam, F. W., Ross, C. A., Torem, M., Coons, P., Dill, D. L., Lowenstein, R. J., & Braun, B. G. (1993). Validity of the Dissociative Experiences Scale in screening for multiple personality disorder: A multicenter study. *American Journal of Psychiatry, 150*(7), 1030–1036.

Chartier, M. J., Walker, J. R., & Naimark, B. (2010). Separate and cumulative effects of adverse childhood experiences in predicting adult health and health care utilization. *Child Abuse & Neglect, 34*(6), 454–464. doi:10.1016/j.chiabu.2009.09.020

Chefetz, R. A. (2015). *Intensive psychotherapy for persistent dissociative processes: The fear of feeling real.* W. W. Norton & Co.

Cheit, R. E., & Krishnaswami, L. A. (2014). *The witch-hunt narrative: Politics, psychology, and the sexual abuse of children.* Oxford University Press.

Chu, J. A. (1988). Ten traps for therapists in the treatment of trauma survivors. *Dissociation, 1*(4), 24–32.

Chu, J. A. (2011). *Rebuilding shattered lives: Treating complex PTSD and dissociative disorders* (2nd ed.). John Wiley & Sons Inc.

Cicchetti, D., Brett, Z. H., Humphreys, K. L., Fleming, A. S., Kraemer, G. W., & Drury, S. S. (2015). Using cross-species comparisons and a neurobiological framework to understand early social deprivation effects on behavioral development. *Development and Psychopathology, 27*(2), 347–367. doi:http://dx.doi.org/10.1017/S0954579415000036

Clark, C., Classen, C. C., Fourt, A., & Shetty, M. (2015). *Treating the trauma survivor: An essential guide to trauma-informed care.* Routledge/Taylor & Francis Group.

Cloitre, M., Courtois, C. A., Ford, J. D., Green, B. L., Alexander, P., Briere, J., Herman, J. L., Lanius, R., Stolbach, B. C., Spinazzola, J., Van der Kolk, B. A., & Van der Hart, O. (2012a). The ISTSS Expert Consensus Treatment Guidelines for Complex PTSD in Adults. https://istss.org/ISTSS_Main/media/Documents/ComplexPTSD.pdf

Cloitre, M., Petkova, E., Wang, J., & Lu Lassell, F. (2012b). An examination of the influence of a sequential treatment on the course and impact of dissociation among women with PTSD related to childhood abuse. *Depression and Anxiety, 29*, 709–717. doi:10.1002/da.21920

Conklin, C. Z., Bradley, R., & Westen, D. (2006). Affect regulation in borderline personality disorder. *Journal of Nervous and Mental Disease, 194*(2), 69–77. doi:10.1097/01.nmd.0000198138.41709.4f

Cook, J. M., Simiola, V., Ellis, A. E., & Thompson, R. (2017). Training in trauma psychology: A national survey of doctoral graduate programs. *Training and Education in Professional Psychology, 11*(2), 108–114. doi:10.1037/tep0000150

Coons, P. M., & Milstein, V. (1990). Self-mutilation associated with dissociative disorders. *Dissociation: Progress in the Dissociative Disorders, 3*(2), 81–87.

Courtois, C. A., & Ford, J. D. (Eds.). (2009). *Treating complex traumatic stress disorders: An evidence-based guide.* Guilford Press.

Courtois, C. A., & Ford, J. D. (2013). *Treatment of complex trauma: A sequenced, relationship-based approach.* Guilford Press.

Courtois, C. A., Ford, J. D., & Cloitre, M. (2009). Best practices in psychotherapy for adults. In C. A. Courtois & J. D. Ford (Eds.), *Treating complex traumatic stress disorders: An evidence-based guide* (pp. 82–103). Guilford Press.

Courtois, C. A., & Gold, S. N. (2009). The need for inclusion of psychological trauma in the professional curriculum: A call to action. *Psychological Trauma: Theory, Research, Practice, and Policy, 1*(1), 3–23.

Cozolino, L. (2017). *The neuroscience of psychotherapy: Healing the social brain.* W. W. Norton & Company.

Dalenberg, C. J. (1996). Accuracy, timing, and circumstances of disclosure in therapy of recovered and continuous memories of abuse. *Journal of Psychiatry and Law, 24*(2), 229–276.

Dalenberg, C. J. (2006). Recovered memory and the Daubert criteria: Recovered memory as professionally tested, peer reviewed, and accepted in the relevant scientific community. *Trauma, Violence, and Abuse, 7*(4), 274–310. doi:10.1177/1524838006294572

Dalenberg, C. J., Brand, B. L., Gleaves, D. H., Dorahy, M. J., Loewenstein, R. J., Cardeña, E., Frewen, P. A., Carlson, E. B., & Spiegel, D. (2012). Evaluation of the evidence for the trauma and fantasy models of dissociation. *Psychological Bulletin*, *138*(3), 550–588. doi:10.1037/a0027447

Dalenberg, C. J., Brand, B. L., Loewenstein, R. J., Gleaves, D. H., Dorahy, M. J., Cardeña, E., Frewen, P. A., Carlson, E. B., & Spiegel, D. (2014). Reality versus fantasy: Reply to Lynn et al. (2014). *Psychological Bulletin*, *140*(3), 911–920.

Dalenberg, C. J., Loewenstein, R., Spiegel, D., Brewin, C., Lanius, R., Frankel, S., Gold, S., Van der Kolk, B., Simeon, D., Vermetten, E., Butler, L., Koopman, C., Courtois, C., Dell, P., Nijenhuis, E., Chu, J., Sar, V., Palesh, O., Cuevas, C., & Paulson, K. (2007). Scientific study of the dissociative disorders. *Psychotherapy and Psychosomatics*, *76*(6), 400–401. doi:10.1159/000107570

Daniels, J. K., McFarlane, A. C., Bluhm, R. L., Moores, K. A., Clark, C. R., Shaw, M. E., Williamson, P. C., Densmore, M., & Lanius, R. A. (2010). Switching between executive and default mode networks in posttraumatic stress disorder: Alterations in functional connectivity. *Journal of Psychiatry & Neuroscience*, *35*(4), 258–266. doi:10.1503/jpn.090175

DeCou, C. R., Comtois, K. A., & Landes, S. J. (2019). Dialectical behavior therapy is effective for the treatment of suicidal behavior: A meta-analysis. *Behavior Therapy*, *50*(1), 60–72. doi:10.1016/j.beth.2018.03.009

Dell, P. F. (1998). Axis II pathology in outpatients with dissociative identity disorder. *Journal of Nervous and Mental Disease*, *186*(6), 352–356.

Dell, P. F. (2002). Dissociative phenomenology of dissociative identity disorder. *Journal of Nervous and Mental Disease*, *190*(1), 10–15.

Dell, P. F. (2006a). The Multidimensional Inventory of Dissociation (MID): A comprehensive measure of pathological dissociation. *Journal of Trauma & Dissociation*, *7*(2), 77–106.

Dell, P. F. (2006b). A new model of dissociative identity disorder. *Psychiatric Clinics of North America*, *29*(1), 1–26.

Dell, P. F. (2009). The phenomena of pathological dissociation. In P. F. Dell & J. A. O'Neil (Eds.), *Dissociation and the dissociative disorders: DSM-5 and beyond* (pp. 225–237). Routledge/Taylor & Francis Group.

Dell, P. F., & O'Neil, J. A. (Eds.). (2009). *Dissociation and the dissociative disorders: DSM-5 and beyond*. Routledge/Taylor & Francis Group.

Dixon-Gordon, K. L., Tull, M. T., & Gratz, K. L. (2014). Self-injurious behaviors in posttraumatic stress disorder: An examination of potential moderators. *Journal of Affective Disorders*, *166*, 359–367. doi:10.1016/j.jad.2014.05.033

Dorahy, M. J., Brand, B. L., Şar, V., Krüger, C., Stavropoulos, P., Martínez-Taboas, A., Lewis-Fernández, R., & Middleton, W. (2014). Dissociative identity disorder: An empirical overview. *Australian and New Zealand Journal of Psychiatry*, *48*(5), 402–417.

Dorahy, M. J., Gorgas, J., Seager, L., & Middleton, W. (2017a). Engendered responses to, and interventions for, shame in dissociative disorders: A survey and experimental investigation. *Journal of Nervous and Mental Disease*, *205*(11), 886–892. doi:10.1097/NMD.0000000000000740

Dorahy, M. J., Lewis-Fernández, R., Krüger, C., Brand, B. L., Şar, V., Ewing, J., Martínez-Taboas, A., Stravropoulos, & Middleton, W. (2017b). The role of clinical experience, diagnosis, and theoretical orientation in the treatment of posttraumatic and dissociative disorders: A vignette and survey investigation. *Journal of Trauma & Dissociation*, 18(2), 206–222. doi:10.1080/15299732.2016.1225626

Dorahy, M. J., Shannon, C., Seagar, L., Corr, M., Stewart, K., Hanna, D., . . . Middleton, W. (2009a). Auditory hallucinations in dissociative identity disorder and schizophrenia with and without a childhood trauma history: Similarities and differences. *Journal of Nervous and Mental Disease*, 197(12), 892–898. doi:10.1097/NMD.0b013e3181c299ea

Dorrepaal, E., Thomaes, K., Smit, J. H., van Balkom, A. J. L. M., Veltman, D. J., Hoogendoorn, A. W., & Draijer, N. (2012). Stabilizing group treatment for complex posttraumatic stress disorder related to child abuse based on psychoeducation and cognitive behavioural therapy: A multisite randomized controlled trial. *Psychotherapy and Psychosomatics*, 81(4), 217–225. doi:10.1159/000335044

Ehlers, A. (2006). More evidence for the role of persistent dissociation in PTSD. *American Journal of Psychiatry*, 163(6), 1112. doi:10.1176/appi.ajp.163.6.1112

Ehlers, A., & Clark, D. M. (2000). A cognitive model of posttraumatic stress disorder. *Behaviour Research and Therapy*, 38(4), 319–345. doi:10.1016/S0005-7967(99)00123-0

Ellason, J. W., & Ross, C. A. (1995). Positive and negative symptoms in dissociative identity disorder and schizophrenia: A comparative analysis. *Journal of Nervous and Mental Disease*, 183(4), 236–241. doi:10.1097/00005053-199504000-00009

Ellason, J. W., Ross, C. A., & Fuchs, D. L. (1996). Lifetime Axis I and II comorbidity and childhood trauma history in dissociative identity disorder. *Psychiatry: Interpersonal and Biological Processes*, 59(3), 255–266.

Emerson, D. (2015). *Trauma-sensitive yoga in therapy: Bringing the body into treatment.* W. W. Norton & Co.

Engelberg, J. C., & Brand, B. L. (2012). The effect of depression on self-harm and treatment outcome in patients with severe dissociative disorders. *Psi Chi Journal of Psychological Research*, 17(3), 115–124.

Espirito-Santo, H., & Pio-Abreu, J. L. (2009). Psychiatric symptoms and dissociation in conversion, somatization and dissociative disorders. *Australian and New Zealand Journal of Psychiatry*, 43(3), 270–276. doi:10.1080/00048670802653307

Evren, C., Şar, V., & Dalbudak, E. (2008). Temperament, character, and dissociation among detoxified male inpatients with alcohol dependency. *Journal of Clinical Psychology*, 64(6), 717–727.

Felitti, V. J., Anda, R. F., Nordenberg, D., Williamson, D. F., Spitz, A. M., Edwards, V., Koss, M. P., & Marks, J. S. (1998). Relationship of childhood abuse and household dysfunction to many of the leading causes of death in adults: The Adverse Childhood Experiences (ACE) study. *American Journal of Preventive Medicine*, 14(4), 245–258.

Fenster, R. J., Lebois, L. A., Ressler, K. J., & Suh, J. (2018). Brain circuit dysfunction in post-traumatic stress disorder: From mouse to man. *Nature Reviews Neuroscience*, 19(9), 535.

Ferdinand, R. F., van der Reijden, M., Verhulst, F. C., Nienhuis, J., & Giel, R. (1995). Assessment of the prevalence of psychiatric disorder in young adults. *British Journal of Psychiatry*, 166(4), 480–488.

Ferry, F. R., Brady, S. E., Bunting, B. P., Murphy, S. D., Bolton, D., & O'Neill, S. M. (2015). The economic burden of PTSD in Northern Ireland. *Journal of Traumatic Stress*, 28(3), 191–197. doi:10.1002/jts.22008

Fisher, J. (2017). *Healing the fragmented selves of trauma survivors: Overcoming internal self-alienation*. Taylor & Francis.

Folger, A. T., Putnam, K. T., Putnam, F. W., Peugh, J. L., Eismann, E. A., Sa, T., Shapiro, R. A., Van Ginkel, J. B., & Ammerman, R. T. (2017). Maternal interpersonal trauma and child social-emotional development: An intergenerational effect. *Paediatric and Perinatal Epidemiology, 31*(2), 99–107. doi:10.1111/ppe.12341

Foote, B., & Orden, K. V. (2016). Adapting dialectical behavior therapy for the treatment of dissociative identity disorder. *American Journal of Psychotherapy, 70*(4), 343–364. doi:10.1176/appi.psychotherapy.2016.70.4.343

Foote, B., Smolin, Y., Kaplan, M., Legatt, M. E., & Lipschitz, D. (2006). Prevalence of dissociative disorders in psychiatric outpatients. *American Journal of Psychiatry, 163*(4), 623–629.

Foote, B., Smolin, Y., Neft, D. I., & Lipschitz, D. (2008). Dissociative disorders and suicidality in psychiatric outpatients. *Journal of Nervous and Mental Disease, 196*(1), 29–36.

Ford, J. D., & Courtois, C. A. (2009). Defining and understanding complex trauma and complex traumatic stress disorders. In C. A. Courtois & J. D. Ford (Eds.), *Treating complex traumatic stress disorders: An evidence-based guide* (pp. 13–30). Guilford Press.

Ford, J. D., & Gómez, J. M. (2015). The relationship of psychological trauma, and dissociative and posttraumatic stress disorders to non-suicidal self-injury and suicidality: A review. *Journal of Trauma & Dissociation, 16*, 232–271. doi:10.1080/15299732.2015.989563

Fraser, G. A., & Raine, D. (1992). *Cost analysis of the treatment of MPD*. Paper presented at the Ninth Annual International Conference on Multiple Personality/Dissociative States, Chicago, Illinois.

Frewen, P. A., Dozois, D. J. A., Neufeld, R. W. J., & Lanius, R. A. (2008). Meta-analysis of alexithymia in posttraumatic stress disorder. *Journal of Traumatic Stress, 21*(2), 243–246. doi:10.1002/jts.20320

Frewen, P. A., Kleindienst, N., Lanius, R., & Schmahl, C. (2014). Trauma-related altered states of consciousness in women with BPD with or without co-occurring PTSD. *European Journal of Psychotraumatology, 5*, 1–10. doi:10.3402/ejpt.v5.24863

Frewen, P. A., & Lanius, R. (2015). *Healing the traumatized self: Consciousness, neuroscience, treatment*. W. W. Norton & Co.

Freyd, J. J. (1996). *Betrayal Trauma: The Logic of Forgetting Childhood Abuse*. Cambridge: Harvard.

Friedl, M. C., Draijer, N., & de Jonge, P. (2000). Prevalence of dissociative disorders in psychiatric in-patients: The impact of study characteristics. *Acta Psychiatrica Scandinavica, 102*(6), 423–428.

Ginzburg, K., Koopman, C., Butler, L. D., Palesh, O., Kraemer, H. C., Classen, C. C., & Spiegel, D. (2006). Evidence for a dissociative subtype of post-traumatic stress disorder among help-seeking childhood sexual abuse survivors. *Journal of Trauma & Dissociation, 7*(2), 7–27.

Gleaves, D. H., & Eberenz, K. P. (1995). Correlates of dissociative symptoms among women with eating disorders. *Journal of Psychiatric Research, 29*(5), 417–426.

Golier, J. A., Yehuda, R., Bierer, L. M., Mitropoulou, V., New, A. S., Schmeidler, J., Silverman, J. M., & Siever, L. J. (2003). The relationship of borderline personality disorder to posttraumatic stress disorder and traumatic events. *American Journal of Psychiatry, 160*(11), 2018–2024. doi:10.1176/appi.ajp.160.11.2018

Grubaugh, A. L., Zinzow, H. M., Paul, L., Egede, L. E., & Frueh, B. C. (2011). Trauma exposure and posttraumatic stress disorder in adults with severe mental illness: A critical review. *Clinical Psychology Review, 31*(6), 883–899. doi:http://dx.doi.org/10.1016/j.cpr.2011.04.003

Halligan, S. L., Michael, T., Clark, D. M., & Ehlers, A. (2003). Posttraumatic stress disorder following assault: The role of cognitive processing, trauma memory, and appraisals. *Journal of Consulting and Clinical Psychology, 71*(3), 419–431. doi:10.1037/0022-006X.71.3.419

Hansen, N. B., Lambert, M. J., & Forman, E. M. (2002). The psychotherapy dose-response effect and its implications for treatment delivery services. *Clinical Psychology: Science and Practice, 9*(3), 329–343. doi:10.1093/clipsy/9.3.329

Harned, M. S., Korslund, K. E., & Linehan, M. M. (2014). A pilot randomized controlled trial of dialectical behavior therapy with and without the dialectical behavior therapy prolonged exposure protocol for suicidal and self-injuring women with borderline personality disorder and PTSD. *Behaviour Research and Therapy, 55*(1), 7–17. doi:10.1016/j.brat.2014.01.008

Harricharan, S., Rabellino, D., Frewen, P. A., Densmore, M., Théberge, J., McKinnon, M. C., Schore, A. N., & Lanius, R. A. (2016). fMRI functional connectivity of the periaqueductal gray in PTSD and its dissociative subtype. *Brain and Behavior, 6*(12), e00579.

Heim, C., & Nemeroff, C. B. (2001). The role of childhood trauma in the neurobiology of mood and anxiety disorders: Preclinical and clinical studies. *Biological Psychiatry, 49*(12), 1023–1039. doi:10.1016/S0006-3223(01)01157-X

Hepworth, I., & McGowan, L. (2013). Do mental health professionals enquire about childhood sexual abuse during routine mental health assessment in acute mental health settings? A substantive literature review. *Journal of Psychiatric and Mental Health Nursing, 20*(6), 473–483. doi:10.1111/j.1365-2850.2012.01939.x

Herman, J. L. (1992). *Trauma and recovery*. Basic Books.

Herman, J. L. (1997). *Trauma and recovery: The aftermath of violence—from domestic abuse to political terror*. Basic Books.

Herman, J. L. (2011). Posttraumatic stress disorder as a shame disorder. In R. L. Dearing & J. P. Tangney (Eds.), *Shame in the therapy hour* (pp. 261–275). American Psychological Association.

Hesse, E., & Main, M. (2000). Disorganized infant, child, and adult attachment: Collapse in behavioral and attentional strategies. *Journal of the American Psychoanalytic Association, 48*(4), 1097–1127. doi:10.1177/00030651000480041101

Hollander, E., Carrasco, J. L., Mullen, L. S., Trungold, S., DeCaria, C. M., & Towey, J. (1992). Left hemispheric activation in depersonalization disorder: A case report. *Biological Psychiatry, 31*(11), 1157–1162.

Holmes, E. A., Brown, R. J., Mansell, W., Fearon, R. P., Hunter, E. C. M., Frasquilho, F., & Oakley, D. A. (2005). Are there two qualitatively distinct forms of dissociation? A review and some clinical implications. *Clinical Psychology Review, 25*(1), 1–23.

Hopper, J. W., Frewen, P. A., Van der Kolk, B. A., & Lanius, R. A. (2007). Neural correlates of reexperiencing, avoidance, and dissociation in PTSD: Symptom dimensions and emotion dysregulation in responses to script-driven trauma imagery. *Journal of Traumatic Stress, 20*(5), 713–725.

Horevitz, R. P., & Braun, B. G. (1984). Are multiple personalities borderline; An analysis of 33 cases. *Psychiatric Clinics of North America, 7*, 69–83.

Howell, E. F. (2011). *Understanding and treating dissociative identity disorder: A relational approach*. Routledge/Taylor & Francis Group.

Huang, L. N., Flatow, R., Biggs, T., Afayee, S., Smith, K., Clark, T., & Blake, M. (2014). *SAMHSA's concept of trauma and guidance for a trauma-informed approach*. Substance Abuse and Mental Health Services Administration.

Hyland, P., Shevlin, M., Fyvie, C., & Karatzias, T. (2018). Posttraumatic stress disorder and complex posttraumatic stress disorder in DSM-5 and ICD-11: Clinical and behavioral correlates. *Journal of Traumatic Stress, 31*(2), 174–180. doi:10.1002/jts.22272

International Society for the Study of Dissociation. (2011). Guidelines for treating dissociative identity disorder in adults, third revision. *Journal of Trauma & Dissociation, 12*(2), 115–187. doi:10.1080/15299732.2011.537247

International Society for the Study of Trauma and Dissociation. (2004). Guidelines for the evaluation and treatment of dissociative symptoms in children and adolescents. *Journal of Trauma & Dissociation, 5*(3), 119–150. doi:10.1300/J229v05n03_09

Jepsen, E. K. K., Langeland, W., Sexton, H., & Heir, T. (2014). Inpatient treatment for early sexually abused adults: A naturalistic 12-month follow-up study. *Psychological Trauma: Theory, Research, Practice, and Policy, 6*(2), 142–151.

Johnson, J. G., Cohen, P., Kasen, S., & Brook, J. S. (2006). Dissociative disorders among adults in the community, impaired functioning, and Axis I and II comorbidity. *Journal of Psychiatric Research, 40*(2), 131–140.

Kandel, E. R., Schwartz, J. H., & Jessell, T. M. (2000). *Principles of neural science*. McGraw-Hill, Health Professions Division.

Karadag, F., Şar, V., Tamar-Gurol, D., Evren, C., Karagoz, M., & Erkiran, M. (2005). Dissociative disorders among inpatients with drug or alcohol dependency. *Journal of Clinical Psychiatry, 66*(10), 1247–1253.

Karpman, S. B. (2011). Fairy tales and script drama analysis. *Group Facilitation: A Research & Applications Journal, 11*, 49–52.

Kessler, R. C. (2000). Posttraumatic stress disorder: The burden to the individual and to society. *Journal of Clinical Psychiatry, 61*(Suppl. 5), 4–14.

Kessler, R. C., Sonnega, A., Bromet, E., Hughes, M., & Nelson, C. B. (1995). Posttraumatic stress disorder in the National Comorbidity Survey. *Archives of General Psychiatry, 52*, 1048–1060.

Kessler, R. C., Warner, C. H., Ivany, C., Petukhova, M. V., Rose, S., Bromet, E. J., Brown, M. 3rd, Cai, T., Colpe, L. J., Cox, K. L., Fullerton, C. S., Gilman, S. E., Gruber, M. J., Heeringa, S. G., Lewandowski-Romps, L., Li, J., Millikan-Bell, A. M., Naifeh, J. A., Nock, M. K., . . . Ursano, R. J.; Army STARRS Collaborators. (2015). Predicting suicides after psychiatric hospitalization in US Army soldiers: The Army Study to Assess Risk and Resilience in Service Members (Army STARRS). *JAMA Psychiatry, 72*(1), 49–57.

Kezelman, C. A., & Stavropoulos, P. A. (2012). *Practice guidelines for treatment of complex trauma and trauma-informed care and service delivery.* Adults Surviving Child Abuse.

Kissee, J. L., Isaacson, L. J., & Miller-Perrin, C. (2014). An analysis of child maltreatment content in introductory psychology textbooks. *Journal of Aggression, Maltreatment & Trauma, 23*(3), 215–228. doi:10.1080/10926771.2014.878891

Klein, B., Mitchell, J., Abbott, J., Shandley, K., Austin, D., Gilson, K., Kiropoulos, L., Cannard, G., & Redman, T. (2010). A therapist-assisted cognitive behavior therapy internet intervention for posttraumatic stress disorder: Pre-, post- and 3-month follow-up results from an open trial. *Journal of Anxiety Disorders, 24*(6), 635–644. doi:10.1016/j.janxdis.2010.04.005

Kleindienst, N., Limberger, M. F., Ebner-Priemer, U. W., Keibel-Mauchnik, J., Dyer, A., Berger, M., Schmahl, C., & Bohus, M. (2011). Dissociation predicts poor response to dialectical behavioral therapy in female patients with borderline personality disorder. *Journal of Personality Disorders, 25*(4), 432–447. doi:10.1521/pedi.2011.25.4.432

Kleindienst, N., Priebe, K., Görg, N., Dyer, A., Steil, R., Lyssenko, L., Winter, D., Schmahl, C., & Bohus, M. (2016). State dissociation moderates response to dialectical behavior therapy for posttraumatic stress disorder in women with and without borderline personality disorder. *European Journal of Psychotraumatology, 7*, 30375. doi:10.3402/ejpt.v7.30375

Kluft, R. P. (Ed.). (1985). *Childhood antecedents of multiple personality disorder.* American Psychiatric Press.

Kluft, R. P. (1987). First-rank symptoms as a diagnostic clue to multiple personality disorder. *American Journal of Psychiatry, 144*(3), 293–298.

Kluft, R. P. (1992). Paradigm exhaustion and paradigm shift: Thinking through the therapeutic impasse. *Psychiatric Annals, 22*(10), 502–508. doi:10.3928/0048-5713-19921001-06

Kluft, R. P. (1993a). Basic principles in conducing the psychotherapy of multiple personality disorder. In R. P. Kluft & C. G. Fine (Eds.), *Clinical perspectives on multiple personality disorder* (pp. 19–50). American Psychiatric Press.

Kluft, R. P. (1993b). Clinical approaches to the integration of personalities. In R. P. Kluft & C. G. Fine (Eds.), *Clinical perspectives on multiple personality disorder* (pp. 101–133). American Psychiatric Press.

Kluft, R. P. (1993c). The initial stages of psychotherapy in the treatment of multiple personality disorder patients. *Dissociation: Progress in the Dissociative Disorders, 6*(2–3), 145–161.

Kluft, R. P. (1994a). Countertransference in the treatment of multiple personality disorder. In J. P. Wilson & J. D. Lindy (Eds.), *Countertransference in the treatment of PTSD* (pp. 122–150). Guilford.

Kluft, R. P. (1994b). Treatment trajectories in multiple personality disorder. *Dissociation, 7*, 63–76.

Kluft, R. P. (2006). Dealing with alters: A pragmatic clinical perspective. *Psychiatric Clinics of North America, 29*(1), 281–304.

Kluft, R. P. (2007). Applications of innate affect theory to the understanding and treatment of dissociative identity disorder. In E. Vermetten, M. Dorahy, D. Spiegel, E.

Vermetten, M. Dorahy, & D. Spiegel (Eds.), *Traumatic dissociation: Neurobiology and treatment* (pp. 301–316). American Psychiatric Publishing, Inc.

Kluft, R. P. (2009). A clinician's understanding of dissociation: Fragments of an acquaintance. In P. F. Dell & J. A. O'Neil (Eds.), *Dissociation and the dissociative disorders: DSM-5 and beyond* (pp. 599–623). Routledge/Taylor & Francis Group.

Kluft, R. P., & Fine, C. G. (1993). *Clinical perspectives on multiple personality disorder.* American Psychiatric Association.

Knaevelsrud, C., & Maercker, A. (2007). Internet-based treatment for PTSD reduces distress and facilitates the development of a strong therapeutic alliance: A randomized controlled clinical trial. *BMC Psychiatry, 7,* Article 13. doi:10.1186/1471-244X-7-13

Korzekwa, M. I., Dell, P. F., & Pain, C. (2009a). Dissociation and borderline personality disorder: An update for clinicians. *Current Psychiatry Reports, 11*(1), 82–88.

Korzekwa, M. I., Dell, P. F., Links, P. S., Thabane, L., & Fougere, P. (2009b). Dissociation in borderline personality disorder: A detailed look. *Journal of Trauma & Dissociation, 10*(3), 346–367. doi:10.1080/15299730902956838

Kozlowska, K., Walker, P., McLean, L., & Carrive, P. (2015). Fear and the defense cascade: Clinical implications and management. *Harvard Review of Psychiatry, 23*(4), 263.

Krüger, C., & Fletcher, L. (2017). Predicting a dissociative disorder from type of childhood maltreatment and abuser-abused relational tie. *Journal of Trauma & Dissociation, 18*(3), 356–372. doi:10.1080/15299732.2017.1295420

Kumar, S. A., Brand, B. L., & Courtois, C. A. (2019). The need for trauma training: Clinicians' reactions to training on complex trauma. *Psychological Trauma: Theory, Research, Practice, and Policy.* Advance online publication. doi:10.1037/tra0000515

Lab, D. D., Feigenbaum, J. D., & De Silva, P. (2000). Mental health professionals' attitudes and practices towards male childhood sexual abuse. *Child Abuse & Neglect, 24*(3), 391–409. doi:10.1016/S0145-2134(99)00152-0

Laddis, A., & Dell, P. F. (2012). Dissociation and psychosis in dissociative identity disorder and schizophrenia. *Journal of Trauma & Dissociation, 13*(4), 397–413. doi:10.1080/15299732.2012.664967

Laddis, A., Dell, P. F., & Korzekwa, M. (2017). Comparing the symptoms and mechanisms of "dissociation" in dissociative identity disorder and borderline personality disorder. *Journal of Trauma & Dissociation, 18*(2), 139–173. doi:10.1080/15299732.2016.1194358

Land, B. B., Bruchas, M. R., Lemos, J. C., Xu, M., Melief, E. J., & Chavkin, C. (2008). The dysphoric component of stress is encoded by activation of the dynorphin κ-opioid system. *Journal of Neuroscience, 28*(2), 407–414.

Langeland, W., Jepsen, E. K. K., Brand, B. L., Kleven, L., Loewenstein, R. J., Putnam, F. W., Schielke, H. J., Myrick, A., Lanius, R. A., & Heir, T. (2020). The economic burden of dissociative disorders: A qualitative systematic review of empirical studies. *Psychological Trauma: Theory, Research, Practice, and Policy, 12*(7), 730–738. doi: 10.1037/tra0000556

Lanius, R. A., Bluhm, R. L., & Frewen, P. A. (2011). How understanding the neurobiology of complex post-traumatic stress disorder can inform clinical practice: A social cognitive and affective neuroscience approach. *Acta Psychiatrica Scandinavica, 124*(5), 331–348. doi:10.1111/j.1600-0447.2011.01755.x

Lanius, R. A., Bluhm, R., Lanius, U., & Pain, C. (2006). A review of neuroimaging studies in PTSD: Heterogeneity of response to symptom provocation. *Journal of Psychiatric Research, 40*(8), 709–729.

Lanius, R. A., Boyd, J. E., McKinnon, M. C., Nicholson, A. A., Frewen, P., Vermetten, E., Jetly, R., & Spiegel, D. (2018). A review of the neurobiological basis of trauma-related dissociation and its relation to cannabinoid- and opioid-mediated stress response: A transdiagnostic, translational approach. *Current Psychiatry Reports, 20*(12), 118.

Lanius, R. A., Brand, B., Vermetten, E., Frewen, P. A., & Spiegel, D. (2012). The dissociative subtype of posttraumatic stress disorder: Rationale, clinical and neurobiological evidence, and implications. *Depression and Anxiety, 29*(8), 701–708. doi:10.1002/da.21889

Lanius, R. A., Frewen, P. A., Tursich, M., Jetly, R., & McKinnon, M. C. (2015). Restoring large-scale brain networks in PTSD and related disorders: A proposal for neuroscientifically-informed treatment interventions. *European Journal of Psychotraumatology, 6*(1), 27313.

Lanius, R. A., Rabellino, D., Boyd, J. E., Harricharan, S., Frewen, P. A., & McKinnon, M. C. (2017). The innate alarm system in PTSD: Conscious and subconscious processing of threat. *Current Opinion in Psychology, 14*, 109–115.

Lanius, R. A., Vermetten, E., Loewenstein, R. J., Brand, B., Christian, S., Bremner, J. D., & Spiegel, D. (2010). Emotion modulation in PTSD: Clinical and neurobiological evidence for a dissociative subtype. *American Journal of Psychiatry, 167*(6), 640–647. doi:10.1176/appi.ajp.2009.09081168

Lanius, R. A., Williamson, P. C., Densmore, M., Boksman, K., Gupta, M. A., Neufeld, R. W., Gati, J. S., & Menon, R. S. (2001). Neural correlates of traumatic memories in posttraumatic stress disorder: A functional MRI investigation. *American Journal of Psychiatry, 158*(11), 1920–1922. doi:10.1176/appi.ajp.158.11.1920

Lanius, R. A., Wolf, E. J., Miller, M. W., Frewen, P. A., Vermetten, E., Brand, B. L., & Spiegel, D. (2014). The dissociative subtype of PTSD. In M. J. Friedman, T. M. Keane, & P. A. Resick (Eds.), *Handbook of PTSD: Science and practice* (2nd ed., pp. 234–250). Guilford Press.

Leichsenring, F., Steinert, C., & Ioannidis, J. P. A. (2019). Toward a paradigm shift in treatment and research of mental disorders. *Psychological Medicine, 49*(13), 2111–2117. doi:10.1017/S0033291719002265

Lemche, E., Surguladze, S. A., Giampietro, V. P., Anilkumar, A., Brammer, M. J., Sierra, M., Chitnis, X., Williams, S. C., Gasston, D., Joraschky, P., David, A. S., & Phillips, M. L. (2007). Limbic and prefrontal responses to facial emotion expressions in depersonalization. *Neuroreport, 18*(5), 473–477.

Leonard, D., Brann, S., & Tiller, J. (2005). Dissociative disorders: Pathways to diagnosis, clinician attitudes and their impact. *Australian and New Zealand Journal of Psychiatry, 39*(10), 940–946.

Lewis, C., Pearce, J., & Bisson, J. I. (2012). Efficacy, cost-effectiveness and acceptability of self-help interventions for anxiety disorders: Systematic review. *British Journal of Psychiatry, 200*(1), 15–21. doi:10.1192/bjp.bp.110.084756

Lewis, C., Roberts, N. P., Simon, N., Bethell, A., & Bisson, J. I. (2019). Internet-delivered cognitive behavioural therapy for post-traumatic stress disorder: Systematic review and meta-analysis. *Acta Psychiatrica Scandinavica, 140*(6), 508–521. doi:10.1111/acps.13079

Lewis, L., Kelly, K., & Allen, J. G. (2004). *Restoring hope and trust: An illustrated guide to mastering trauma*. Sidran Press.

Lieb, R., Pfister, H., Mastaler, M., & Wittchen, H.-U. (2000). Somatoform syndromes and disorders in a representative population sample of adolescents and young adults: Prevalence, comorbidity and impairments. *Acta Psychiatrica Scandinavica, 101*(3), 194–208.

Lilly, M. M., London, M. J., & Bridgett, D. J. (2014). Using SEM to examine emotion regulation and revictimization in predicting PTSD symptoms among childhood abuse survivors. *Psychological Trauma: Theory, Research, Practice, and Policy, 6*(6), 644–651. doi:10.1037/a0036460

Linehan, M. M. (1993). *Cognitive-behavioral treatment of borderline personality disorder*. Guilford Press.

Linehan, M. (2014). *DBT skills training manual*. Guilford Publications.

Liotti, G. (1992). Disorganized/disoriented attachment in the etiology of the dissociative disorders. *Dissociation: Progress in the Dissociative Disorders, 5*(4), 196–204.

Liotti, G. (1999). Disorganization of attachment as a model for understanding dissociative psychopathology. In J. Solomon & C. George (Eds.), *Attachment disorganization* (pp. 291–317). Guilford Press.

Liotti, G. (2004). Trauma, dissociation, and disorganized attachment: Three strands of a single braid. *Psychotherapy: Theory, Research, Practice, Training, 41*(4), 472–486. doi:10.1037/0033-3204.41.4.472

Lloyd, C. S., Lanius, R. A., Brown, M. F., Neufeld, R. J., Frewen, P. A., & McKinnon, M. C. (2019). Assessing posttraumatic tonic immobility responses: The Scale for Tonic Immobility Occurring Post-Trauma. *Chronic Stress, 3*. doi:2470547018822492

Lloyd, M. (2011). How investing in therapeutic services provides a clinical cost saving in the long term. *Health Service Journal*.

Lloyd, M. (2016). Reducing the cost of dissociative identity disorder: Measuring the effectiveness of specialised treatment by frequency of contacts with mental health services. *Journal of Trauma & Dissociation, 17*(3), 362–370. doi:10.1080/15299732.2015.1108947

Loewenstein, R. J. (1991). An office mental status examination for complex chronic dissociative symptoms and multiple personality disorder. *Psychiatric Clinics of North America, 14*(3), 567–604.

Loewenstein, R. J. (1993). Dissociative and posttraumatic aspects of transference and countertransference in the treatment of multiple personality disorder. In R. P. Kluft & C. G. Fine (Eds.), *Clinical perspectives on multiple personality disorder* (pp. 51–85). American Psychiatric Press.

Loewenstein, R. J. (1994). Diagnosis, epidemiology, clinical course, treatment, and cost effectiveness of treatment for Dissociative Disorders and MPD: Report submitted to the Clinton Administration Task Force on Health Care Financing Reform. *Dissociation: Progress in the Dissociative Disorders, 7*(1), 3–11.

Loewenstein, R. J. (2005). Psychopharmacologic treatments for dissociative identity disorder. *Psychiatric Annals, 35*(8), 666–673.

Loewenstein, R. J. (2006). DID 101: A hands-on clinical guide to the stabilization phase of dissociative identity disorder treatment. *Psychiatric Clinics of North America, 29*(1), 305–332.

Loewenstein, R. J., & Putnam, F. W. (1990). The clinical phenomenology of males with MPD: A report of 21 cases. *Dissociation: Progress in the Dissociative Disorders, 3*(3), 135–143.

Longden, E., Madill, A., & Waterman, M. G. (2012). Dissociation, trauma, and the role of lived experience: Toward a new conceptualization of voice hearing. *Psychological Bulletin, 138*(1), 28–76. doi:10.1037/a0025995

Lu, S., Pan, F., Gao, W., Wei, Z., Wang, D., Hu, S., Huang, M., Xu, Y., & Li, L. (2017). Neural correlates of childhood trauma with executive function in young healthy adults. *Oncotarget, 8*(45), 79843.

Ludascher, P., Valerius, G., Stiglmayr, C., Mauchnik, J., Lanius, R. A., Bohus, M., & Schmahl, C. (2010). Pain sensitivity and neural processing during dissociative states in patients with borderline personality disorder with and without comorbid posttraumatic stress disorder: A pilot study. *Journal of Psychiatry & Neuroscience, 35*(3), 177–184. doi:10.1503/jpn.090022

Lynch, S. M., Forman, E., Mendelsohn, M., & Herman, J. (2008). Attending to dissociation: Assessing change in dissociation and predicting treatment outcome. *Journal of Trauma & Dissociation, 9*(3), 301–319. doi:10.1080/15299730802139063

Lynn, S. J., Lilienfeld, S. O., Merckelbach, H., Giesbrecht, T., McNally, R. J., Loftus, E. F., Bruck, M., Garry, M., & Malaktaris, A. (2014). The trauma model of dissociation: Inconvenient truths and stubborn fictions: Comment on Dalenberg et al. (2012). *Psychological Bulletin, 140*(3), 896–910. doi:10.1037/a0035570

Lyons-Ruth, K., Dutra, L., Schuder, M. R., & Bianchi, I. (2006). From infant attachment disorganization to adult dissociation: Relational adaptations or traumatic experiences? *Psychiatric Clinics of North America, 29*(1), 63–86.

Lyssenko, L., Schmahl, C., Bockhacker, L., Vonderlin, R., Bohus, M., & Kleindienst, N. (2018). Dissociation in psychiatric disorders: A meta-analysis of studies using the Dissociative Experiences Scale. *American Journal of Psychiatry, 175*(1), 37–46. doi:10.1176/appi.ajp.2017.17010025

MacLean, P. D. (1990). *The triune brain in evolution: Role in paleocerebral functions.* Springer Science & Business Media.

Main, M., & Hesse, E. (1990). Parents' unresolved traumatic experiences are related to infant disorganized attachment status: Is frightened and/or frightening parental behavior the linking mechanism? In M. T. Greenberg, D. Cicchetti, E. M. Cummings, M. T. Greenberg, D. Cicchetti, & E. M. Cummings (Eds.), *Attachment in the preschool years: Theory, research, and intervention* (pp. 161–182). University of Chicago Press.

Mansfield, A. J., Kaufman, J. S., Marshall, S. W., Gaynes, B. N., Morrissey, J. P., & Engel, C. C. (2010). Deployment and the use of mental health services among U.S. army wives. *New England Journal of Medicine, 362*(2), 101–109. doi:10.1056/NEJMoa0900177

Mayou, R. A., Ehlers, A., & Bryant, B. (2002). Posttraumatic stress disorder after motor vehicle accidents: 3-year follow-up of a prospective longitudinal study. *Behaviour Research and Therapy, 40*(6), 665–675. doi:10.1016/S0005-7967(01)00069-9

McFetridge, M., Hauenstein Swan, A., Heke, S., Karatzias, T., Greenberg, N., Kitchiner, N., & Morley, R. (2017). *Guideline for the treatment and planning of services for complex post-traumatic stress disorder in adults.* UK Psychological Trauma Society.

McGowan, P. O., Sasaki, A., D'Alessio, A. C., Dymov, S., Labonte, B., Szyf, M., Turecki, G., & Meaney, M. J. (2009). Epigenetic regulation of the glucocorticoid receptor in human brain associates with childhood abuse. *Nature Neuroscience, 12*(3), 342–348. doi: 10.1038/nn.2270

McKinnon, M. C., Boyd, J. E., Frewen, P. A., Lanius, U. F., Jetly, R., Richardson, J. D., & Lanius, R. A. (2016). A review of the relation between dissociation, memory, executive functioning and social cognition in military members and civilians with neuropsychiatric conditions. *Neuropsychologia, 90,* 210–234. doi:10.1016/j.neuropsychologia.2016.07.017

McTavish, J. R., Sverdlichenko, I., MacMillan, H. L., & Wekerle, C. (2019). Child sexual abuse, disclosure and PTSD: A systematic and critical review. *Child Abuse & Neglect, 92,* 196–208. doi:10.1016/j.chiabu.2019.04.006

Mendelsohn, M., Herman, J. L., Schatzow, E., Coco, M., Kallivayalil, D., & Levitan, J. (2011). *The trauma recovery group: A guide for practitioners.* Guilford Press.

Menon, V. (2011). Large-scale brain networks and psychopathology: A unifying triple network model. *Trends in Cognitive Sciences, 15*(10), 483–506.

Merckelbach, H., & Patihis, L. (2018). Why "trauma-related dissociation" is a misnomer in courts: A critical analysis of Brand et al. (2017a, b). *Psychological Injury and Law, 11,* 370–376. doi:10.1007/s12207-018-9328-8

Michael, T., Schanz, C. G., Mattheus, H. K., Issler, T., Frommberger, U., Köllner, V., & Equit, M. (2019). Do adjuvant interventions improve treatment outcome in adult patients with posttraumatic stress disorder receiving trauma-focused psychotherapy? A systematic review. *European Journal of Psychotraumatology, 10*(1), 1634938. doi:10.1080/20008198.2019.1634938

Michelson, L., June, K., Vives, A., Testa, S., & Marchione, N. (1998). The role of trauma and dissociation in cognitive-behavioral psychotherapy outcome and maintenance for panic disorder with agoraphobia. *Behaviour Research and Therapy, 36*(11), 1011–1050. doi:10.1016/S0005-7967(98)00073-4

Morland, L. A., Mackintosh, M.-A., Greene, C. J., Rosen, C. S., Chard, K. M., Resick, P., & Frueh, B. C. (2014). Cognitive processing therapy for posttraumatic stress disorder delivered to rural veterans via telemental health: A randomized noninferiority clinical trial. *Journal of Clinical Psychiatry, 75*(5), 470–476. doi:10.4088/JCP.13m08842

Morrison, K. H., Bradley, R., & Westen, D. (2003). The external validity of controlled clinical trials of psychotherapy for depression and anxiety: A naturalistic study. *Psychology and Psychotherapy: Theory, Research and Practice, 76*(2), 109–132. doi:10.1348/147608303765951168

Mosquera, D. (2019). *Working with voices and dissociative parts: A trauma-informed approach.* Instituto INTRA-TP, S.L.

Mosquera, D., & Ross, C. (2017). A psychotherapy approach to treating hostile voices. *Psychosis, 9*(2), 167–175.

Mueller, C., Moergeli, H., Assaloni, H., Schneider, R., & Rufer, M. (2007). Dissociative disorders among chronic and severely impaired psychiatric outpatients. *Psychopathology, 40*(6), 470–471.

Mueller-Pfeiffer, C., Rufibach, K., Perron, N., Wyss, D., Kuenzler, C., Prezewowsky, C., Pitman, R. K., & Rufer, M. (2012). Global functioning and disability in dissociative disorders. *Psychiatry Research, 200*(2–3), 475–481.

Mychailyszyn, M. P., Brand, B. L., Webermann, A. R. Şar, V., & Draijer, N. (2021). Differentiating dissociative from non-dissociative disorders: A meta-analysis of the

Structured Clinical Interview for DSM Dissociative Disorders (SCID-D). *Journal of Trauma & Dissociation, 22*(1), 19–34. doi:10.1080/15299732.2020.1760169

Myrick, A. C., Brand, B. L., McNary, S. W., Classen, C. C., Lanius, R., Loewenstein, R. J., Pain, C., & Putnam, F. W. (2012). An exploration of young adults' progress in treatment for dissociative disorder. *Journal of Trauma & Dissociation, 13*(5), 582–595.

Myrick, A. C., Brand, B. L., & Putnam, F. W. (2013). For better or worse: The role of revictimization and stress in the course of treatment for dissociative disorders. *Journal of Trauma & Dissociation, 14*(4), 375–389.

Myrick, A. C., Chasson, G. S., Lanius, R. A., Leventhal, B., & Brand, B. L. (2015). Treatment of complex dissociative disorders: A comparison of interventions reported by community therapists versus those recommended by experts. *Journal of Trauma & Dissociation, 16*(1), 51–67. doi:10.1080/15299732.2014.949020

Myrick, A. C., Webermann, A. R., Langeland, W., Putnam, F. W., & Brand, B. L. (2017a). Treatment of dissociative disorders and reported changes in inpatient and outpatient cost estimates. *European Journal of Psychotraumatology, 8*(1), 1375829. doi:10.1080/20008198.2017.1375829

Myrick, A. C., Webermann, A. R., Loewenstein, R. J., Lanius, R., Putnam, F. W., & Brand, B. L. (2017b). Six-year follow-up of the treatment of patients with dissociative disorders study. *European Journal of Psychotraumatology, 8*(1), 1344080. doi:10.1080/20008198.2017.1344080

Najavits, L. M., & Hien, D. (2013). Helping vulnerable populations: A comprehensive review of the treatment outcome literature on substance use disorder and PTSD. *Journal of Clinical Psychology, 69*(5), 433–479. doi:10.1002/jclp.21980

Najavits, L. M., & Walsh, M. (2012). Dissociation, PTSD, and substance abuse: An empirical study. *Journal of Trauma & Dissociation, 13*(1), 115–126.

Narang, D. S., & Contreras, J. M. (2005). The relationships of dissociation and affective family environment with the intergenerational cycle of child abuse. *Child Abuse & Neglect, 29*(6), 683–699. doi:10.1016/j.chiabu.2004.11.003

Nester, M. S., Boi, C., Brand, B. L., & Schielke, H. J. (2022). The reasons dissociative disorder patients self-injure. *European Journal of Psychotraumatology, 13*(1), 2026738. doi:10.1080/20008198.2022.2026738

Nester, M. S., Hawkins, S. L., & Brand, B. L. (2022). Barriers to accessing and continuing mental health treatment among individuals with dissociative symptoms. *European Journal of Psychotraumatology, 13*(1), 2031594. doi:10.1080/20008198.2022.2031594

Nicholson, A. A., Friston, K. J., Zeidman, P., Harricharan, S., McKinnon, M. C., Densmore, M., Neufeld, R. W. J., Théberge, J., Corrigan, F., Jetly, R., Spiegel, D., & Lanius, R. A. (2017). Dynamic causal modeling in PTSD and its dissociative subtype: Bottom-up versus top-down processing within fear and emotion regulation circuitry. *Human Brain Mapping, 38*(11), 5551–5561.

Nijenhuis, E. R. S. (2010). The scoring and interpretation of the SDQ-20 and SDQ-5. *Activitas Nervosa Superior, 52*(1), 24–28.

Nijenhuis, E. R. S., Spinhoven, P., vn Dyck, R., van der Hart, O., & Vanderlinden, J. (1996). The development and psychometric characteristics of the Somatoform Dissociation Questionnaire (SDQ-20). *Journal of Nervous and Mental Disease, 184*(11), 688–694. doi:10.1097/00005053-199611000-00006

Nijenhuis, E. R. S., Spinhoven, P., van Dyck, R., van der Hart, O., & Vanderlinden, J. (1998a). Psychometric characteristics of the Somatoform Dissociation Questionnaire: A replication study. *Psychotherapy and Psychosomatics, 67*(1), 17–23.

Nijenhuis, E. R. S., & van der Hart, O. (2011). Dissociation in trauma: A new definition and comparison with previous formulations. *Journal of Trauma & Dissociation, 12*(4), 416–445. doi:10.1080/15299732.2011.570592

Nijenhuis, E. R. S., van der Hart, O., Kruger, K., & Steele, K. (2004). Somatoform dissociation, reported abuse and animal defence-like reactions. *Australian and New Zealand Journal of Psychiatry, 38*(9), 678–686. doi:10.1111/j.1440-1614.2004.01441.x

Nijenhuis, E. R. S., Vanderlinden, J., & Spinhoven, P. (1998b). Animal defensive reactions as a model for trauma-induced dissociative reactions. *Journal of Traumatic Stress, 11*(2), 243–260. doi:10.1023/A:1024447003022

Noll, J. G., Trickett, P. K., Harris, W. W., & Putnam, F. W. (2009). The cumulative burden borne by offspring whose mothers were sexually abused as children: Descriptive results from a multigenerational study. *Journal of Interpersonal Violence, 24*(3), 424–449. doi:10.1177/0886260508317194

Nummenmaa, L., Glerean, E., Hari, R., & Hietanen, J. K. (2014). Bodily maps of emotions. *Proceedings of the National Academy of Sciences of the United States of America, 111*(2), 646–651. doi:10.1073/pnas.1321664111

Ogawa, J. R., Sroufe, L. A., Weinfield, N. S., Carlson, E. A., & Egeland, B. (1997). Development and the fragmented self: Longitudinal study of dissociative symptomatology in a nonclinical sample. *Development and Psychopathology, 9*(4), 855–879. doi:10.1017/S0954579497001478

Ogden, P., Minton, K., & Pain, C. (2006a). *Trauma and the body: A sensorimotor approach to psychotherapy.* W. W. Norton & Company.

Ogden, P., Pain, C., & Fisher, J. (2006b). A sensorimotor approach to the treatment of trauma and dissociation. *Psychiatric Clinics of North America, 29*(1), 263–279.

Olivé, I., Densmore, M., Harricharan, S., Théberge, J., McKinnon, M. C., & Lanius, R. (2018). Superior colliculus resting state networks in post-traumatic stress disorder and its dissociative subtype. *Human Brain Mapping, 39*(1), 563–574.

Ozer, E. J., Best, S. R., Lipsey, T. L., & Weiss, D. S. (2003). Predictors of posttraumatic stress disorder and symptoms in adults: A meta-analysis. *Psychological Bulletin, 129*(1), 52–73.

Panksepp, J. (2004). *Affective neuroscience: The foundations of human and animal emotions.* Oxford University Press.

Pasquini, P., Liotti, G., Mazzotti, E., Fassone, G., & Picardi, A. (2002). Risk factors in the early family life of patients suffering from dissociative disorders. *Acta Psychiatrica Scandinavica, 105*(2), 110–116.

Passardi, S., Peyk, P., Rufer, M., Plichta, M. M., Mueller-Pfeiffer, C., Wingenbach, T. S. H., Hassanpour, K., Schnyder, U., & Pfaltz, M. C. (2018). Impaired recognition of positive emotions in individuals with posttraumatic stress disorder, cumulative traumatic exposure, and dissociation. *Psychotherapy and Psychosomatics, 87*(2), 118–120. doi:10.1159/000486342

Pietrzak, R. H., Naganawa, M., Huang, Y., Corsi-Travali, S., Zheng, M. Q., Stein, M. B., Henry, S., Lim, K., Ropchan, J., Lin, S. F., Carson, R. E., & Neumeister, A. (2014). Association of in vivo κ-opioid receptor availability and the transdiagnostic dimensional expression of trauma-related psychopathology. *JAMA Psychiatry, 71*(11), 1262–1270.

Polak, A. R., Witteveen, A. B., Denys, D., & Olff, M. (2015). Breathing biofeedback as an adjunct to exposure in cognitive behavioral therapy hastens the reduction of PTSD symptoms: A pilot study. *Applied Psychophysiology and Biofeedback, 40*(1), 25–31. doi:10.1007/s10484-015-9268-y

Pollock, B. E., Macfie, J., & Elledge, L. C. (2017). Evidence for phase-based psychotherapy as a treatment for dissociative identity disorder comorbid with major depressive disorder and alcohol dependence. *Journal of Trauma & Dissociation, 18*(4), 595–609.

Price, M., Kearns, M., Houry, D., & Rothbaum, B. O. (2014). Emergency department predictors of posttraumatic stress reduction for trauma-exposed individuals with and without early intervention. *Journal of Consulting & Clinical Psychology, 82*(2), 336–341. doi:10.1037/a0035537

Price, M., Spinazzola, J., Musicaro, R., Turner, J., Suvak, M., Emerson, D., & van der Kolk, B. (2017). Effectiveness of an extended yoga treatment for women with chronic posttraumatic stress disorder. *Journal of Alternative and Complementary Medicine, 23*(4), 300–309. doi:10.1089/acm.2015.0266

Putnam, F. W. (1985). Dissociation as a response to extreme trauma. In R. P. Kluft (Ed.), *Childhood antecedents of multiple personality* (pp. 65–97). American Psychiatric Press.

Putnam, F. W. (1989). *Diagnosis and treatment of multiple personality disorder.* Guilford.

Putnam, F. W. (1997). *Dissociation in children and adolescents: A developmental model.* Guilford.

Putnam, F. W. (2016). *The way we are: How states of mind influence our identities, personality, and potential for change.* International Psychoanalytic Books.

Putnam, F. W., Guroff, J. J., Silberman, E. K., Barban, L., & Post, R. M. (1986). The clinical phenomenology of multiple personality disorder: A review of 100 recent cases. *Journal of Clinical Psychiatry, 47*, 285–293.

Rabellino, D., Densmore, M., Harricharan, S., Jean, T., McKinnon, M. C., & Lanius, R. A. (2018a). Resting-state functional connectivity of the bed nucleus of the stria terminalis in post-traumatic stress disorder and its dissociative subtype. *Human Brain Mapping, 39*(3), 1367–1379.

Rabellino, D., Densmore, M., Théberge, J., McKinnon, M. C., & Lanius, R. A. (2018b). The cerebellum after trauma: Resting-state functional connectivity of the cerebellum in posttraumatic stress disorder and its dissociative subtype. *Human Brain Mapping, 39*(8), 3354–3374.

Reinders, A. A T. S., Nijenhuis, E. R. S., Quak, J., Korf, J., Haaksma, J., Paans, A. M. J., Willemsen, A. T. M., & den Boer, J. A. (2006). Psychobiological characteristics of dissociative identity disorder: A symptom provocation study. *Biological Psychiatry, 60*(7), 730–740. doi:10.1016/j.biopsych.2005.12.019

Resick, P. A., Suvak, M. K., Johnides, B. D., Mitchell, K. S., & Iverson, K. M. (2012). The impact of dissociation on PTSD treatment with cognitive processing therapy. *Depression and Anxiety, 29*, 718–730. doi:10.1002/da.21938 B

Rodewald, F., Wilhelm-Gößling, C., Emrich, H. M., Reddemann, L., & Gast, U. (2011). Axis-I comorbidity in female patients with dissociative identity disorder and dissociative identity disorder not otherwise specified. *Journal of Nervous and Mental Disease, 199*(2), 122–131.

Roesler, T. A., & Wind, T. W. (1994). Telling the secret: Adult women describe their disclosures of incest. *Journal of Interpersonal Violence, 9*(3), 327–338. doi:10.1177/088626094009003003

Romano, E., Moorman, J., Ressel, M., & Lyons, J. (2019). Men with childhood sexual abuse histories: Disclosure experiences and links with mental health. *Child Abuse & Neglect, 89*, 212–224. doi:10.1016/j.chiabu.2018.12.010

Ross, C. A. (1991). Epidemiology of multiple personality disorder and dissociation. *Psychiatric Clinics of North America*, *14*(3), 503–517.

Ross, C. A. (n.d.). The Dissociative Disorders Interview Schedule—DSM-5 version. http://www.rossinst.com/downloads/DDIS-DSM-5.pdf

Ross, C. A., & Dua, V. (1993). Psychiatric health care costs of multiple personality disorder. *American Journal of Psychotherapy*, *47*(1), 103–112.

Ross, C. A., & Ellason, J. W. (2005). Discriminating between different diagnostic categories using the Dissociative Disorders Interview Schedule. *Psychological Reports*, 96, 445–453.

Ross, C. A., Ferrell, L., & Schroeder, E. (2014). Co-occurrence of dissociative identity disorder and borderline personality disorder. *Journal of Trauma & Dissociation*, *15*(1), 79–90. doi:10.1080/15299732.2013.834861

Ross, C. A., Heber, S., Norton, G. R., & Anderson, D. (1989a). The Dissociative Disorders Interview Schedule: A structured interview. *Dissociation: Progress in the Dissociative Disorders*, *2*(3), 169–189.

Ross, C. A., Miller, S. D., Bjornson, L., Reagor, P., Fraser, G. A., & Anderson, G. (1991). Abuse histories in 102 cases of multiple personality disorder. *Canadian Journal of Psychiatry*, *36*, 97–101.

Ross, C. A., Miller, S. D., Reagor, P., Bjornson, L., Fraser, G. A., & Anderson, G. (1990). Schneiderian symptoms in multiple personality disorder and schizophrenia. *Comprehensive Psychiatry*, *31*, 111–118.

Ross, C. A., & Norton, G. R. (1989). Suicide and parasuicide in multiple personality disorder. *Psychiatry: Interpersonal and Biological Processes*, *52*(3), 365–371.

Ross, C. A., Norton, G. R., Fraser, G. A., & Anderson, G. (1989b). Somatic symptoms in multiple personality disorder. *Psychosomatics*, *30*(2), 154–160.

Rossiter, A., Byrne, F., Wota, A. P., Nisar, Z., Ofuafor, T., Murray, I., Byrne, C., & Hallahan, B. (2015). Childhood trauma levels in individuals attending adult mental health services: An evaluation of clinical records and structured measurement of childhood trauma. *Child Abuse & Neglect*, *44*, 36–45. doi:10.1016/j.chiabu.2015.01.001

Rothschild, B. (2000). *The body remembers: The psychophysiology of trauma and trauma treatment*. W. W. Norton & Company.

Rufer, M., Held, D., Cremer, J., Fricke, S., Moritz, S., Peter, H., & Hand, I. (2006). Dissociation as a predictor of cognitive behavior therapy outcome in patients with obsessive-compulsive disorder. *Psychotherapy and Psychosomatics*, *75*(1), 40–46.

Sack, M., Sachsse, U., Overkamp, B., & Dulz, B. (2013). Trauma-related disorders in patients with borderline personality disorders: Results of a multicenter study. *Der Nervenarzt*, *84*(5), 608–614. doi:10.1007/s00115-012-3489-6

Şar, V., Akyüz, G., & Doğan, O. (2007). Prevalence of dissociative disorders among women in the general population. *Psychiatry Research*, *149*(1-3), 169–176.

Şar, V., Akyuz, G., Kugu, N., Ozturk, E., & Ertem-Vehid, H. (2006). Axis I dissociative disorder comorbidity in borderline personality disorder and reports of childhood trauma. *Journal of Clinical Psychiatry*, *67*(10), 1583–1590.

Şar, V., Kundakci, T., Kiziltan, E., Yargic, I. L., Tutkun, H., Bakim, B., Bozkurt, O., Özpulat, T., Keser, V., & Özdemir, Ö. (2003). The Axis-I dissociative disorder comorbidity of borderline personality disorder among psychiatric outpatients. *Journal of Trauma & Dissociation*, *4*(1), 119–136. doi:10.1300/J229v04n01_08

Saxe, G. N., Chinman, G., Berkowitz, R., Hall, K., Lieberg, G., Schwartz, J., & van der Kolk, B. A. (1994). Somatization in patients with dissociative disorders. *American Journal of Psychiatry*, *151*(9), 1329–1334.

Schauer, M., & Elbert, T. (2010). Dissociation following traumatic stress: Etiology and treatment. *Zeitschrift für Psychologie/Journal of Psychology*, *218*(2), 109–127.

Schiavone, F. L., Frewen, P., McKinnon, M., & Lanius, R. A. (2018a). The dissociative subtype of PTSD: An update of the literature. *PTSD Research Quarterly*, *29*(3), 1–4.

Schiavone, F. L., McKinnon, M. C., & Lanius, R. A. (2018b). Psychotic-like symptoms and the temporal lobe in trauma-related disorders: Diagnosis, treatment, and assessment of potential malingering. *Chronic Stress*, *2*. doi:10.1177/2470547018797046

Schielke, H. J., & Brand, B. L. (2019, April). Therapists' and patients' change in knowledge: Did TOP DD Network Study participants' knowledge related to symptom management and stabilization change over the course of the study? Paper presented at the 36th Annual Conference of the International Society for the Study of Trauma and Dissociation, New York, NY.

Schielke, H. J., Brand, B. L., & Lanius, R. A. (2020). *The Finding Solid Ground workbook: Overcoming obstacles in trauma treatment*. Oxford University Press.

Schielke, H. J., Brand, B. L., & Marsic, A. (2017). Assessing therapeutic change in patients with severe dissociative disorders: The Progress in Treatment Questionnaire, therapist and patient measures. *European Journal of Psychotraumatology*, *8*(1), 12. doi:10.1080/20008198.2017.1380471

Schlumpf, Y. R., Nijenhuis, E. R. S., Chalavi, S., Weder, E. V., Zimmermann, E., Luechinger, R., La Marca, R., Reinders, A. A. T. S., & Jäncke, L. (2013). Dissociative part-dependent biopsychosocial reactions to backward masked angry and neutral faces: An fMRI study of dissociative identity disorder. *NeuroImage: Clinical*, *3*(0), 54–64. doi:http://dx.doi.org/10.1016/j.nicl.2013.07.002

Schore, A. N. (2003). *Affect dysregulation and disorders of the self*. W. W. Norton & Company.

Schlumpf, Y. R., Nijenhuis, E. R. S., Klein, C., Jäncke, L., & Bachmann, S. (2019). Functional reorganization of neural networks involved in emotion regulation following trauma therapy for complex trauma disorders. *Neuroimage Clinical*, *23*, 101807. doi:10.1016/j.nicl.2019.101807

Shin, L. M., Orr, S. P., Carson, M. A., Rauch, S. L., Macklin, M. L., Lasko, N. B., Peters, P. M., Metzger, L. J., Dougherty, D. D., Cannistraro, P. A., Alpert, N. M., Fischman, A. J., & Alpert, N. M. (2004). Regional cerebral blood flow in the amygdala and medial prefrontal cortex during traumatic imagery in male and female Vietnam veterans with PTSD. *Archives of General Psychiatry*, *61*(2), 168–176.

Siegel, D. J. (1999). *The Developing Mind*: Guilford Press.

Siegel, D. J. (2007). *The mindful brain: Reflection and attunement in the cultivation of well-being*. W. W. Norton & Company.

Siegel, D. J. (2010). *Mindsight: The new science of personal transformation*. Bantam.

Siegel, D. J. (2015). *The developing mind: How relationships and the brain interact to shape who we are*. Guilford Press.

Sijbrandij, M., Kunovski, I., & Cuijpers, P. (2016). Effectiveness of internet-delivered cognitive behavioral therapy for posttraumatic stress disorder: A systematic review and meta-analysis. *Depression and Anxiety*, *33*(9), 783–791. doi:10.1002/da.22533

Simeon, D., & Loewenstein, R. J. (2009). Dissociative disorders. In B. J. Sadock, V. A. Sadock, & P. Ruiz (Eds.), *Comprehensive textbook of psychiatry* (9th ed., Vol. 1, pp. 1965–2026). Wolters Kluwer/Lippincott Williams & Wilkens.

Simon, N., McGillivray, L., Roberts, N. P., Barawi, K., Lewis, C. E., & Bisson, J. I. (2019). Acceptability of internet-based cognitive behavioural therapy (i-CBT) for post-traumatic stress disorder (PTSD): A systematic review. *European Journal of Psychotraumatology, 10*(1), 1646092. doi:10.1080/20008198.2019.1646092

Spiegel, D. (1984). Multiple personality as a post-traumatic stress disorder. *Psychiatric Clinics of North America, 7*, 101–110.

Spiegel, D. (1991). Dissociation and trauma. In A. Tasman & S. Goldfinger (Eds.), *American Psychiatric Press annual review of psychiatry* (Vol. 10, pp. 261–275). American Psychiatric Press.

Spiegel, D., Loewenstein, R. J., Lewis-Fernández, R., Şar, V., Simeon, D., Vermetten, E., Cardeña, E., Brown, R. J., & Dell, P. F. (2011). Dissociative disorders in DSM-5. *Depression and Anxiety, 28*(12), E17–E45. doi:10.1002/da.20923

Steele, K., Boon, S., & van der Hart, O. (2017). *Treating trauma-related dissociation: A practical, integrative approach.* W. W. Norton & Co.

Steele, K., van der Hart, O., & Nijenhuis, E. R. (2001). Dependency in the treatment of complex posttraumatic stress disorder and dissociative disorders. *Journal of Trauma & Dissociation, 2*(4), 79–116.

Stein, D. J., Koenen, K. C., Friedman, M. J., Hill, E. M., McLaughlin, K. A., Petukhova, M., Ruscio, A. M., Shahly, V., Spiegel, D., Borges, G., Bunting, B., Caldas-de-Almeida, J. M., de Girolamo, G., Demyttenaere, K., Florescu, S., Haro, J. M., Karam, E. G., Kovess-Masfety, V., Lee, S., . . . Kessler, R. C. (2013). Dissociation in posttraumatic stress disorder: Evidence from the world mental health surveys. *Biological Psychiatry, 73*(4), 302–312.

Steinberg, M. (1994). *The Structured Clinical Interview for DSM-IV Dissociative Disorders—revised (SCID-D-R).* American Psychiatric Press.

Steinberg, M. (2000). Advances in the clinical assessment of dissociation: The SCID-D-R. *Bulletin of the Menninger Clinic, 64*(2), 146–163.

Steinberg, M. (in press). *The SCID-D Interview: Diagnostic and therapeutic assessment for dissociative symptoms and disorders.* American Psychiatric Association Publishing.

Steuwe, C., Lanius, R. A., & Frewen, P. A. (2012). Evidence for a dissociative subtype of PTSD by latent profile and confirmatory factor analyses in a civilian sample. *Depression and Anxiety, 29*(8), 689–700. doi:10.1002/da.21944

Stevens, N. R., Gerhart, J., Goldsmith, R. E., Heath, N. M., Chesney, S. A., & Hobfoll, S. E. (2013). Emotion regulation difficulties, low social support, and interpersonal violence mediate the link between childhood abuse and posttraumatic stress symptoms. *Behavior Therapy, 44*(1), 152–161. doi:10.1016/j.beth.2012.09.003

Stiglmayr, C. E., Ebner-Priemer, U. W., Bretz, J., Behm, R., Mohse, M., Lammers, C. H., Anghelescu, I. G., Schmahl, C., Schlotz, W., Kleindienst, N., & Bohus, M. (2008). Dissociative symptoms are positively related to stress in borderline personality disorder. *Acta Psychiatrica Scandinavica, 117*(2), 139–147.

Stiglmayr, C. E., Shapiro, D. A., Stieglitz, R. D., Limberger, M. F., & Bohus, M. (2001). Experience of aversive tension and dissociation in female patients with borderline personality disorder: A controlled study. *Journal of Psychiatric Research, 35*(2), 111–118. doi:10.1016/S0022-3956(01)00012-7

Tanner, J., Zeffiro, T., Wyss, D., Perron, N., Rufer, M., & Mueller-Pfeiffer, C. (2019). Psychiatric symptom profiles predict functional impairment. *Frontiers in Psychiatry*, *10*, 37. doi:10.3389/fpsyt.2019.00037

Terpou, B. A., Harricharan, S., McKinnon, M. C., Frewen, P., Jetly, R., & Lanius, R. A. (2019). The effects of trauma on brain and body: A unifying role for the midbrain periaqueductal gray. *Journal of Neuroscience Research*, *97*(9), 1110–1140.

van der Hart, O., Nijenhuis, E. R. S., & Steele, K. (2006). *The haunted self: Structural dissociation and the treatment of chronic traumatization*. W. W. Norton & Co.

van der Kolk, B. (1989). Compulsion to repeat the trauma: Re-enactment, revictimization, and masochism. *Psychiatric Clinics of North America*, *12*, 389–411.

van der Kolk, B. A. (2005). Developmental trauma disorder: Toward a rational diagnosis for children with complex trauma histories. *Psychiatric Annals*, *35*(5), 401–408.

Van der Kolk, B. (2014). *The body keeps the score: Mind, brain and body in the transformation of trauma*. Penguin UK.

van der Kolk, B., Pelcovitz, D., Roth, S., Mandel, F. S., McFarlane, A., & Herman, J. L. (1996). Dissociation, somatization, and affect dysregulation: The complexity of adaptation to trauma. *American Journal of Psychiatry*, *153*(Suppl.), 83–93.

van der Velden, P. G., & Wittmann, L. (2008). The independent predictive value of peritraumatic dissociation for PTSD symptomatology after type I trauma: A systematic review of prospective studies. *Clinical Psychology Review*, *28*(6), 1009–1020. doi:10.1016/j.cpr.2008.02.006

Waelde, L. C., Silvern, L., & Fairbank, J. A. (2005). A taxometric investigation of dissociation in Vietnam veterans. *Journal of Traumatic Stress*, *18*(4), 359–369.

Wagner, A. W., Rizvi, S. L., & Harned, M. S. (2007). Applications of dialectical behavior therapy to the treatment of complex trauma-related problems: When one case formulation does not fit all. *Journal of Traumatic Stress*, *20*(4), 391–400.

Waller, N. G., & Ross, C. A. (1997). The prevalence and biometric structure of pathological dissociation in the general population: Taxometric and behavioral genetic findings. *Journal of Abnormal Psychology*, *106*, 499–510.

Wang, C.-T., & Holton, J. (2007). Total estimated cost of child abuse and neglect in the United States. Chicago: Prevent Child Abuse America.

Weathers, F. W., Blake, D. D., Schnurr, P. P., Kaloupek, D. G., Marx, B. P., & Keane, T. M. (2013). The Life Events Checklist for DSM-5 (LEC–5). U.S. Department of Veterans Affairs. https://www.ptsd.va.gov/professional/assessment/te-measures/life_events_checklist.asp

Webermann, A. R., Brand, B. L., & Chasson, G. S. (2014). Childhood maltreatment and intimate partner violence in dissociative disorder patients. *European Journal of Psychotraumatology*, *5*. doi:10.3402/ejpt.v5.24568

Webermann, A. R., Brand, B. L., Schielke, H. J., Kumar, S., & Myrick, A. C. (2017). Depression and culture in the TOP DD Network study: Assessing depressive symptoms, self-harm, and hospitalization among dissociative patients across four cultures. *Acta Psychopathologica*, *3*, 39. doi:10.4172/2469-6676.100111

Weiss, N. H., Walsh, K., DiLillo, D. D., Messman-Moore, T. L., & Gratz, K. L. (2019). A longitudinal examination of posttraumatic stress disorder symptoms and risky sexual behavior: Evaluating emotion dysregulation dimensions as mediators. *Archives of Sexual Behavior*, *48*(3), 975–986. doi:10.1007/s10508-019-1392-y

Wilgus, S. J., Packer, M. M., Lile-King, R., Miller-Perrin, C. L., & Brand, B. L. (2016). Coverage of child maltreatment in abnormal psychology textbooks: Reviewing the adequacy of the content. *Psychological Trauma: Theory, Research, Practice, and Policy*, 8(2), 188–197. doi:10.1037/tra0000049

Williams, L. M. (1995). Recovered memories of abuse in women with documented child sexual victimization histories. *Journal of Traumatic Stress*, 8(4), 649–673. doi:10.1002/jts.2490080408

Wolf, E. J., Lunney, C. A., Miller, M. W., Resick, P. A., Friedman, M. J., & Schnurr, P. P. (2012a). The dissociative subtype of PTSD: A replication and extension. *Depression and Anxiety*, 29(8), 679–688. doi:10.1002/da.21946

Wolf, E. J., Miller, M., Reardon, A. F., Ryabchenko, K. A., Castillo, D., & Freund, R. (2012b). A latent class analysis of dissociation and posttraumatic stress disorder: Evidence for a dissociative subtype. *Archives of General Psychiatry*, 69(7), 698–705. doi:10.1001/archgenpsychiatry.2011.1574

World Health Organization. (2020). *ICD-11: International statistical classification of diseases and related health problems* (11th ed.). https://icd.who.int/

Xiao, C. L., Gavrilidis, E., Lee, S., & Kulkarni, J. (2016). Do mental health clinicians elicit a history of previous trauma in female psychiatric inpatients? *Journal of Mental Health*, 25(4), 359–365.

Yang, B., & Lester, D. (2007). Recalculating the economic cost of suicide. *Death Studies*, 31(4), 351–361. doi:10.1080/07481180601187209

Yeager, C. A., & Lewis, D. O. (1996). The intergenerational transmission of violence and dissociation. *Child and Adolescent Psychiatric Clinics of North America*, 5(2), 393–430.

Yehuda, R., Hoge, C. W., McFarlane, A. C., Vermetten, E., Lanius, R. A., Nievergelt, C. M., Hobfoll, S. E., Koenen, K. C., Neylan, T. C., & Hyman, S. E. (2015). Post-traumatic stress disorder. *Nature Reviews Disease Primers*, 1(1), 1–22.

Zanarini, M. C., Frankenburg, F. R., Dubo, E. D., Sickel, A. E., Trikha, A., Levin, A., & Reynolds, V. (1998). Axis I comorbidity of borderline personality disorder. *American Journal of Psychiatry*, 155(12), 1733–1739.

Zanarini, M. C., Gunderson, J. G., Marino, M. F., Schwartz, E. O., & Frankenburg, F. R. (1989). Childhood experiences of borderline patients. *Comprehensive Psychiatry*, 30(1), 18–25.

Zittel Conklin, C., & Westen, D. (2005). Borderline personality disorder in clinical practice. *American Journal of Psychiatry*, 162(5), 867–875. doi:10.1176/appi.ajp.162.5.867

Zlotnick, C., Mattia, J. I., & Zimmerman, M. (2001). The relationship between posttraumatic stress disorder, childhood trauma and alexithymia in an outpatient sample. *Journal of Traumatic Stress*, 14(1), 177–188. doi:10.1023/A:1007899918410

Zlotnick, C., Shea, M. T., Pearlstein, T., Simpson, E., Costello, E., & Begin, A. (1996). The relationship between dissociative symptoms, alexithymia, impulsivity, sexual abuse, and self-mutilation. *Comprehensive Psychiatry*, 37(1), 12–16. doi:10.1016/S0010-440X(96)90044-9 doi.org/10.1007/s11920-018-0983-y

ABOUT THE AUTHORS

Bethany L. Brand, Ph.D., Professor at Towson University, is an expert in trauma disorders and dissociation. She serves on international and national task forces developing guidelines for the assessment and treatment of trauma disorders. Dr. Brand's research focuses on a series of international dissociative disorders treatment studies (TOP DD studies), assessment methods for distinguishing dissociative disorders from other conditions including malingering, training therapists about treating trauma, and the assessment of the accuracy and adequacy of textbooks' coverage of trauma. In her private practice, Dr. Brand treats complex trauma patients and serves as a forensic expert in trauma-related cases.

Hugo J. Schielke, Ph.D., is Trauma Services Development Lead for Homewood Health Centre and the Centre's Traumatic Stress Injury & Concurrent Program in Guelph, Ontario. He specializes in the assessment and treatment of trauma-related disorders, and his work is informed by his post-doctoral fellowship at The Trauma Disorders Program at Sheppard Pratt Health System and his involvement with the California Department of State Hospitals' Trauma-Informed Care Project. His research is focused on the treatment of trauma-related disorders, psychotherapy process, and the relational components of psychotherapy.

Francesca Schiavone, M.D., FRCPC., is a staff psychiatrist at the Centre for Addiction and Mental Health in Toronto, Ontario, Canada, in the Borderline Personality Disorder Clinic, and the Women's Trauma Program. She is also Lecturer at the University of Toronto. Her work includes providing diagnostic assessment and treatment of a range of trauma-related disorders as well as teaching and supervision of postgraduate trainees.

Ruth A. Lanius, M.D., Ph.D., is Psychiatry Professor and Harris-Woodman Chair at Western University of Canada, where she directs the Clinical Research Program for PTSD. Ruth has over 25 years of clinical and research experience with trauma-related disorders. Ruth has received numerous research and teaching awards, including the Banting Award for Military Health Research. She has published over 150 research articles and book chapters focusing on brain adaptations to psychological trauma and novel adjunct treatments for PTSD. Ruth has co-authored *The Effects of Early Life Trauma on Health and Disease: The Hidden Epidemic* and *Healing the Traumatized Self: Consciousness, Neuroscience, Treatment.*

For the benefit of digital users, indexed terms that span two pages (e.g., 52–53) may, on occasion, appear on only one of those pages.

Tables, figures, and boxes are indicated by *t*, *f*, and *b* following the page number

ACE score, 119–20
Adult Attachment Interview, 5
Adverse Childhood Experiences (ACE)
    questions, 119–20
Ainsworth, M., 4
alexithymia, 28, 112–13. *See also* emotion
amygdala, 53–54, 55*b*
anxiety disorders as comorbidity, 12
arousal, dysregulated, 48–53, 51*f*, 61, 102
assessment
    borderline personality disorder, 35–36
    comorbidity profiles, 30
    depersonalization/derealization, 24
    differential diagnosis, 34–36
    for dissociation, 23
    dissociative amnesia/fugue (*see*
        dissociative amnesia/fugue)
    of dysregulation, 27–28
    headline level discussion, 22
    identity alteration, 25–27, 34
    informed consent process, 21
    interview content sequencing, 19–20
    interviews, 33–34
    patient education, 21
    protocol, 19–21
    psychological testing, 36–37
    psychotic disorders, 34–35, 35n.1, 56,
        58*b*
    of relational functioning, 22, 27, 36, 90
    safety, 28–30
    self-report measures, 30–33
    of trauma history, 21–23
    trauma-related reactions, triggering,
        21–22
    treatment progress, 37–38
attachment resources, 105, 135–36
attachment styles, treatment impacts, 92–93

attachment–trauma–dissociation links,
    4–6
attachment type D, in infants. *See*
    disorganized attachment
attention neurobiology, 59–60
autonomic nervous system, 40–42, 44*b*–45
awareness/acceptance improvement,
    165–66

bed nucleus/stria terminalis (BNST),
    53–55
behavior/appearance contradictions, 26
Bessel van der Kolk, xvii
between-session contact, 88–89
blinking, 26
body awareness, 101–2, 105
body-oriented therapies, 88
body representations, dissociative, 8–9
borderline personality disorder, 10–11,
    35–36, 57, 66–67, 126
Bowlby, J., 4
breathing exercises, 111–12
Brown, D. P., 5–6

central executive network, 59–60
central nervous system (CNS), 42, 44*b*–45
cerebellum, 53–54, 56, 57
cerebral cortex, 43–44, 56
Cheit, R., 15
child sexual abuse, 15–16, 64, 113–14
claustrum, 54–55
clergy abuse study, 5–6
clinicians attitudes/training, 16–18
cognition neurobiology, 59–60
collaboration, 17, 131–32, 134, 157
communication, 5, 33, 52, 56–57, 84–85,
    131–32, 134

comorbidity profiles, 30
compartmentalization, 8–9
compassion, 16, 30, 63, 67, 83, 103, 132,
      134, 159
contact, between-session, 88–89
cooperation, 132, 166
corticolimbic inhibition model, 53–55, 55b
corticolimbic model of dissociation, 6–7

DDIS (Dissociative Disorders Interview), 33
default mode network, 59–60
defense cascade model, 2, 45–48, 47f, 48b
Dell, P., 26
depersonalization/derealization disorder,
      11–12
depersonalization disorder, 53–54
depression as comorbidity, 12
DES-II (Dissociative Experiences Scale),
      31–32
detachment/depersonalization speech, 26
difficulties with absences role play, 93–94
difficulty ending session role play, 94–95
discrete behavioral model, 6–7
disorganized attachment, 4, 5, 92–93, 126
dissociation vs. grounding, 164–65
dissociative amnesia/fugue
      assessment, 23, 24–25
      characterization, 8–9, 11–12
      etiology, 7–8
dissociative detachment, 9
dissociative disorder not otherwise
      specified (DDNOS). See other
      specified dissociative disorder
      (OSDD)
dissociative disorders, characterization,
      11–12
dissociative identity disorder (DID)
      assessment for, 23
      assessment tools, 31–32, 33
      association/integration failures, 8
      BPD vs., 66–67
      characterization, viii, 11–12
      concepts, definitions, 6–9
      derealization, 8–9
      diagnosis/under-diagnosis, 16
      differential diagnosis, 34–36, 56, 58b, 126
      emotion regulation, 65–67
      etiology of, 1–3, 3n.1, 5–6

identity alteration assessment, 25–27, 34
      neurobiology, 56–58
      parent–child dyad longitudinal studies, viii
      psychological testing, 36–37
      recognition of, vii, 15
      treatment frames, ISSTD guidelines,
            86–87
      treatment/prevention of, 17–18
dissociative PTSD
      characterization, 9–10
      continuum of dissociation, 8
      diagnostic criteria, 20
      neurobiology, 56–58
      recognition of, vii–viii
dissociative self-states/intrusions
      amnesia/memory loss role play, 138–39
      angry/critical self-states treatment, 133–35
      assessment, 5, 25–27
      attachment styles, treatment impacts,
            92–93
      awareness/acceptance improvement,
            165–66
      boundary management, 87
      change-fighting self-state underlying
            concerns, 137–38
      characterization, 124–30
      childlike self-states role play, 139–40
      common, 132–36
      compartmentalization in, 128
      functions of, 127–28
      parts language, 125, 131
      relational patterns of, 128–30
      in relation to safety role play, 136–37
      role plays, 131, 136–40
      role/social context effects, 124–25
      separateness/autonomy of, 126, 127
      traumatic intrusions management, 163–64
      treatment of, 130–32
      unsafe behaviors assessment, 29–30, 130
      young self-states treatment, 135–36
DSS, 9, 17, 124–25, 124–27, 127–28, 128,
      128–30, 130–32, 132–33, 133–34, 134,
      136, 138, 140, 163, 165–66, 168
dynorphins, 54–55

eating disorders as comorbidity, 12
Elbert, T., 2, 45–46
Elliott, D. S., 6

emotion
    bottom-up processing, 43
    challenges related to, 112–13
    disruptions in, 8–9
    dysregulation assessment, 27–28
    happiness, inability to feel, 116
    positive affect tolerance, 113–15
    positive emotions/ungrounded states
        association, 115–16
    regulation development, 7
    regulation neurobiology, 43–44, 53–55
    regulation skills, xiv, 67
    regulation treatment, 65–67, 79
    role plays, 113
    safety stabilization, 63–65
    shutdown/collapse, 2–3, 45–53, 47f,
        48b, 61
    tolerance/effective use of, 167–69
    top-down processing, 43
    unsafe behaviors assessment, 29–30, 130
emotional flashbacks, 163–64
emotional neglect, 6, 64
extended amygdala, 53–54
eye fluttering/rolling, 26

Fantasy Model of Dissociation, 3n.1
fearfulness management role play, 98–99
fight or flight, 2, 40–41, 45–53, 47f, 48b,
    52b–53b, 61, 102–3
Finding Solid Ground program. See also
    TOP DD Network study
    awareness/acceptance improvement,
        165–66
    background, 150–51
    clinical considerations, 159–60
    core skill sets, xiv–xv
    development of, xi–xii, 76, 77–78, 79
    dissociation vs. grounding, 164–65
    emotional tolerance/effective use,
        167–69
    fear-driven ambivalence resolution,
        161–63
    goals of, xii–xiv, 74–75, 151, 152
    in group settings, 156–59
    in individual settings, 156
    patient selection, 79
    principles, techniques of, 76–77, 151–56,
        152t

safety stabilization, 63–65, 166–67
    schedules, adapting, 159
    self-understanding/self-compassion
        skills, 160–61
    traumatic intrusions management,
        163–64
first-person plural references, 26
flight/avoidance state, 129
flight/interruption state, 129
flooding emotion, xiii
4-D model of dissociation, 6–7
freezing. See tonic immobility
Frewen, P. A., 107n.2

getting healthy needs met safely skills, xiv,
    67–68
going along/submission, 2–3
grounding strategies
    attachment resources, 105
    attending to need for, 104
    awareness/acceptance improvement,
        165–66
    barriers to, 107–9
    breathing exercises, 111–12
    described, xiv, 67, 152
    dissociation vs. grounding, 164–65
    identification of need for, 101–4, 102f
    positive emotions/ungrounded states
        association, 115–16
    protocol, 100–1
    reorientation, 106–7
    role plays in, 109–11
    script, 181–82
    technique variation by patient, 104–7
    time frame by patient, 107, 107n.2
    ungrounded state perceived advantages,
        108–9

Herman, J., 15
Hesse, E., 4
highway hypnosis, 23
hospitalization. See also treatment
    economic costs, 73–74, 80–81
    inpatient, 12, 65, 73–74
    quality of life impairment, 80
    TOP DD longitudinal study, 72–73
    TOP DD naturalistic study, 71–72
    TOP DD Network study, 78

treatment benefits, ix, 72, 80
hyperarousal/hypoarousal, 102–4, 106–7,
    109–11

identification/Stockholm syndrome, 2–3
identify/identification state, 129
identity alteration assessment, 25–27, 34
identity disruptions, 8–9
immobilizing defenses, 2–3, 45–53, 47f,
    48b, 52b–53b, 61, 102–3, 110, 129
incidental touch, 88
informed consent, 21, 85–86
innate alarm system neurobiology, 50, 53b,
    61
insecure-ambivalent attachment, 4, 5
insecure-avoidant attachment, 4, 5
interpersonal violence role plays, 146–47
interviews, 33–34
intrinsic connectivity networks, 59–60, 61

Karpman's triangle, 84, 92–93, 134–35, 144

Lanius, R., 107n.2
lateness role play, 94
LEC-5 (Life Events Checklist/DSM 5), 31
limbic system, 53–54
Liotti, G., 92–93
Loewenstein, R. J., 26

MacLean, P. D., 42
Main, M., 4
Mansfield, A. J., 14
MDI (Multiscale Dissociation Inventory), 32
medial prefrontal cortex, 53–54
memory
    amnesia/memory loss role
        play, 138–39
    false/recovered, of child abuse, 15–16
    neurobiology, 59–60
    trauma effects on, xiv, 3, 7–9
micro-dissociations, 26
MID-6 (Multidimensional Inventory of
    Dissociation 6.0), 32
misdiagnosis, 11, 124
motor control/behavior disruptions, 8–9

neomammalian complex/triune brain
    model, 43

neurobiology of trauma
    arousal, dysregulated, 48–53, 51f,
        61, 102
    attention, 59–60
    brain activation patterns, viii, 40, 66
    cognition, 59–60
    defense cascade model, 45–48, 47f, 48b
    defensive/survival responses, 44
    fear networks, 168–69
    functional connectivity, 52, 59–60
    innate alarm system, 50, 53b, 61
    intrinsic connectivity
        networks, 59–60, 61
    memory, 59–60
    nervous system structure, 40–45,
        44b–45
    paleomammalian complex/triune brain
        model, 42, 53–55
    perceptual abnormalities, 56–58, 58b
    relational functioning, 53
    reptilian complex/triune brain model,
        42, 48–53, 51f
    triune brain model, 40–45, 61
90/10 reactions, 163–64
nonattendance/cancellation policies, 86–87
nonsuicidal self-injury (NSSI). See also
    unsafe behaviors
    assessment, 21
    emotion regulation, 65–67, 112
    risky/unhealthy behaviors,
        understanding, 64–65
    safety assessment, 28–30
    TOP DD naturalistic study, 72–73
    treatment benefits, xii, 79–80

opioid neuromodulatory system, 54–55
other specified dissociative disorder
    (OSDD)
    characterization, 11–12
    continuum of dissociation, 8
    diagnostic criteria, 20
    differential diagnosis, 34–36, 126
    functional impairment, 13
    psychological testing, 36–37
    TOP DD naturalistic study, 71

paleomammalian complex/triune brain
    model, 42, 53–55

parietal lobe, 56
passive influence phenomena, 26
patients asking for hug role play, 96, 139
PCL-5 (PTSD Checklist/DSM 5), 31
perceptual abnormalities neurobiology,
    56–58, 58b
periaqueductal gray matter (PAG), 50–52,
    51f, 53–54
peritraumatic dissociation, 1–2
phasic trauma treatment, 14–15
physical health outcomes, 119–22
physical touch, 88, 96, 139
polypharmacy, 120–21
posttraumatic stress disorder. See PTSD
Progress in Treatment Questionnaires
    (PITQ), 37–38, 79, 171–79
psychiatric medications, 120–21
psychological testing, 36–37
psychotic disorders assessment, 34–35,
    35n.1, 56, 58b
PTSD
    assessment, 31
    comorbidities, 12
    complex, 10, 126
    dissociative (see dissociative PTSD)
    neurobiology, 59–60
    positive affect tolerance, 113–15
    predictive factors, 1–2
    recognition of, vii, 15
    treatment, ix, 79
Putnam, F., 6–7, 164

reenactment, 82, 84,
relational functioning
    assessment of, 22, 27, 36, 90
    attachment styles, treatment impacts, 92–93
    between-session contact, 88–89
    boundaries/boundary violations, 83,
        84–85, 87
    boundary management, 85–87
    collaboration dynamic establishment, 91
    difficulty ending session, 94–95
    in dissociative self-states/intrusions,
        128–30
    fearfulness management, 98–99
    Karpman's triangle, 84, 92–93, 134–35,
        144

lateness, 94
neurobiology, 53
patients asking for hug, 96, 139
physical touch, 88, 96, 139
reenactments, 82–83, 84–85
response to abuser, 2–3
role plays addressing TRD impacts,
    93–99
therapeutic relationship, 82–85
too-frequent calls/not accepting advice,
    96–98
transparency dynamic
    establishment, 91
treatment, 62–63, 70, 70f, 90–92
treatment frames, 85–87
triggering by therapist, 89–92
reorientation, 106–7
reptilian complex/triune brain model, 42,
    48–53, 51f
rest and digest, 40–41
revictimization, 64–67, 72
role plays
    addressing TRD impacts, 93–99
    amnesia/memory loss/DSS, 138–39
    change-fighting self-state underlying
        concerns, 137–38
    childlike self-states, 139–40
    difficulty ending session, 94–95
    dissociative self-states/intrusions, 131,
        136–40
    emotion, 113
    fearfulness management, 98–99
    in grounding strategies, 109–11
    happiness, inability to feel, 116
    interpersonal violence, 146–47
    lateness, 94
    medically unexplained symptoms, 122
    patients asking for hug, 96, 139
    positive emotions/ungrounded states
        association, 115–16
    in relation to safety, 136–37
    sexually provocative clothing/
        interpersonal safety, 147
    shame/self-criticism, 118–19
    too-frequent calls/not accepting advice,
        96–98
    unsafe behaviors, 146–47

safety
    assessment, 28–30
    assessment, TOP DD Network study,
        28–29
    emotion regulation, 65–67
    role plays in relation to, 136–37
    sexually provocative clothing/
        interpersonal safety role plays, 147
    stabilization of, 63–65, 166–67
    treatment benefits, 79–80
    in treatment dynamic, 91–92
    unsafe behaviors assessment, 29–30, 130
salience network, 59–60
Scale for Tonic Immobility Occurring Post
    Trauma (STOP), 3
Schauer, M., 2, 45–46
schizophrenia, 35, 35n.1, 56, 58b
SCID-D-R (Structured Clinical Interview/
    DSM-IV), 33
SDQ-20/SDQ-5 (Somatoform Dissociation
    Questionnaire), 32
secure attachment, 4, 5
self-compassion, 67, 76, 77, 150–51,
    160–63, 166
self-destructiveness as comorbidity, 12. See
    also nonsuicidal self-injury (NSSI)
self-injury. See nonsuicidal self-injury (NSSI)
self-report measures, 30–33
self-states. See dissociative self-states/
    intrusions
separating past from present skills, xiv, 67
sexually provocative clothing/
    interpersonal safety role plays, 147
shame/self-criticism
    assessment of, 27, 29
    child development and, 7–8
    chronic, 114, 116–19
    dissociation timing and, 68
    neurobiology of, 43–44, 46–47, 49–51,
        53–55, 55b, 60
    reduction of, in therapy, 40, 43–44, 60,
        76–77, 82–83, 86–87, 90, 155, 169
    role plays, 94, 118–19
    safety maintenance, 66
    somatic indicators of, 118
    trauma response as source of, 43–44,
        46–47, 49–50
    triggering, 117

social media, 85–86
somatization disorders/somatic symptoms,
    119–22
staring, fixed, 26
Stockholm syndrome, 2
STOP (Scale for Tonic Immobility
    Occurring Post-Trauma), 32–33
Strange Situation measure, 4, 5
structural model of dissociation, 6–7
Structured Clinical Interview for
    Dissociative Disorders (SCID-D), 5
submit/submission state, 129
suicidality. See also unsafe behaviors
    as comorbidity, 12, 13–14
    emotion regulation, 65–67
    prevalence of, 14
    risky/unhealthy behaviors,
        understanding, 64–65
    safety assessment, 28–30
    TOP DD naturalistic study, 73
sympathetic nervous system, 40–42

temporal lobe, 36–37, 56, 57
tonic immobility, xiii, 2, 45–53, 47f, 48b,
    52b–53b, 61, 102–3, 110, 129
too-frequent calls/not accepting advice
    role play, 96–98
TOP DD Network study
    background, xi–xii
    benefits of, ix
    characterization, 74–80
    clinicians' interventions vs, expert
        recommendations, 69–71, 70f
    cross-cultural applicability, xiii
    development/design of, 75–78
    discontinuation of treatment, 74
    economic costs, 14–15, 73
    expert survey, 69
    follow-up data, 73–74
    naturalistic study, 71–74, 120–21
    procedure, 78
    psychiatric comorbidities, 12
    psychiatric medications, 120–21
    results, 78–80
    safety assessment, 28–29
    summary/implications, 80–81
touch, 88, 96, 139
Trauma Model of Dissociation, 3n.1

trauma-related altered states of
consciousness (TRASC), 11
trauma-related disorders (TRDs)
assessment of (see assessment)
attachment difficulties, 4–6
comorbidities, 9–12
diagnosis/under-diagnosis, 12–15, 16
disability/quality of life impediments,
12–15, 80
economic costs of, 14–15, 73
etiology of, 1–3
posttraumatic effects generally, ix–8,
39–40, 60–61, 149–50
potentially traumatic situations
responses, 2–3
predictors of impairment studies, 13
prevalence, 9–12
screening in diagnosis of, 17
treatment/prevention of, ix, 17–18
treatment. See also hospitalization
attachment styles impacts, 92–93
clinicians' interventions vs, expert
recommendations, 69–71, 70f
collaboration dynamic establishment, 91
difficulties with absences role play,
93–94
difficulty ending session role play, 94–95
emotion regulation, 65–67
expert recommendations, 68–71, 70f
fearfulness management role play, 98–99
grounding strategies (see grounding
strategies)
lateness role play, 94
patients asking for hug role play, 96, 139
phasic trauma, 14–15, 64
positive emotions/ungrounded states
association, 115–16
processing phase, 63
progress assessment, 37–38
reconnection phase, 63
relational functioning, 62–63, 70, 70f,
90–92
risky/unhealthy behaviors,
understanding, 64–65
safety stabilization, 63–65

survivor skills, 67–68
symptom management/stabilization
phase, 62–63, 77
timing of dissociation as predictive, 68
too-frequent calls/not accepting advice
role play, 96–98
transparency dynamic establishment, 91
of trauma-related disorders generally,
ix, 17–18
Treatment of Patients with Dissociative
Disorders. See TOP DD Network
study
triggering
grounding strategies, xiv, 67, 100–1,
104–9
identifying, 101–4
90/10 reactions, 163–64
shame/self-criticism, 117
by therapist, 89–92
trauma-related reactions, 21–22
triune brain model, 40–45, 61

unsafe behaviors
addictions model approach to, 142–43
assessment, 29–30, 130
autonomy emphasis in therapy, 145
collaborative, harm-reduction approach,
145–46
functions of, 144–45
interpersonal violence role plays, 146–47
Karpman's triangle, 84, 92–93, 134–35,
144
relapse, 143–44
role plays, 146–47
sexually provocative clothing/
interpersonal safety, 147
stabilization of, 142–46
unspecified dissociative disorder (UDD),
11–12

vermis, 53–54
vestibular system, 56–57
victim blaming, 16

window of tolerance model, 102–3, 102f